Especially for

....

From

....

Date

....

GOD
CALLING

STUDENT EDITION

The Classic Daily Devotional

GOD
CALLING

STUDENT EDITION

Edited by

A.J. RUSSELL

BARBOUR
PUBLISHING

Member of the
Evangelical Christian
Publishers Association

Introduction

Very few books, even number-one bestsellers, are read with much passion a decade after their release. In twenty or thirty years, most are largely forgotten.

So there must be something special about a book that is not only read but revered more than seventy years after its first publication. *God Calling* is such a volume.

It began in the fall of 1932 when two British women met to pray, share fellowship with each other, and to write down what they thought God was saying to them through His Son, Jesus Christ. Ultimately, they generated a year's worth of writings, which were then edited for publication by A. J. Russell, a London newspaperman.

The two women, who have always remained anonymous, were "poor, brave [and] courageously fighting against sickness and penury," in Russell's words. "They were facing a hopeless future and one of them even longed to be quit of this hard world for good," he wrote in his original introduction. But then God spoke to their hearts, and *God Calling* was born.

Over the decades, the anonymous friends' work has become one of the most read and beloved daily devotionals of all time. Millions of copies have been printed and sold, read personally, and given as gifts, in Great Britain and the United States. The book has also been translated for use around the world.

Its literary approach—*God Calling* is written as if Jesus Himself is speaking to the reader—resonates with both men and women, of varying ages and cultures. "Open this book at any page and taste its beauty," Russell wrote. "Dwell lovingly on its tender phrases. Let its wonderful quality sink deep into your spirit."

Those tender phrases and wonderful qualities are reproduced completely and without change in this new edition. Everything that makes *God Calling* so powerful will be found in these pages, along with exciting new "expanded edition" features presented in colored type. For example, a carefully selected scripture has been added to every entry. Throughout the book, you'll also find:

- relevant hymn lyrics and other verses
- thought-provoking quotations
- helpful prayer starters
- "consider" questions for further thought.

We hope this expanded edition of *God Calling* will provide challenge, encouragement, and inspiration for your Christian walk. Read on to meet your loving Savior.

THE PUBLISHER

Between the Years

Therefore do not worry about tomorrow, for tomorrow will worry about its own things. Sufficient for the day is its own trouble.
MATTHEW 6:34

Our Lord and our God. We joy in Thee. Without Thy Help we could not face unafraid the year before us.

I stand between the years. The Light of My Presence is flung across the year to come—the radiance of the Sun of Righteousness. Backward, over the past year, is My Shadow thrown, hiding trouble and sorrow and disappointment.

Dwell not on the past—only on the present. Only use the past as the trees use My Sunlight to absorb it, to make from it in after days the warming fire-rays. So store only the blessings from Me, the Light of the World. Encourage yourselves by the thought of these.

Bury every fear of the future, of poverty for those dear to you, of suffering, of loss. Bury all thought of unkindness and bitterness, all your dislikes, your resentments, your sense of failure, your disappointment in others and in yourselves, your gloom, your despondency, and let us leave them all, buried, and go forward to a new and risen life.

Remember that you must not see as the world sees. I hold the year in My Hands—in trust for you. But I shall guide you one day at a time.

Leave the rest with Me. You must not anticipate the gift by fears or thoughts of the days ahead.

And for each day I shall supply the wisdom and the strength.

Arm of Love

Bear one another's burdens, and so fulfill the law of Christ.
GALATIANS 6:2

You are to help to save others. Never let one day pass when you have not reached out an arm of Love to someone outside your home—a note, a letter, a visit, help in some way.

Be full of Joy. Joy saves. Joy cures. Joy in Me. In every ray of sunlight, every smile, every act of kindness, or love, every trifling service—joy.

Each day do something to lift another soul out of the sea of sin, or disease or doubt into which man has fallen. I still walk today by the lakeside and call My Disciples to follow Me and to become fishers of men.

The helping hand is needed that raises the helpless to courage, to struggle, to faith, to health. Love. Laugh. Love and laughter are the beckoners to faith and courage. Trust on, love on, joy on.

Refuse to be downcast. Refuse to be checked in your upward climb. Love and laugh. I am with you. I bear your burdens. Cast your burden upon Me and I will sustain thee. And then in very lightheartedness you turn and help another with the burden that is pressing too heavily upon him or her.

How many burdens can you lighten this year? How many hearts can you cheer? How many souls can you help?

And in giving you gain: "Good measure, pressed down, and running over." I your Lord have said it.

The Way Will Open

But they that wait upon the LORD shall renew their strength.
ISAIAH 40:31 KJV

You must be renewed, remade. Christ, Christ, Christ. Everything must rest on Me. Force is born of rest. Only Love is a conquering force. Be not afraid, I will help you.

Be channels both of you. My Spirit shall flow through and My Spirit shall, in flowing through, sweep away all the bitter past.

Take heart. God loves, God helps, God fights, God wins. You shall see. You shall know. The way will open. All My Love has ever planned, all My Love has ever thought, you shall see each day unfold. Only be taught. Just be a child. A child never questions plans. It accepts gladly.

CONSIDER:
If God, in His great love, has planned beautiful things for me,
should I hesitate to reach out and place my hand in His?
Although I might not understand the way that He is leading me,
why would I want to avoid what He desires for my life?
If God wishes to remake me, won't I be a better person?

PRAY:
*Give me the heart of a child, Lord, one that never questions the abundant
love and grace You've sent my way. Give me the heart of a child,
never doubting the goodness You've bestowed on me.*

Do Not Plan

A man's heart plans his way, but the Lord directs his steps.
PROVERBS 16:9

Shew us Thy Way, O Lord, and let us walk in Thy Paths.
Lead us in Thy Truth and teach us.

All is well. Wonderful things are happening. Do not limit God at all. He cares and provides.

Uproot self—the channel-blocker. Do not plan ahead; the way will unfold step by step. Leave tomorrow's burden. Christ is the Great Burden-bearer. You cannot bear His load and He only expects you to carry a little day-share.

Help me to cast off my worries,
To only take thought of today,
To bear just the portion You give me,
And walk with trust in Your way.

Wonderful things are now happening!
Marvelous things will soon be!
Lord Jesus, You bear all my burdens,
And give but a day-share to me.

God doesn't often reveal the details of where He's taking you
because He wants you to trust Him for every step.
STORMIE OMARTIAN
JUST ENOUGH LIGHT FOR THE STEP I'M ON

Hoard Nothing

"And do not seek what you should eat or what you should drink,
nor have an anxious mind. For all these things the nations of the
world seek after, and your Father knows that you need these things."
LUKE 12:29–30

L ove Me and do My Will. No evil shall befall you. Take no thought
for tomorrow. Rest in My Presence brings Peace. God will help
you. Desire brings fulfillment. Peace like a quiet flowing river cleanses,
sweeps all irritants away.

You shall be taught, continue these prayer times, even if they seem
fruitless. The devil will try by any means to stop them. Heed him not.
He will say evil spirits may enter in. Heed him not.

Rest your nerves. Tired nerves are a reflection on, not of, God's
Power. Hope all the time.

Do not be afraid of poverty. Let money flow freely. I will let it flow
in, but you must let it flow out. I never send money to stagnate—only to
those who pass it on. Keep nothing for yourself. Hoard nothing. Only
have what you need and use. This is My Law of Discipleship.

PRAY:
Father, help me to be faithful to spend time with You,
even though I see nothing happening. May I not become
frustrated when my prayers go unanswered. Lord, I also pray:
help me not to cling to my money out of fear of poverty.

Sharp and Ready

Be diligent to present yourself approved to God, a worker who does not need to be ashamed, rightly dividing the word of truth.
2 TIMOTHY 2:15

Guide me, O Thou Great Jehovah,
Pilgrim through this foreign land.
I am weak but Thou art mighty,
Guide me with Thy powerful Hand.

You must pray. The way will open. God cares and His plans unfold. Just love and wait.

Love is the Key. No door is too difficult for it to open.

What cause have you to fear? Has He not cared for and protected you? Hope on. Hope gladly. Hope with certainty. Be calm, calm in My Power.

Never neglect these times. Pray and read your Bible and train and discipline yourself. That is your work—Mine to use you. But My instruments must be sharp and ready. Then I use them.

Discipline and perfect yourselves at all costs. Do this, for soon every fleeting thought will be answered, every wish gratified, every deed used. It is a fearful Power, a mighty Power. Oh! be careful that you ask nothing amiss—nothing that is not according to My Spirit.

All thoughts harmful must be turned out. See how necessary I have made the purity and goodness of your own lives to you. Soon, you shall ask and at once it will come. Welcome the training. Without it I dare not give you this Power.

Do not worry about others' lives. You must perfect yourselves first in My Strength.

The Secret Pearl

Therefore, having these promises, beloved, let us cleanse ourselves from all filthiness of the flesh and spirit, perfecting holiness in the fear of God.
2 CORINTHIANS 7:1

Look upon us with Thy favor, O Lord, while we behold "the land that is very far off" and yet so near to the seeing eye and the listening ear.

Wait. Wonders are unfolding. Tremble with awe. No man can stand upon the threshold of Eternity unshaken. I give unto you Eternal Life. A free gift, a wonderful gift—the Life of the Ages.

Silently comes the Kingdom. No man can judge when It enters the heart of man, only in results. Listen quietly. Sometimes you may get no message. Meet thus all the same. You will absorb an atmosphere.

Cultivate silence. "God speaks in silences." A silence, a soft wind. Each can be a message to convey My meaning to the heart, though by no voice, or even word.

Each word or thought of yours can be like a pearl that you drop into the secret place of another heart, and in some hour of need, lo! the recipient finds the treasure and realizes for the first time its value.

Do not be too ready to *do*, just *be*. I said, "*Be* ye therefore perfect" not "do" perfect things. Try and grasp this. Individual efforts avail nothing. It is only the work of the Universal Spirit—My Spirit—that counts.

Dwell in thought on this more and more; saints have taken a lifetime to grasp it.

Love Bangs the Door

*Therefore we do not lose heart. Even though our outward man
is perishing, yet the inward man is being renewed day by day.
For our light affliction, which is but for a moment, is working
for us a far more exceeding and eternal weight of glory.*
2 CORINTHIANS 4:16–17

L ife with Me is not immunity *from* difficulties, but peace *in* difficulties. My guidance is often by *shut* doors. Love bangs as well as opens.

Joy is the result of faithful trusting acceptance of My Will, when it seems *not* joyous.

St. Paul, My servant, learnt this lesson of the banged doors when he said "our light affliction, which is but for a moment, worketh for us a far more exceeding and eternal weight of glory." Expect rebuffs until this is learned—it is the only way.

Joy is the daughter of calm.

CONSIDER:
*What difficult circumstances has God allowed into my life,
and what anxious situations does He want me to be calm in?
Do I believe God truly knows how these things test my faith?*

PRAY:
*Dear God, I know that You allow difficulties in my life for a reason.
Please show me what lesson You want me to learn through them.*

No Strain

*"Come to Me, all you who labor and are heavy laden, and I
will give you rest. Take My yoke upon you and learn from Me,
for I am gentle and lowly in heart, and you will find rest for
your souls. For My yoke is easy and My burden is light."*
MATTHEW 11:28–30

Be calm, no matter what may befall you. Rest in Me. Be patient,
and let patience have her perfect work. Never think things
overwhelming. How can you be overwhelmed when I am with you?

Do not feel the strain of life. There is no strain for My children. Do
you not see I am a Master Instrument-maker? Have I not fashioned
each part? Do I not know just what it can bear without a strain? Would
I, the maker of so delicate an instrument, ask of it anything that could
destroy or strain?

No! The strain is only when you are serving another master, the
world, fame, the good opinion of men—or carrying two days' burden on
the one day.

Remember that it must not be.

PRAY:
*O God! Help me, I pray! I confess that I feel overwhelmed at times.
Help me to remember that You are with me. Plant that knowledge
deep within me. Whisper it constantly in my ear. Help me to know
that You're the One I'm serving, You're the One I'm living for.*

CONSIDER:
*What burdens am I straining under? What can
I let go of that isn't mine to handle anyway?*

Influence

"So shall My word be that goes forth from My mouth;
it shall not return to Me void, but it shall accomplish what
I please, and it shall prosper in the thing for which I sent it."
Isaiah 55:11

When you come to Me, and I give you that Eternal Life I give to all who believe in Me, it alters your whole existence, the words you speak, the influences you have.

These are all eternal. They *must* be. They spring from the life within you, My Life, Eternal Life, so that they, too, live forever. Now, you see how vast, how stupendous, is the work of any soul that has Eternal Life. The words, the influence, go on down the ages forever.

You must ponder on these truths I give you. They are not surface facts, but the secrets of My Kingdom, the hidden pearls of rare price.

Meditate upon them. Work at them in your minds and hearts.

Thy Word is a lamp to my feet,
A light to my path alway,
To guide and to save me from sin,
And show me the heavenly way.

Thy Word have I hid in my heart,
That I might not sin against Thee;
That I might not sin, that I might not sin,
Thy Word have I hid in my heart.
Ernest Orlando Sellers (1869–1952)

PRAY:
God, help me to ponder Your truth, that I may be transformed by You.

The Ache of Love

All the ends of the world shall remember and turn to the LORD,
and all the families of the nations shall worship before You.
For the kingdom is the LORD's, and He rules over the nations.
PSALM 22:27–28

Cry unto me, and I will her you and bless you. Use My unlimited stores for your needs and those of others. Seek My wonderful truths and you *shall* find.

But there was a time in the Upper Room, after My Ascension, when My disciples had to comfort themselves by saying, "Did He not speak to us by the way?"

There may come times when you sit in silence, when it seems as if you were left alone. Then, I command you to remember I have spoken to you.

You will have the consciousness of My Presence when you hear no voice. Abide in that Presence. "I am the light of the world," but sometimes in tender pity, I withhold too glaring a light, lest, in its dazzling brightness, you should miss your daily path and work.

Not until Heaven is reached do souls sit and drink in the ecstasy of God's revelation to His Own. At the moment you are pilgrims and need only your daily marching orders and strength and guidance for the day.

Oh! Listen to My Voice, eagerly, joyfully. Never crowd it out. I have no rival claimants, and if men seek the babble of the world, then I withdraw.

Life has hurt you. Only scarred lives can really save.

You cannot escape the discipline. It is the hallmark of discipleship. My children, trust Me always. Never rebel.

The trust given to Me today takes away the ache of rejection of My love that I suffered on earth and have suffered through the ages. "I died for you, My children, and could ye treat Me so?"

Thanks for Trials

Be kindly affectionate to one another with brotherly love, in honor giving preference to one another; not lagging in diligence, fervent in spirit, serving the Lord; rejoicing in hope, patient in tribulation, continuing steadfastly in prayer; distributing to the needs of the saints, given to hospitality.
ROMANS 12:10–13

You must say "Thank You" for everything, even seeming trials and worries.

Joy is the whole being's attitude of "Thank You" to Me. Be glad. Rejoice. A father loves to see his children happy.

I am revealing so much to you. Pass it on. Each Truth is a jewel. Some poor spirit-impoverished friend will be glad of it. Drop one here and there.

Seek to find a heart-home for each Truth I have imparted to you. More Truths will flow in. Use *all* I give you. Help others. I ache to find a way into each life and heart, for all to cry expectantly, "Even so, come, Lord Jesus."

Thanks to God for my Redeemer,
Thanks for all Thou dost provide!
Thanks for times now but a memory,
Thanks for Jesus by my side!
Thanks for pleasant, balmy springtime,
Thanks for dark and stormy fall!
Thanks for tears by now forgotten,
Thanks for peace within my soul!
AUGUST LUDVIG STORM (1862–1914)

PRAY:
Oh Lord, I am Yours to use. Line me up with Your will.

> *"I will bring the one-third through the fire, will refine them as silver is refined, and test them as gold is tested. They will call on My name, and I will answer them. I will say, 'This is My people'; And each one will say, 'The LORD is my God.'"*
> ZECHARIAH 13:9

Never despair, never despond. Be just a channel of helpfulness for others.

Have more sympathy. Feel more tenderness toward others. Your lives shall not be all care. *Gold* does not *stay* in the crucible—*only* until it is refined. Already I hear the music and the marching of the unseen host, rejoicing at your victory.

No follower of Mine would ever err or fall, if once the veil were withdrawn which prevents him seeing how these slips delight the evil spirits, and the pain and disappointment of those who long for him to conquer in My Strength and Name, and the ecstasy of rejoicing when victory is won.

My Strength is *the same* as that in which I conquered Satan in the Wilderness—depression and sorrow in the Garden, and even death on Calvary.

Think of that.

CONSIDER:

Scripture says that all the angels of heaven rejoice when one soul is saved, and that they long to look into the mystery of my salvation, but have I ever imagined the hosts of heaven playing triumphant music and marching in a victory parade when I gain a major victory?

Mighty and Marvelous

*For I delight in the law of God according to the inward man. But I see
another law in my members, warring against the law of my mind,
and bringing me into captivity to the law of sin which is in my members.
O wretched man that I am! Who will deliver me from this body of death?
I thank God—through Jesus Christ our Lord! So then, with the mind
I myself serve the law of God, but with the flesh the law of sin.*

ROMANS 7:22–25

Glad indeed are the souls with whom I walk. Walking with Me is
security. The coming of My Spirit into a life and Its working are
imperceptible, but the result is mighty.

Learn of Me. Kill the self. Every blow to self is used to shape the
real, eternal, imperishable you.

Be very candid and rigorous with yourselves. "Did *self* prompt
that?" and if it did, oust it at all costs.

When I died on the Cross, I died embodying all the human self.
Once that was crucified, I could conquer even death.

When I bore your sins in My own body on the Tree I bore the
self-human nature of the world. As you, too, kill self, you gain the
overwhelming power I released for a weary world, and you, too, will be
victorious.

It is not life and its difficulties you have to conquer, only the self
in you. As I said to My disciples, "I have many things to say to you, but
you cannot bear them now." You could not understand them. But as you
go on obeying Me and walking with Me and listening to Me, you will,
and then you will see how glorious, how marvelous, My revelations are,
and My teachings.

Relax

*The work of righteousness will be peace, and the effect of righteousness,
quietness and assurance forever. My people will dwell in a peaceful
habitation, in secure dwellings, and in quiet resting places.*
ISAIAH 32:17–18

Relax, do not get tense, have no fear. All is for the best. How can you fear change when your life is hid with Me in God, who changeth not—and I am the same yesterday, today, and forever.

You must learn poise, soul-balance and poise, in a vacillating, changing world.

Claim My power. The same power with which I cast out devils is yours today. Use it. If not, I withdraw it. Use it ceaselessly.

You cannot ask too much. Never think you are too busy. As long as you get back to Me and replenish after each task, no work can be too much. My Joy I give you. Live in it. Bathe your Spirit in it. Reflect it.

CONSIDER:
*Do I sometimes have the feeling that I'm asking God too much?
Or, on the opposite extreme, am I so busy that I don't take
time with God, and don't ask Him to replenish me?*

PRAY:
*Father, I am yours! Here are my concerns,
my needs, my praise. I give them all to You.*

Friend in Drudgery

But let all those rejoice who put their trust in You; let them ever shout for joy,
because You defend them; let those also who love Your name be joyful in You.
PSALM 5:11

It is the daily strivings that count, not the momentary heights. The obeying of My Will day in, day out, in the wilderness plains, rather than the occasional Mount of Transfiguration.

Perseverance is nowhere needed so much as in the religious life. The drudgery of the Kingdom it is that secures My intimate Friendship. I am the Lord of little things, the Divine Control of little happenings.

Nothing in the day is too small to be a part of My scheme. The little stones in a mosaic play a big part.

Joy in Me. Joy is the God-given cement that secures the harmony and beauty of My mosaic.

I know that my Redeemer lives,
And ever prays for me;
A token of His love He gives,
A pledge of liberty.
CHARLES WESLEY (1707–1788)

PRAY:
Oh God, my joy, my life, keep my head above the rough
waters of my circumstances so that I can stay aware
of You at all times. Help me never to give up hope.

God's Rush to Give

"Give, and it will be given to you: good measure, pressed down,
shaken together, and running over will be put into your bosom.
For with the same measure that you use, it will be measured back to you."
LUKE 6:38

Silence. Be silent before Me. Seek to *know* and then to do My will in all things.

Abide in My Love, an atmosphere of loving understanding to all men. This is *your* part to carry out, and then *I* surround you with a protective screen that keeps all evil from you. It is fashioned by your own attitude of mind, words, and deeds toward others.

I want to give you all things, good measure, pressed down and running over. Be quick to learn. You know little yet of the Divine Impatience which longs to rush to give. Does one worrying thought enter your mind, one impatient thought? Fight it at once.

Love and Trust are the solvents for the worry and cares and frets of a life. Apply them *at once*. You are channels, and though the channel may not be altogether blocked, fret and impatience and worry corrode, and in time would become beyond your help.

Persevere, oh! persevere. Never lose heart. All is well.

CONSIDER:
Do I believe that God rejoices to do good to me
and bless me? Can I stretch my faith a little further and
believe that God is eager to bless me? Why are love and
trust important parts of receiving blessing from God?

Faith–Works

*Knowing that a man is not justified by the works of the law but
by faith in Jesus Christ, even we have believed in Christ Jesus,
that we might be justified by faith in Christ and not by the works
of the law; for by the works of the law no flesh shall be justified.*
GALATIANS 2:16

Pray daily for Faith. It is My Gift.

It is your only requisite for the accomplishment of mighty deeds. Certainly you have to work, you have to pray, but upon Faith alone depends the answer to your prayers—your works.

I give it you in response to your prayer, because it is the necessary weapon for you to possess for the dispersion of evil—the overcoming of all adverse conditions, and the accomplishment of all good in your lives, and then you having Faith, give it back to Me. It is the envelope in which every request to Me should be placed.

And yet "Faith without works is dead." So you need works, too, to feed your Faith in Me. As you seek to do, you feel your helplessness. You then turn to Me. In knowing Me, your faith grows—and that faith is all you need for My Power to work.

PRAY:

*Give me faith, O Lord, so I can fight Your fight in
Your strength. Give me faith so I may honor You.
Give me faith so I can live out Your will on earth.*

Love Anticipates

"Or what man is there among you who, if his son asks for bread, will give him a stone? Or if he asks for a fish, will he give him a serpent? If you then, being evil, know how to give good gifts to your children, how much more will your Father who is in heaven give good things to those who ask Him!"

MATTHEW 7:9–11

Lord, I will seek Thee.

None ever sought Me in vain. I wait, wait with a hungry longing to be called upon; and I, who have already seen your hearts' needs before you cried upon Me, before perhaps you were conscious of those needs yourself, I am already preparing the answer.

It is like a Mother, who is setting aside suitable gifts for her daughter's wedding, before Love even has come into the daughter's life.

The *Anticipatory Love* of God is a thing mortals seldom realize. Dwell on this thought. Dismiss from your minds the thought of a grudging God, who had to be petitioned with sighs and tears and much speaking before reluctantly He loosed the desired treasures. Man's thoughts of Me need revolutionizing.

Try and see a Mother preparing birthday or Christmas delights for her child—the while her Mother-heart sings: "Will she not love that? How she will love this!" and anticipates the rapture of her child, her own heart full of the tenderest joy. Where did the Mother learn all this preparation-joy? From Me—a faint echo this of My preparation-joy.

Try to see this as plans unfold of My preparing. It means much to Me to be understood, and the understanding of Me will bring great joy to you.

At One with God

*Finally, brethren, whatever things are true, whatever things are noble,
whatever things are just, whatever things are pure, whatever things are
lovely, whatever things are of good report, if there is any virtue and
if there is anything praiseworthy—meditate on these things.*
PHILIPPIANS 4:8

One with Me. I and My Father are one. One with the Lord of the whole Universe!

Could human aspiration reach higher? Could man's demands transcend this? One with Me.

If you realize your high privilege, you have only to think and immediately the object of your thought is called into being. Indeed, well may I have said, "Set your affection on things above, not on things on the earth."

To dwell in thought on the material, when once you live in Me— is to call it into being. So you must be careful only to think of and desire that which will help, not hinder, your spiritual growth. The same law operates, too, on the spiritual plane.

Think Love, and Love surrounds you, and all about whom you think. Think thoughts of *ill-will*, and ill surrounds you, and those about whom you think. Think health—health comes. The physical reflects the mental and spiritual.

CONSIDER:
What's running through my mind when I wake up?
What do I think about when I travel?
What occupies my thoughts throughout the day?

A Crowded Day

I will be glad and rejoice in You;
I will sing praise to Your name, O Most High.
PSALM 9:2

Believe that I am with you and controlling all. When My Word has gone forth, *all* are powerless against it.

Be calm. Never fear. You have much to learn. Go on until you can take the most crowded day with a song. "Sing unto the Lord." The finest accompaniment to a Song of Praise to Me is a very crowded day. Let Love be the motif running through all.

Be glad all the time. Rejoice exceedingly. Joy in Me. Rest in Me. Never be afraid. Pray more. Do not get worried. I am thy Helper. "Underneath are the Everlasting Arms." You cannot get below that. Rest in them, as a tired child rests.

PRAY:

Lord, sometimes I'm so busy that I'm just about run off my feet. I don't have time to rest and catch my breath, or barely even to take time to pray. I ask You right now to keep me from getting frustrated and burning out. Help me to rest in You even if, physically, I have to keep moving all day.

Gray Days

*Enter into His gates with thanksgiving, and into His
courts with praise. Be thankful to Him, and bless His name.*
PSALM 100:4

Be not afraid. I am your God, your Deliverer. From all evil, I will deliver you. Trust Me. Fear not.

Never forget your "Thank You." Do you not see it is a lesson? You *must* say "Thank You" on the grayest days. You *must* do it. All cannot be light unless you do. There is gray-day practice. It is absolutely necessary.

My death upon the Cross was not only necessary to save a world, it was necessary if only to train My disciples. It was all a part of their training: My entering Jerusalem in triumph; My washing the disciples' feet; My sorrow-time in Gethsemane; My being despised, judged, crucified, buried. Every step was necessary to their development— and so with you.

If a gray day is not one of thankfulness, the lesson has to be repeated until it is. Not to everyone is it so. But only to those who ask to serve Me well and to do much for Me. A great work requires a great and careful training.

CONSIDER:
*What kind of "gray day" do I have the most difficulty giving
God thanks for? Do I honestly think that God can use
such difficult times as part of my spiritual training?*

How Power Comes

You prepare a table before me in the presence of my enemies;
You anoint my head with oil; my cup runs over.
PSALM 23:5

Lord, Thou art our Refuge. Our God, in Thee
do we trust. O Master, come and talk with us.

All power is given unto Me. It is Mine to give, Mine to withhold, *but* even I have to acknowledge that I cannot withhold it from the soul that dwells near Me, because it is then not a gift, but passes insensibly from Me to My disciples.

It is breathed in by the soul who lives in My Presence.

Learn to shut yourself away in My Presence—and then, without speaking, you have those things you desire of Me, Strength—Power—Joy—Riches.

I love to steal awhile away
From every cumbering care,
And spend the hours of closing day
In humble, grateful, prayer.
PHOEBE HINSDALE BROWN (1783–1861)

Your Great Reward

Jesus said to him, "If you can believe, all things are possible to him who believes." Immediately the father of the child cried out and said with tears, "Lord, I believe; help my unbelief."
MARK 9:23–24

You pray for Faith, and you are told to do so. But I make provision in the House of My Abiding for those who turn toward Me and yet have weak knees and hearts that faint. Be not afraid. I am your God. Your Great Reward. Yours to look up and say, "All is well."

I am your Guide. Do not want to see the road ahead. Go just one step at a time. I very rarely grant the long vista to My disciples, especially in personal affairs, for one step at a time is the best way to cultivate Faith.

You are in uncharted waters. But the Lord of all Seas is with you, the Controller of all Storms is with you. Sing with joy. You follow the Lord of Limitations, as well as the God in whose service is perfect freedom.

He, the God of the Universe, confined Himself within the narrow limits of a Baby-form and, in growing Boyhood and young Manhood, submitted to your human limitations, and you have to learn that your vision and power, boundless as far as spiritual things are concerned, must in temporal affairs submit to limitations, too.

But I am with you. It was when the disciples gave up effort after a night of fruitless fishing that I came and the nets broke with the overabundance of supply.

Way of Happiness

The thief does not come except to steal, and to kill,
and to destroy. I have come that they may have life,
and that they may have it more abundantly.
JOHN 10:10

Complete surrender of every moment to God is the *foundation* of happiness; the *superstructure* is the joy of Communion with Him. And that is, for each, the place, the mansion, I went to prepare for you.

My followers have misunderstood that and looked too often upon that promise as referring only to an After-Life, and too often—far too often—upon this life as something to be struggled through in order to get the reward and the joy of the next.

Seek to carry out all I say, and such understanding, insight, vision, and joy will be yours as shall pass indeed all understanding. The plans of God are very wonderful—beyond your highest hopes.

Cling to thoughts of protection, safety, guidance.

CONSIDER:
Have I allowed the thief, the enemy of my soul, to rob me
of my joy and peace—even a little bit? Or am I living
the abundant life in the Spirit, right here and now?

PRAY:
Lead me today, O God. Give me the courage to follow.
May I seek to do all that You tell me.

Keep Calm

Casting all your care upon Him, for He cares for you.
1 PETER 5:7

Keep your Spirit-Life calm and unruffled. Nothing else matters. Leave all to Me. This is your great task, to get calm in My Presence, not to let one ruffled feeling stay for one moment. Years of blessing may be checked in one moment by that.

No matter *who* frets you or what, yours is the task to stop all else until absolute calm comes. Any block means My Power diverted into other channels.

Pour forth—pour forth—pour forth—I cannot bless a life that does not act as a channel. My Spirit brooks no stagnation, not even rest. Its Power must flow on. Pass on everything, every blessing. Abide in Me.

See how many you can bless each day. Dwell much in My Presence.

I've got peace like a river,
I've got peace like a river,
I've got peace like a river in my soul,
I've got peace like a river,
I've got peace like a river,
I've got peace like a river in my soul.
TRADITIONAL

PRAY:
Give me not to fear and worry.
Give me only to Your strength.

Height of the Storm

Lord, to whom shall we go?
thou hast the words of eternal life.
JOHN 6:68 KJV

I am with you both. Go forward unafraid. Health and strength, peace and happiness and joy—they are all My gifts. Yours for the asking. In the spiritual (as in the material) world there is no empty space, and as self and fears and worries depart out of your lives, it follows that the things of the Spirit, that you crave so, rush in to take their places. All things are yours, and ye are Christ's, and Christ is God's. What a wonderful cycle, because ye are God's.

Be not afraid. Fear not. It is to the drowning man the Rescuer comes. To the brave swimmer who can fare well alone He comes not. And no rush of Joy *can* be like that of a man towards his Rescuer.

It is a part of My method to wait till the storm is at its full violence. So did I with My disciples on the Lake. I could have bidden the first angry wave be calm, the first gust of wind be still, but what a lesson unlearned. What a sense of tender nearness of refuge and safety would have been lost.

Remember this—My disciples thought that in sleep I had forgotten them. Remember how mistaken they were. Gain strength and confidence and joyful dependence and anticipation from that.

Never fear. Joy is yours, and the radiant joy of the rescued shall be yours.

Low Ambitions

*"The Spirit of the LORD is upon Me, because He has anointed Me to preach
the gospel to the poor; He has sent Me to heal the brokenhearted,
to proclaim liberty to the captives and recovery
of sight to the blind, to set at liberty those who are oppressed."*
LUKE 4:18

Fear not. Do not fear to be busy. You are the servant of all. "He that would be the greatest among you, let him be the servant of all."

Service is the word of My disciples. I served indeed, the humblest, the lowliest. I was at their command. My highest powers were at their service.

Be used. Be used by all, by the lowest, the smallest. How best you can serve? Let that be your daily seeking, not how best can you be served.

Look around you. Do the aims and ambitions that man strives for bring peace, or the world's awards bring heart-rest and happiness? No! indeed, man is at war with man. Those whom the world has most rewarded, with name, fame, honor, wealth, are weary and disappointed.

And yet, to the listening ear, above the jangle of the world's discordant cries, there echoes down the 1900 years My message, "Come unto Me, all ye that are weary and heavy laden and I will give you rest."

And the weary and disappointed who listen and turn to Me find indeed that rest. Joy of the Weary I am, Music to the Heart I am, Health to the Sick, Wealth to the Poor, Food to the Hungry, Home to the Wanderer, Rapture to the Jaded, Love to the Lonely.

There is not *one* want of the soul that I do not supply for the asking, and to you, too, I long to be all.

I Clear the Path

Wait on the LORD.
PSALM 27:14 KJV

I am thy shield. Have no fear. You must know that "All is well." I will never let anyone do to you both, other than My Will for you.

I can see the future. I can read men's hearts. I know better than you what you need. Trust Me absolutely. You are not at the mercy of Fate, or buffeted about by others. You are being led in a very definite way, and others, who do not serve your purpose, are being moved out of your Path by Me.

Never fear, whatever may happen. You are both being led. Do not try to plan. I have planned. You are the builder, *not* the Architect.

Go very quietly, very gently. All is for the very best for you.

Trust me for all. Your very extremity will ensure My activity for you. And having your foundation on the Rock—Christ, Faith in Him, and "being rooted and grounded in Him," and having belief in My Divinity as your Corner Stone, it is yours to build, knowing all is well.

Literally, you have to depend on Me for everything—everything. It was out of the depths that David cried unto Me, and I heard his voice. All is well.

The Soul at War

They reel to and fro, and stagger like a drunken man, and are
at their wits' end. Then they cry out to the LORD in their trouble,
and He brings them out of their distresses. He calms the storm,
so that its waves are still. Then they are glad because they
are quiet; so He guides them to their desired haven.
PSALM 107:27–30

No evil can befall you if I am with you. "All that He blesses is our good." Every time of being laid aside is a time of retreat into the quiet place with Me. Never fear but in that place you shall find restoration and power and joy and healing.

Plan both of your retreat days now and then—days when you live apart with Me, and arise rested and refreshed—physically, mentally, and spiritually, to carry on the work I have given to you. I will never give you a load greater than you can bear.

Love, Joy, Peace—welcome these. Let no personal feelings, no thoughts of self banish these. Singly, they are miracle-producing in a life, but together, they can command all that is needed on the physical, mental, and spiritual planes.

It is in these wonder-realm attributes all success lies. You have to see your inner lives are all they should be, and then the work is accomplished. Not in rushing and striving on the material plane, but on the battlefield of the Soul are these things won.

Suffering Redeems

For as the sufferings of Christ abound in us, so our consolation also abounds through Christ. Now if we are afflicted, it is for your consolation and salvation, which is effective for enduring the same sufferings which we also suffer. Or if we are comforted, it is for your consolation and salvation.
2 CORINTHIANS 1:5–6

A ll sacrifice and all suffering is redemptive: to teach the individual or to be used to raise and help others.

Nothing is by chance.

Divine Mind, and its wonder working, is beyond your finite mind to understand.

No detail is forgotten in My Plans, already perfect.

O let me hear Thee speaking
In accents clear and still,
Above the storms of passion,
The murmurs of self-will.

O speak to reassure me,
To hasten, or control;
O speak, and make me listen,
Thou Guardian of my soul!

CONSIDER:
What do I think about my difficulties? Do I accept
the fact that God can use them to mold me?

Another Start

Through the LORD's mercies we are not consumed,
because His compassions fail not. They are new
every morning; great is Your faithfulness.
LAMENTATIONS 3:22–23

Take courage. Do not fear. Start a new life tomorrow. Put the old mistakes away, and start anew. I give you a fresh start. Be not burdened. Be not anxious. If My forgiveness were for the righteous only and those who had not sinned, where would be its need?

Remember as I said, "To whom much is forgiven, the same loveth much."

Why do you fret and worry so? I wait to give you all that is lovely, but your lives are soiled with worry and fret. You would crush My treasures. I can only bless glad, thankful hearts.

You *must* be glad and joyful.

Renewal and restoration are not luxuries; they are essentials.
Being alone and resting for a while is not selfish; it is Christlike.
CHARLES SWINDOLL
MAN TO MAN

PRAY:

It's a new day, Father, to love You and be loved by You, to listen to You and to be heard by You, to find and seek. Old things have been washed away! All things have become new! For this, I am grateful.

Practice Love

And if you lend to those from whom you hope to receive back,
what credit is that to you? For even sinners lend to sinners to receive
as much back. But love your enemies, do good, and lend, hoping for
nothing in return; and your reward will be great, and you will be
sons of the Most High. For He is kind to the unthankful and evil.
Therefore be merciful, just as your Father also is merciful.
LUKE 6:34–36

Watch over and protect us.

Want of Love will block the way. You *must* love all. Those that fret you and those who do not.

Practice Love. It is a great lesson, and you have a great Teacher. You *must* love; how otherwise can you dwell in Me, where nothing unloving can come? Practice this and I will bless you exceedingly, above all you cannot only ask, but imagine.

No limit to My Power. Do all you can and leave to Me the rest. Peace will come and Trust. Fear not, I am your Advocate, your Mediator.

CONSIDER:
Who would have imagined that failure to love an enemy could
block God's blessing in my life? What enemy do I need to love?
What family member or former friend do I need to forgive?

PRAY:
O God, give me Your supernatural love. Fill my heart with
Your Holy Spirit. "God is love," so I need more of You in my life!

If Men Oppose

*The king's heart is in the hand of the LORD, like the
rivers of water; He turns it wherever He wishes.*
PROVERBS 21:1

Only believe. The walls of Jericho fell down. Was it axes or human implements that brought them down? Rather the Songs of Praise of the people and My Thought carried out in action.

All walls shall fall before you, too. There is no earth-power. It falls like a house of paper at My miracle-working touch. Your faith and My power—the only two essentials. Nothing else is needed.

So, if man's petty opposition still holds good, it is only because I choose to let it stand between you and what would be a mistake for you. If not—a word—a thought—from Me, and it is gone. The hearts of Kings are in My rule and governance. All men can be moved at My wish.

Rest in this certainty. Rely on Me.

CONSIDER:
*Do I believe that God can bring down
every wall that stands against me?*

PRAY:
*Dear Lord, if what I desire is Your will, let no man stand against it.
Open a door that no man can shut. However, I yield to You if
what I want isn't Your will—at least not at this time.*

Drop Your Crutch

When my father and my mother forsake me, then the
LORD will take care of me. Teach me Your way, O LORD,
and lead me in a smooth path, because of my enemies.
PSALM 27:10–11

Just go step by step. My will shall be revealed as you go. You will never cease to be thankful for this time when you felt at peace and trustful and yet had no human security.

That is the time of the True learning of trust in Me. "When thy father and mother forsake thee, then the Lord will take thee up." This is a literal dependence on Me.

When human support or material help of any kind is removed, then My power can become operative. I cannot teach a man to walk who is trusting to a crutch. Away with your crutch, and My power shall so invigorate you that you shall indeed walk on to victory. Never limit My power. It is limitless.

CONSIDER:
Do I truly believe that God's power is limitless—even now, today—
or do I believe that He only did miracles back in Bible days? Do I
limit Him with a skeptical attitude and lack of faith? Why, before
God does miracles, does He so often first allow me to get into
predicaments that no person can, or is willing to, get me out of?

PRAY:
Thank You for the support You have given me in friends and
family, but help me remember that my true help comes from You.
People can and will fail me, but You, Lord, will never fail me.

You Shall Know

*Trust in the LORD with all your heart, and lean not on your own
understanding; in all your ways acknowledge Him, and He shall direct
your paths. Do not be wise in your own eyes; fear the LORD and depart
from evil. It will be health to your flesh, and strength to your bones.*
PROVERBS 3:5–8

Walk with Me. I will teach you. Listen to Me and I will speak.
Continue to meet Me, in spite of all opposition and every
obstacle, in spite of days when you may hear no voice, and there may
come no intimate heart-to-heart telling.

As you persist in this, and make a life-habit of it, in many
marvelous ways I will reveal My will to you. You shall have more sure
knowing of both the present and the future. But that will be only the
reward of the regular coming to meet Me.

Life is a school. There are many teachers. Not to everyone do I
come personally. Believe literally that the problems and difficulties of
your lives can be explained by Me more clearly and effectually than by
any other.

CONSIDER:
*Do I sometimes pray for days—or even weeks—without
hearing God's voice, without feeling that He loves me,
without even sensing His presence? Why is it vital to persist in
prayer even when it seems, in the natural, that God is ignoring me?*

PRAY:
*Lord, I will love You and seek You even when You
are silent, because I know that You do hear me.*

God's Longing

Therefore the LORD will wait, that He may be gracious to you;
and therefore He will be exalted, that He may have mercy on you.
For the LORD is a God of justice; blessed are all those who wait for Him.
ISAIAH 30:18

To the listening ear I speak, to the waiting heart I come. Sometimes I may not speak. I may ask you merely to wait in My Presence, to know that I am with you.

Think of the multitudes who thronged Me when I was on earth all eager for something. Eager to be healed or taught or fed.

Think as I supplied their many wants, and granted their manifold requests what it meant to Me, to find amid the crowd, some one or two who followed Me just to be near Me, just to dwell in My Presence. How some longing of the Eternal Heart was satisfied thereby.

Comfort Me awhile by letting Me know that you would seek Me just to dwell in My Presence, to be near Me, not even for teaching, not for material gain, not even for a message—but for Me. The longing of the human heart to be loved for itself is something caught from the Great Divine Heart.

I bless you. Bow your heads.

PRAY:
Father, thank You for Your presence. May there
be times that I draw near to You, not because of
anything I need, but simply because I love You.

Light Ahead

> *I will bring the one-third through the fire, will refine them*
> *as silver is refined, and test them as gold is tested. They will call on*
> *My name, and I will answer them. I will say, "This is My people";*
> *and each one will say, "The LORD is my God."*
> ZECHARIAH 13:9

Trust and be not afraid. Life is full of wonder. Open child-trusting eyes to all I am doing for you. Fear not.

Only a few steps more and then My Power shall be seen and known. You are, yourselves, now walking in the tunnel-darkness. Soon, you yourselves shall be lights to guide feet that are afraid.

The cries of your sufferings have pierced even to the ears of God Himself—My Father in Heaven, your Father in Heaven. To hear, with God, is to answer. For only a cry from the heart, a cry to Divine Power to help human weakness, a trusting cry, ever reaches the Ear Divine.

Remember, trembling heart, that with God, to hear is to answer. Your prayers, and they have been many, are answered.

CONSIDER:
Do I believe God will hear and answer me? Do I look for
His response? Do I know He has my best interests at heart?

PRAY:
Lord, I have shared my heart's desires with You.
Please help me. But most of all, whatever the answers You give,
make me like You, because I know that is Your heart's desire.

On Me Alone

*Whom have I in heaven but You? And there is none upon
earth that I desire besides You. My flesh and my heart fail;
but God is the strength of my heart and my portion forever.*
PSALM 73:25–26

I am your Lord, your Supply. You *must* rely on Me. Trust to the last
uttermost limit. Trust and be not afraid. You must depend on Divine
Power *only*. I have not forgotten you. Your help is coming. You shall
know and realize My Power.

Endurance is faith tried almost to the breaking point. You must
wait and trust and hope and joy in Me. You must not depend on man
but on Me—on Me, your Strength, your Help, your Supply.

This is the great test. Am *I* your supply or not? Every great work
for Me has had to have this great test-time.

Possess your souls in patience and rejoice. You must wait until I
show the way. Heaven itself cannot contain more joy than that soul
knows, when, after the waiting-test, I crown it Victor, but no disciple
of Mine can be victor, who does not wait until I give the order to start.
You cannot be anxious if you *know* that I am your supply.

*If God is the Creator and we are the creation,
we have to depend on him for life and provision.*
HENRY CLOUD AND JOHN TOWNSEND
HOW PEOPLE GROW

The Voice Divine

Now we have received, not the spirit of the world, but the Spirit who is from God, that we might know the things that have been freely given to us by God. These things we also speak, not in words which man's wisdom teaches but which the Holy Spirit teaches, comparing spiritual things with spiritual.
1 CORINTHIANS 2:12–13

The Divine Voice is not always expressed in words. It is made known as a heart-consciousness.

I hear Thy welcome voice
That calls me, Lord, to Thee,
For cleansing in Thy precious blood
That flowed on Calvary.

I am coming Lord!
Coming now to Thee!
Wash me, cleanse me in the blood
That flowed on Calvary!

'Tis Jesus calls me on
To perfect faith and love,
To perfect hope and peace and trust,
For earth and heav'n above.

'Tis Jesus Who confirms
The blessed work within,
By adding grace to welcomed grace,
Where reigned the power of sin.
UNKNOWN

The Lifeline

*If you abide in Me, and My words abide in you, you will ask what
you desire, and it shall be done for you. By this My Father is
glorified, that you bear much fruit; so you will be My disciples.*
JOHN 15:7–8

I am your Savior, your Savior from sins' thralls, your Savior from all the
cares and troubles of life, your Savior from disease.

I speak in all to you both. Look to Me for salvation. Trust in Me
for help. Did not My servant of old say, "All Thy waves and Thy billows
are gone over me?" But not all the waters of affliction could drown him.
For of him was it true, "He came from above, He took me, He drew me
out of many waters."

The lifeline, the line of rescue, is the line from the soul to God,
faith, and power. It is a strong line, and no soul can be overwhelmed
who is linked to Me by it. Trust, trust, trust. Never be afraid.

Think of My trees stripped of their beauty, pruned, cut, disfigured,
bare, but through the dark, seemingly dead branches flows silently,
secretly, the spirit-life-sap, till, lo! with the sun of Spring comes new
life, leaves, bud, blossom, fruit, but oh! fruit a thousand times better for
the pruning.

Remember that you are in the hands of a Master-Gardener. He
makes no mistakes about His pruning. Rejoice. Joy is the Spirit's
reaching out to say its thanks to Me. It is the new life—sap of the tree,
reaching out to Me to find such beautiful expression later. So never
cease to joy. Rejoice.

The Difficult Path

*Wait on the LORD; be of good courage, and He shall
strengthen your heart; wait, I say, on the LORD!*
PSALM 27:14

Your path is difficult, difficult for you both. There is no work
in life so hard as waiting, and yet I say wait. Wait until I show
you My Will. Proof it is of My Love and of My certainty of your true
discipleship, that I give you both hard tasks.

Again, I say wait. All motion is more easy than calm waiting.
So many of My followers have marred their work and hindered the
progress of My Kingdom by activity.

Wait. I will not overtry your spiritual strength. You are both like
two persons, helpless on a raft in mid-ocean. But, lo! there cometh
toward you One walking on the waters, like unto the Son of Man.
When He comes and you receive Him, it will be with you, as it was
with My Disciples when I was on earth, that straightway you will be at
the place where you would be.

All your toil in rowing and all your activity could not have
accomplished the journey so soon. Oh, wait and trust. Wait,
and be not afraid.

Meet Me Everywhere

*You have turned for me my mourning into dancing; You have
put off my sackcloth and clothed me with gladness, to the
end that my glory may sing praise to You and not be silent.
O LORD my God, I will give thanks to You forever.*
PSALM 30:11–12

L ife is really consciousness of Me.

Have no fear. A very beautiful future lies before you. Let it be
a new life, a new existence, in which in every single happening, event,
plan, you are conscious of Me.

"And this is life eternal, that they might know thee, and Jesus
Christ, whom thou hast sent."

Get this ever-consciousness and you have Eternal Life—the Life
of the Ages. Be in all things led by the Spirit of God and trust Me in
all. And the consciousness of Me must bring Joy. Give Me not only
trust but gladness.

CONSIDER:
*It's natural to be conscious of my own thoughts, desires, and needs—
so natural, in fact, that it takes a special effort to become conscious
of God's thoughts and desires for my life. Am I willing to take the
time to quiet my spirit, to "be still and know that He is God"?
How often do I dwell in His presence? How well do I know God?*

PRAY:
*Teach me of eternal life, the life that only You can give.
Teach me how to follow You and live the life You'd have me live.*

Near the Goal

Brethren, I do not count myself to have apprehended;
but one thing I do, forgetting those things which are behind and
reaching forward to those things which are ahead, I press toward
the goal for the prize of the upward call of God in Christ Jesus.
PHILIPPIANS 3:13–14

In a race it is not the start that hurts, not the even pace of the long stretch. It is when the goal is in sight that heart and nerves and courage and muscles are strained almost beyond human endurance, almost to the breaking point.

So with you now the goal is in sight, you need your final cry to Me. Can you not see by the nerve and heart rack of the past few days that your race is nearly run? Courage, courage. Heed My voice of encouragement. Remember that I am by your side, spurring you on to victory.

In the annals of heaven, the saddest records are those that tell of the many who ran well, with brave, stout hearts, until in sight of the goal, of victory, and then their courage failed. The whole host of heaven longed to cry out how near the end was, to implore the last spurt, but they fell out, never to know until the last day of revealing how near they were to victory.

Would that they had listened to Me in the silence as you two meet with Me. They would have known. There must be the listening ear, as well as the still small voice.

In My Presence

For a day in Your courts is better than a thousand.
I would rather be a doorkeeper in the house of my God
than dwell in the tents of wickedness. For the LORD God
is a sun and shield; the LORD will give grace and glory;
no good thing will He withhold from those who walk uprightly.
PSALM 84:10–11

You do not realize that you would have broken down under the weight of your cares but for the renewing time with Me. It is not what I say; it is I, Myself. It is not the hearing Me so much as the being in My Presence. The strengthening and curative powers of this you cannot know. Such knowledge is beyond your human reckoning.

This would cure the poor sick world, if every day each soul or group of souls waited before Me. Remember that you must never fail to keep this time apart with Me. Gradually you will be transformed, physically, mentally, spiritually, into My likeness. All who see you or have contact with you will be, by this communion with you, brought near to Me, and gradually the influence will spread.

You are making one spot of earth a Holy Place, and though you must work and spend yourself ceaselessly because that is for the present your appointed task, yet the greatest work either of you can do, and are doing, is done in this time apart with Me. Are you understanding that?

Do you know that every thought, every activity, every prayer, every longing of the day is gathered up and offered to Me, now? Oh! Joy that I am with you. For this I came to earth, to lead man back to spirit-converse with his God.

Inspiration—Not Aspiration

*And whatever you do, do it heartily, as to the Lord
and not to men, knowing that from the Lord you will receive
the reward of the inheritance; for you serve the Lord Christ.*
COLOSSIANS 3:23–24

You shall be used. The Divine Force is never less. It is sufficient for all the work in the world. I only need the instruments for Me to use. To know that would remake the world.

The world does not need supermen, but supernatural men. Men who will persistently turn the self out of their lives and let Divine Power work through them. England could be saved tomorrow if only her politicians just let Me use them.

Let inspiration take the place of aspiration. All unemployment would cease. I have always plenty of work to be done and always pay My workpeople well as you will see, as more and more you get the right attitude of thought about the work being Mine only.

CONSIDER:
*Am I allowing God's divine power to work through me?
How can I change my attitude so that I let His
inspiration take the place of my aspiration?*

PRAY:
*Dear God, help me become more of a supernatural person—
to depend upon Your power rather than striving in my limited power.*

Never Ruffled

But know that the LORD has set apart for Himself him who is godly;
the LORD will hear when I call to Him. Be angry, and do not sin.
Meditate within your heart on your bed, and be still. Selah.
Offer the sacrifices of righteousness, and put your trust in the LORD.
PSALM 4:3–5

Even were I never to speak to you, you would be well rewarded for setting apart this time, if you only sat still and longed for Me, if you just drew hungering breaths for Me, as you do for the fresh pure air of the open.

Be still, be calm. Wait before Me. Learn of Me, patience, humility, peace. When will you be absolutely unruffled whatever happens? You are slow to learn your lesson. In the rush and work and worry, the very seeking of silence must help.

In bustle so little is accomplished. You must learn to take the calm with you in the most hurried days.

God, let me simply long for You
Without a word of uttered prayer.
Let me breathe Your presence in,
Just as I would the morning air.
May I approach Your Throne of Grace
And just rest with You there.

Psychic Powers

Not forsaking the assembling of ourselves together,
as is the manner of some, but exhorting one another,
and so much the more as you see the Day approaching.
HEBREWS 10:25

Psychic powers are not necessarily Spiritual Powers. Do not seek the spiritual through material means. Could you but see, it is weighing beautiful spirit-wings down with earth's mud.

Seek *this* time as a time of communion with Me—not as a time to ask questions and have them answered. And meet Me in Communion. It is soul-food that I have provided.

Do not expect a perfect Church, but find in a church the means of coming very near to Me. That alone matters, then the much, that is husk, falls away. Hold it of no account. Grasp the truth and find Me—the true Bread of Life. The lesson of the grain is the lesson of My Church and Me. The real life is all that matters, the outward Church is the husk; but the husk was necessary to present the life-grain to man.

CONSIDER:
Am I unsatisfied with my present church? Should I seek
another church, or seek God and draw near to Him where I am?

PRAY:
Lord, help me to feast on the Bread of Life, and to take
no account of the husks, the outer forms, it's delivered in.

Let Me Do It

"If a son asks for bread from any father among you, will he give him a stone? Or if he asks for a fish, will he give him a serpent instead of a fish? Or if he asks for an egg, will he offer him a scorpion? If you then, being evil, know how to give good gifts to your children, how much more will your heavenly Father give the Holy Spirit to those who ask him!"
LUKE 11:11–13

Never miss these times. It is not what I reveal to you so much as the linking up of your frail natures with the limitless Divine Powers. Already, forces are set in motion. Only My Will is coming to pass. And now God is blessing you very richly.

You think that there is much to *do* in a crisis like this. There is only *one* thing to do. Link your lives onto the Divine Forces, and then, it is as much My work to see those lives and their affairs run in an orderly right manner as to see that tomorrow's sun rises.

It is not passionate appeal that gains the Divine Ear so much as the quiet placing of the difficulty and worry in the Divine Hands. So trust and be no more afraid than a child would be, who places its tangled skein of wool in the hands of a loving mother and runs out to play, pleasing the mother more by its unquestioning confidence than if it went down on its knees and implored her help, which would pain her the rather, as it would imply she was not eager to help when help was needed.

Endure

*You therefore must endure hardship
as a good soldier of Jesus Christ.*
2 TIMOTHY 2:3

Do not forget to meet all your difficulties with love and laughter. Be assured that I am with you. Remember, remember it is the last few yards that tell. Do not fail Me. I *cannot* fail you. Rest in My love.

How many of the world's prayers have gone unanswered because My children who prayed did not endure to the end. They thought it was too late, and that they must act for themselves, that I was not going to act for them. Remember My words: "He that endureth to the end shall be saved."

Can *you* endure to the end? If so, *you* shall be saved. But endure with courage, with Love and laughter. Oh! My children, is My training too hard?

For you, My children, I will unlock the secret treasures hidden from so many. Not one of your cries is unheard. I am with you indeed to aid you. Go through all I have said to you, and live in every detail as I have enjoined you. As you follow implicitly all I say, success—spiritual, mental, and physical—shall be yours. Wait in silence awhile, conscious of My presence, in which you must live to have rest unto your souls, and Power and Joy and Peace.

Claim Your Rights

*Be anxious for nothing, but in everything by prayer and
supplication, with thanksgiving, let your requests be made known
to God; and the peace of God, which surpasses all understanding,
will guard your hearts and minds through Christ Jesus.*
PHILIPPIANS 4:6–7

"In every thing by prayer and supplication let your requests be made known unto God."

But do not beg. Rather, come just as a business manager bringing to the owner the needs, checks to be signed, etc., and knowing that to lay the matter before him means immediate supply.

I long to supply, but the asking—or the faith-assurance from you, is necessary, because to you that contact with Me is vital.

CONSIDER:

*Does my spirit resonate with the picture of me as a business manager
bringing God checks to sign—or does that seem impersonal?
Do I feel that the Owner of the Universe loves me and desires
to fulfill my requests, or do I feel that I have a distant relationship
where I'm compelled to beg for my needs?*

Nothing Can Hurt

*I have taught you in the way of wisdom; I have led you
in right paths. When you walk, your steps will not be
hindered, and when you run, you will not stumble.*
PROVERBS 4:11–12

The way is plain.

You do not need to see far ahead. Just one step at a time
with Me. The same light to guide you as the Hosts of Heaven
know—the Son of Righteousness Himself.

Only self can cast a shadow on the way. Be more afraid of
Spirit-unrest, of soul-disturbance, of any ruffling of the Spirit,
than of earthquake or fire or any outside forces.

When you feel the absolute calm has been broken—come away
alone with Me until your heart sings and all is strong and calm.

These are the only times when evil can find an entrance. The forces
of evil surround the city of man-soul and are keenly alert for one such
unguarded spot through which an arrow can pierce and do havoc.

Remember all that you have to do is to keep calm and happy. God
does the rest. No evil force can hinder My Power—only you yourself
have power to do that. Think when all God's mighty forces are arrayed
to aid you—and your poor, puny self impedes their onward march.

You Must Trust

So the Lord said, "If you have faith as a mustard seed,
you can say to this mulberry tree, 'Be pulled up by the roots
and be planted in the sea,' and it would obey you."
LUKE 17:6

You *must* trust Me wholly. This lesson has to be learnt. You shall be helped, you shall be led, guided, continually. The children of Israel would long before have entered the Promised Land—only their doubts and fears continually drove them back into the wilderness. Remember always, doubts delay. Are you trusting all to Me or not?

I have told you how to live, and you must do it. My children, I love you. Trust My tender Love. It will never fail you, but you must learn not to fail it.

Oh! could you see, you would understand. You have much to learn in turning out fear and being at peace. All your doubts arrest My work. You must not doubt. I died to save you from sin and doubt and worry. You must believe in Me absolutely.

Why should I make a man my trust?
Princes must die and turn to dust;
Happy the man whose hopes rely
On Israel's God: He made the sky,
And earth, and seas, with all their train;
His truth for ever stands secure,
He saves th'oppressed, He feeds the poor,
And none shall find His promise vain.
ISAAC WATTS (1674–1748)

PRAY:
Please increase my faith in You,
my God and my Provider.

Secret of Healing

Behold, I will do a new thing, now it shall spring forth; shall you not know it? I will even make a road in the wilderness and rivers in the desert.
ISAIAH 43:19

Love the busy life. It is a joy-filled life. I love you both and bid you be of good cheer. Take your fill of joy in the Spring.

Live outside whenever possible. Sun and air are My great healing forces, and that inward Joy that changes poisoned blood to a pure, healthy, life-giving flow.

Never forget that real healing of body, mind, and Spirit comes from within, from the close loving contact of your spirit with My Spirit.

When you see a beautiful painting, praise the artist.
When you hear a beautiful song, praise the composer.
When you experience beauty in nature, praise the Creator.
BRUCE BICKEL AND STAN JANTZ
GOD IS IN THE SMALL STUFF

CONSIDER:
Even secular studies agree that positive thoughts and laughter
are great healing forces, so why would I not embrace peaceful,
joyful attitudes, since God in His Word commands me to?

PRAY:
God, remind me of all the ways You work in the world,
Your Spirit within and Your handiwork all around.

Share Everything

Command those who are rich in this present age not to be haughty,
nor to trust in uncertain riches but in the living God, who gives us
richly all things to enjoy. Let them do good, that they be rich in good works,
ready to give, willing to share, storing up for themselves a good foundation
for the time to come, that they may lay hold on eternal life.
1 TIMOTHY 6:17–19

Silently the work of the Spirit is done.

Already Love is drawing others to you. Take *all* who come as sent by Me, and give them a royal welcome. It will surprise you, all that I have planned for you.

Welcome all who come with the love of both your hearts. *You* may not see the work. Today they may not need you. Tomorrow they may need you. I may send you strange visitors. Make each desire to return. Nobody must come and feel unwanted.

Share your Love, your Joy, your Happiness, your time, your food gladly with all. Such wonders will unfold. You see it all but in bud now—the glory of the open flower is beyond all your telling. Love, Joy, Peace, in richest abundance—only believe. Give out Love and all you can with a glad free heart and hand. Use all you can for others, and back will come such countless stores and blessings.

How to Conquer

But thanks be to God, who gives us the
victory through our Lord Jesus Christ.
1 CORINTHIANS 15:57

Joy is the sovereign balm for all the ills of the world, the spirit-cure for every ailment. There is nothing that Joy and Love cannot do.

Set your standard very high. Aim at conquering a world, the world all around you. Just say, "Jesus conquers"—"Jesus saves"—in the face of every doubt, every sin, every evil, every fear.

No evil can stand against that, for there is "none other Name under Heaven given among men, whereby men can be saved." To every thought of want or lack, "Jesus saves from poverty," to every fear, "Jesus saves from fear."

Do this to every ill and it will vanish, as night when sun arises.

CONSIDER:
Do I raise my standard, my battle flag, high? Do I believe that,
through Jesus, I can conquer the world around me? Do I have the
faith that I can overcome every doubt, every sin, every evil, every fear,
every financial shortcoming? How do I obtain such power?

PRAY:
God, give me the stamina to face the difficulties of this life with Your power
strengthening me. Help me to believe, deep in my spirit, that Your Son, Jesus,
has the power to conquer everything in life, and save me in all situations.

Swift Help

There is nothing lacking in your lives, because really all is yours, only you lack the faith to know it. You are like a King's daughters who sit in rags, and yet around them are stores of all they could desire.

Pray for more faith, as a thirsty man in a desert prays for rain, for water. Swift comes My help, swift and strong. Do you know what it is to feel sure that I can never fail you? As sure as you are that you still breathe? How poor is man's faith! So poor. Do you trust Me as much as you would a friend if that friend came and said he would send you help? Pray daily and most diligently that your faith may increase.

CONSIDER:

Jesus' closest disciples said to Him, "Increase our faith."
If those three words were their prayer then, shouldn't they be my heart's prayer now? The Bible also says that "without faith it is impossible to please Him," so shouldn't I pray for more faith?

PRAY:

Oh God, give me faith in You, Your power, Your love.

Spirit Sounds

Watch and pray, lest you enter into temptation.
The spirit indeed is willing, but the flesh is weak.
MATTHEW 26:41

Take time for prayer. Take more time to be alone with Me. So only will you prosper.

Realize that the hearing of Spirit Sounds is more than the hearing of all earth's noises. I am with you. Let that content you, nay, more, let that fill you with rapture.

Seek sometimes not even to hear Me. Seek a silence of spirit-understanding with Me. Be not afraid. All is well. Dwell much on what I did, as well as what I said.

Remember, I "touched her hand, and the fever left her." Not many words, just a moment's contact, and all fever left her. She was well, whole, calm, able to arise and "minister unto them."

My touch is still a potent healer. Just feel that touch. Sense My Presence, and the fever of work and care and fear just melts into nothingness—and health, joy, peace, take its place.

CONSIDER:
What do I fear in the days ahead? What do I need help with?
What requests should I take before my heavenly Father?

Perfect Work

Confess your trespasses to one another, and pray for one another, that you may be healed. The effective, fervent prayer of a righteous man avails much.
JAMES 5:16

S pend more time alone with Me.

A strength and a Joy come from such times that will add much to your friendship and much to your work.

Times of prayer are times of growth. Cut those times short and many well-filled hours of work may be profitless. Heaven's values are so different from the values of earth.

Remember that from the point of view of the Great Worker, one poor tool, working *all* the time, but doing *bad* work, is of small value compared with the sharp, keen, perfect instrument used only a short time but which turns out perfect work.

UPHILL

Does the road wind
uphill all the way?
Yes, to the very end.
Will the journey take
the whole long day?
From morn to night, my friend.
C. G. ROSSETTI

PRAY:

Father, help me remember to seek You and to not get caught in the hectic whirlwind of life. Help me remain convinced that time spent with You is time well spent.

Draw Near

*But it is good for me to draw near to God; I have put my
trust in the Lord GOD, that I may declare all Your works.*
PSALM 73:28

How little man knows and senses My need! My need of Love and
Companionship.

I came "to draw men unto Me," and sweet it is to feel hearts
drawing near in Love, not for help, as much as for tender comradeship.
Many know the need of man; few know the need of Christ.

*Today, as you hunger after His bread, remember that God
is seeking the hungry; as you long for living waters, remember
that He invites the thirsty to drink; as you seek His presence,
remember that He bids you to draw near; as you commit to
walk in His ways, remember that He is always on the alert,
looking for those who are totally committed to Him.*
ROY LESSIN
TODAY IS YOUR BEST DAY

PRAY:
*Dear Lord Jesus, I hear You calling me to Yourself.
Help me listen to that call, and respond to Your invitation.*

Shower Love

Trust in the LORD, and do good; dwell in the land, and feed on His faithfulness. Delight yourself also in the LORD, and He shall give you the desires of your heart. Commit your way to the LORD, trust also in Him, and He shall bring it to pass. He shall bring forth your righteousness as the light, and your justice as the noonday.

PSALM 37:3–6

I always hear your cry. No sound escapes Me.

Many, many in the world cry to Me, but oh! how few wait to hear Me speak to them, and yet to the soul, My speaking to it matters so much.

My words are Life. Think then, to hear Me speak is to find Life and healing and strength. Trust Me in all things. Love showered on all brings truly a quick return.

Just carry out My wishes and leave Me to carry out yours. Treat Me as Savior and King, but also with the tender intimacy of One much beloved.

Keep to the rules I have laid down for you, persistently, perseveringly, lovingly, patiently, hopefully, and in faith, and every mountain of difficulty shall be laid low, the rough places of poverty shall be made smooth, and all who know you shall know that I, your Lord, am the Lord.

Shower love.

CONSIDER:

What a thought: "Just carry out My wishes and leave Me to carry out yours." Jesus promises that if I obey Him and seek first His Kingdom, that all things I need will be given to me. If I delight myself in God, He shall give me the desires of my heart. What promises! How much do I believe them?

Spirit Words

Simon Peter answered and said, "You are the Christ, the Son of the living God." Jesus answered and said to him, "Blessed are you, Simon Bar-Jonah, for flesh and blood has not revealed this to you, but my Father who is in heaven. And I also say to you that you are Peter, and on this rock I will build My church, and the gates of Hades shall not prevail against it. And I will give you the keys of the kingdom of heaven, and whatever you bind on earth will be bound in heaven, and whatever you loose on earth will be loosed in heaven."

MATTHEW 16:16–19

The words that I speak unto you, they are spirit, and they are life." Just as much as the words I spoke to My disciples of old. This is your reward for not seeking spirit-communication through a medium. Those who do it can never know the ecstasy, the wonder, of spirit-communication as you know it.

Life, Joy, Peace, and Healing are yours in very full measure. You will see this as you go on. At first, you can hardly credit the powers I am bestowing on you.

I sent My disciples out two by two and gave them power over unclean spirits and to heal all manner of diseases.

Wonderful indeed must it have been to St. Peter to feel suddenly that His Lord's power was his.

Spirit, strength of all the weak,
Giving courage to the meek,
Teaching faltering hopes to speak;
Hear us, Holy Spirit.
THOMAS BENSON POLLOCK (1836–1896)

CONSIDER:

Am I ready to receive God's power? Am I prepared for His Spirit to work through me? When He calls, will I answer?

Grow Like Me

For whom He foreknew, He also predestined to be conformed to the
image of His Son, that He might be the firstborn among many brethren.
Moreover whom He predestined, these He also called; whom He called, these
He also justified; and whom He justified, these He also glorified. What then
shall we say to these things? If God is for us, who can be against us?
ROMANS 8:29–31

Think of Me. Look at Me often, and unconsciously you will grow
like Me.

You may never see it. The nearer you get to Me, the more will you
see your unlikeness to Me. So be comforted, My children.

Your very deep sense of failure is a sure sign that you are growing
nearer to Me. And if you desire to help others to Me, then that prayer-
desire is answered.

Remember, too, it is only struggle that hurts. In sloth, spiritual, or
mental, or physical, there is no sense of failure or discomfort, but with
action, with effort, you are conscious not of strength but of weakness—
at least, at first.

That again is a sign of Life, of spiritual growth.

And remember, My Strength is made perfect in weakness.

CONSIDER:
Am I ashamed of my weaknesses? Do I try to hide them—
even, foolishly, from God? Do I want to grow to be more like
Him even if it means my weaknesses being exposed in the process?

PRAY:
Father, I want to run from my weaknesses, instead of running to Your
strength. Give me the wisdom to trust in You rather than myself.

Key to Holiness

*And not only that, but we also glory in tribulations, knowing that
tribulation produces perseverance; and perseverance, character; and
character, hope. Now hope does not disappoint, because the love of God has
been poured out in our hearts by the Holy Spirit who was given to us.*
ROMANS 5:3–5

Draw near to Me, My children. Contact with Me is the panacea for
all ills.

Remember that Truth is many-sided. Have much tender Love and
Patience for all who do not see as you do.

The elimination of self is the key to holiness and happiness, and
can only be accomplished with My help. Study My life more. Live in
My Presence. Worship Me.

I said in Gethsemane, "If it be possible let this cup pass." I did *not*
say that there was no cup of sorrow to drink. I was scourged and spat
upon and nailed to the Cross, and I said, "Father, forgive them; for they
know not what they do."

I did *not* say that they did not do it. When My disciple, Peter,
urged Me to escape the Cross, I said, "Get thee behind Me, Satan."

When My disciples failed to help the epileptic boy, I said, "This
kind cometh not out but by Prayer and Fasting." I did *not* say, "You
imagined that he was ill. Nothing is wrong."

When the Bible says, "God has purer eyes than to behold evil," it
means to impute evil to His people. He always sees the good in people,
but remember that I "beheld the city, and wept over it."

Fear Is Evil

*Love has been perfected among us in this: that we may have boldness
in the day of judgment; because as He is, so are we in this world.
There is no fear in love; but perfect love casts out fear, because fear
involves torment. But he who fears has not been made perfect in love.*
1 JOHN 4:17–18

Have no fear. Fear is evil and "perfect Love casts out fear." There
is no room for fear in the heart in which I dwell. Fear destroys
Hope. It cannot exist where Love is or where Faith is.

Fear is the curse of the world. Man is afraid—afraid of poverty,
afraid of loneliness, afraid of unemployment, afraid of sickness.

Many, many are man's fears. Nation is afraid of nation. Fear, fear,
fear, everywhere. Fight fear as you would a plague. Turn it out of your
lives and home. Fight it singly. Fight it together. Never inspire fear. It is
an evil ally. Fear of punishment, fear of blame.

No work that employs this enemy of Mine is work for Me. Banish
it. There must be another and better way.

Ask Me, and I will show it to you.

CONSIDER:
*What am I afraid of today? What do I think that I don't
have enough of? How can I walk in faith rather than fear?*

PRAY:
*Show me the way out of fear, O Lord. Unmask the lies
that I'm tempted to believe. Help me to see the truth
of who You are and what You have promised.*

Love and Laugh

*The wind blows where it wishes, and you hear the
sound of it, but cannot tell where it comes from and
where it goes. So is everyone who is born of the Spirit.*
JOHN 3:8

Work for Me, with Me, through Me. All work to last must be
done in My Spirit. How silently My Spirit works. How gently
and gradually souls are led into My Kingdom.

Love and Laughter form the plough that prepares the ground for
the seed. Remember this. If the ground is hard, seed will not grow there.

Prepare the ground, prepare it as I say.

*Perhaps today there are loving words
Which Jesus would have me speak,
There may be now, in the paths of sin,
Some wand'rer whom I should seek;
O Savior, if Thou wilt be my guide,
Tho dark and rugged the way,
My voice shall echo the message sweet,
I'll say what You want me to say.*
CHARLES E. PRIOR (1856–1926)

CONSIDER:

*Do I realize how much my love for others prepares their
hearts to receive the truth? How does my laughter help
the process? Do I have a reason to laugh or to be joyful?*

Surprises

*But let all those rejoice who put their trust in You; let them
ever shout for joy, because You defend them; let those also who
love Your name be joyful in You. For You, O LORD, will bless the righteous;
with favor You will surround him as with a shield.*
PSALM 5:11–12

Many there are who think that I test and train and bend to My Will. I, who bade the disciples take up the cross, I loved to prepare a feast for them by the lakeside—a little glad surprise, not a necessity, as the feeding of the multitude may have seemed. I loved to give the wine-gift at the marriage feast.

As you love to plan surprises for those who understand, and joy in them, so with Me. I love to plan them for those who see My Love and tender Joy in them.

Dear to the heart of My Father are those who see not only My tears, the tears of a Savior, but the smile, the joy-smile of a friend.

---

*We need the whole song, all the verses and the
choruses to serve us as our own story unfolds
because—trust me—life is hard, but God is good.*
GLORIA GAITHER
THEN SINGS MY SOUL, BOOK 2

CONSIDER:
*Do I have difficulty seeing Jesus rejoicing over me?
What about over others?*

Heaven–Life

In this manner, therefore, pray: Our Father in heaven, hallowed be Your name. Your kingdom come. Your will be done on earth as it is in heaven.
MATTHEW 6:9–10

The Joy of the Spring shall be yours in full measure. Revel in the earth's joy. Do not you think that Nature is weary, too, of her long months of travail? There will come back a wonderful joy, if you share in her Joy now.

Nature is the embodied Spirit of My Thoughts of beauty for this world. Treat her as such—as truly My servant and messenger, as any saint who has ever lived. To realize this will bring to you both new life-joy. Share her joys and travails, and great blessings will be yours.

This is all-important, because it is not only believing certain things *about* Me that helps and heals, but knowing Me, sensing My Presence in a flower, My message in its beauty and perfume.

You can truly live a life not of earth—a heaven-life here and now. Joy—Joy—Joy.

CONSIDER:
What kind of life am I living? A heaven-life?
Am I joyful? Am I plugged into God's promises?

Nothing Is Small

*Though I speak with the tongues of men and of angels, but have not love,
I have become sounding brass or a clanging cymbal. And though I have the gift
of prophecy, and understand all mysteries and all knowledge, and though I have
all faith, so that I could remove mountains, but have not love, I am nothing.*
1 CORINTHIANS 13:1–2

Nothing is small to God. In His sight a sparrow is of greater
value than a palace, one kindly word of more importance than
a statesman's speech.

It is the Life in all that has value and the quality of the life that
determines the value. I came to give Eternal Life.

*To lead an unexamined life means to rush from
task to busy task, but not call enough time-outs
to reflect on life's larger meaning and purpose.*
PATRICK MORLEY
UNDERSTANDING YOUR MAN IN THE MIRROR

CONSIDER:
Am I living my moments as if they are a part of eternity?

PRAY:
*Father, help me see You in the little things. Teach me to experience
You in every moment and to worship You with my every breath.*

Fruit of Joy

And these things we write to you
that your joy may be full.
1 JOHN 1:4

You have to hush the heart and bid all your senses be still before you can be attuned to receive Heaven's music.

Your five senses are your means of communication with the material world, the links between your real Spirit-Life and the material manifestations around you, but you must sever all connection with them when you wish to hold Spirit-communication. They will hinder, not help.

See the good in everybody. Love the good in them. See your unworthiness compared with their worth. Love, laugh, make the world, your little world, happy.

As the ripples caused by a flung stone stir the surface of a whole pond, so your joy-making shall spread in ever-widening circles, beyond all your knowledge, all anticipation. Joy in Me. Such Joy is eternal.

Centuries after, it is still bearing Joy's precious fruit.

CONSIDER:
What can I do to bring smiles to my corner of the world today?
How can I share cheerfulness with others?

PRAY:
Father, please hush my heart
and prepare me to receive Your joy!

Seek Beauty

He has made everything beautiful in its time.
ECCLESIASTES 3:11

Draw Beauty from every flower and Joy from the song of the birds and the color of the flowers.

I am with you. When I wanted to express a beautiful thought, I made a lovely flower.

When I want to express to man what I am—what My Father is—I strive to make a very beautiful character.

Think of yourselves as My expression of attributes, as a lovely flower is My expression of thought, and you will strive in all, in Spiritual beauty, in Thought—power, in Health, in clothing, to be as fit an expression for Me as you can.

Absorb Beauty. As soon as the beauty of a flower or a tree is impressed upon your soul, it leaves an image there which reflects through your actions. Remember that no thought of sin and suffering, of the approaching scorn and Crucifixion, ever prevented My seeing the beauty of the flowers.

Look for beauty and joy in the world around. Look at a flower until its beauty becomes part of your very soul. It will be given back to the world again by you in the form of a smile or a loving word.

Listen to a bird. Take the song as a message from My Father. Let it sink into your soul. That, too, will be given back to the world in ways I have said. Laugh more, laugh often. Love more. I am with you. I am your Lord.

Simplicity

*"Whoever receives one of these little children in My name receives Me;
and whoever receives Me, receives not Me but Him who sent Me."*
MARK 9:37

Simplicity is the keynote of My Kingdom. Choose simple things always.

Love and reverence the humble and the simple.

Have only simple things here. Your standard must never be the world's standard.

*Simple means unpretentious. It means just being me.
It means no more playing proud mind-games.
It means taking my mask off and being real.
It means being free to say what I think. . .in love.
I think I could stand being simpler.*

CONSIDER:
*Jesus could have been born in a palace,
but He chose the simple surroundings of a stable.*

PRAY:
*Father, thank You for simple things. May I never complicate
my relationship with You, my family, and my friends.*

Spiritualism

*So Saul died for his unfaithfulness which he had committed
against the LORD, because he did not keep the word of the LORD,
and also because he consulted a medium for guidance.*
1 CHRONICLES 10:13

Wait before Me, gently breathing in My Spirit.

That Spirit which, if given a free entrance and not barred out by self, will enable you to do the same works as I did, which being interpreted is, will enable Me to do the same works, and even greater than I did when on earth—through you.

Spiritualism is wrong. No man should ever be a medium for any spirit other than Mine.

All you should know, all it is well for you to know of My Spirit-Kingdom, I will tell you when and how I see best. The limit is set by your own spiritual development. Follow My injunctions in all things.

Peace—Peace—Peace.

CONSIDER:

*When so many people today want a "quick answer" that
they're tempted to visit a medium or read their horoscope,
am I willing to patiently wait for God to answer?*

God's Touch

But those who wait on the LORD shall renew their strength;
they shall mount up with wings like eagles, they shall run
and not be weary, they shall walk and not faint.
ISAIAH 40:31

Near, all broodingly near, as some tender mother bird anxious over its young, I am here. I am your Lord, Life of your body and mind and soul—renewer of your youth.

You do not know all that this time of converse with Me will mean to you. Did not My servant Isaiah say, "They that wait upon the LORD shall renew their strength; they shall mount up with wings as eagles; they shall run and not be weary; they shall walk and not faint."

Persevere in all I tell you to do. The persistent carrying out of My commands, My desires, will unfailingly bring you, as far as spiritual, mental, and temporal things are concerned, to that place where you would be.

If you look back over My Words to you, you will see that My leading has been very gradual, and that only as you have carried out My wishes have I been able to give you more clear and definite teaching and guidance.

Man's ecstasy is God's touch on quickened, responsive spirit-nerves. Joy—Joy—Joy.

Your Cross Is You

Then He said to them all, "If anyone desires to come after Me,
let him deny himself, and take up his cross daily, and follow Me."
LUKE 9:23

Remember, you are only an instrument. Not yours to decide how or when or where you act. I plan all that. Make yourself very fit to do My work. All that hinders your activity must be cured.

Mine is the Cross on which the burdens of the world are laid. How foolish is any one of My disciples who seeks to bear his own burdens, when there is only one place for them—My Cross.

It is like a weary man on a hot and dusty road, bearing a heavy load, when all plans have been made for its carriage. The road, the scenery, flowers, beauty around—all are lost.

But, My children, you may think I did say, "Take up your cross daily, and follow Me."

Yes, but the cross given to each one of you is only a cross provided on which you can crucify the self of yours that hinders progress and Joy and prevents the flow through your being of My invigorating Life and Spirit.

Listen to Me, love Me, joy in Me. Rejoice.

Reflect Me

*For this reason I bow my knees to the Father of our Lord Jesus Christ,
from whom the whole family in heaven and earth is named, that He
would grant you, according to the riches of His glory, to be strengthened
with might through His Spirit in the inner man.*
EPHESIANS 3:14–16

My children, I am here beside you. Draw near in spirit to Me. Shut out the distractions of the world. I am your Life, the very breath of your soul. Learn what it is to shut yourself in the secret place of your being, which is My secret place, too.

True it is, I wait in many a heart, but so few retire into that inner place of the being to commune with Me. Wherever the soul is, I am. Man has rarely understood this. I *am* actually at the center of every man's being, but, distracted with the things of the sense-life, he finds Me not.

Do you realize that I am telling you *truths*, revealing them, not repeating oft-told facts. Meditate on all I say. Ponder it. Not to draw your own conclusions, but to absorb Mine.

All down the ages, men have been too eager to say what they thought about My truth, and so doing, they have grievously erred. Hear Me. Talk to Me. Reflect Me. Do not say what you think *about* Me. My words need none of man's explanation. I can explain to each heart.

Make Me real, and leave Me to do My own work. To lead a soul to Me is one thing, to seek to stay with it to interpret mars the first great act. So would it be with human communion. How much more then, when it is a question of the soul, and Me, its Maker, and only real Spirit that understands it.

No Greater Joy

Jesus answered and said to him, "Most assuredly, I say to you, unless one is born again, he cannot see the kingdom of God." Nicodemus said to Him, "How can a man be born when he is old? Can he enter a second time into his mother's womb and be born?" Jesus answered, "Most assuredly, I say to you, unless one is born of water and the Spirit, he cannot enter the kingdom of God."

JOHN 3:3–5

Withdraw into the calm of communion with Me. Rest—rest, rest in that calm and Peace. Life knows no greater joy than you will find in converse and companionship with Me.

You are Mine. When the soul finds its home of rest in Me, then it is that its real Life begins. Not in years, as man counts it, do we measure in My Kingdom.

We count only from his second birth, that new birth of which I spoke to Nicodemus when I said, "Ye must be born again." We know no life but Eternal Life, and when a man enters into that, then he lives.

And this is Life, Eternal, to know God, My Father and Me, the Son sent by Him. So immature, so childish, so empty is all so-called living before that. I shower Love on you. Pass Love on.

Do not fear. To fear is as foolish as if a small child with a small coin but a rich father fretted about how rent and rates should be paid and what he or she would do about it. Is this work Mine or not? You need to trust Me for everything.

Your Resolutions

Then the disciples came to Jesus privately and said, "Why could we not cast it out?" So Jesus said to them, "Because of your unbelief; for assuredly, I say to you, if you have faith as a mustard seed, you will say to this mountain, 'Move from here to there,' and it will move; and nothing will be impossible for you."
MATTHEW 17:19–20

Listen, listen, I am your Lord. Before Me there is none other. Just trust Me in everything. Help is here all the time.

The difficult way is nearly over, but you have learnt in it lessons you could learn in no other way. "The kingdom of heaven suffereth violence, and the violent take it by force." Wrest from Me, by firm and simple trust and persistent prayer, the treasures of My Kingdom.

Such wonderful things are coming to you, Joy—Peace—Assurance—Security—Health—Happiness—Laughter.

Claim big, really big, things now. Remember, nothing is too big. Satisfy the longing of My Heart to give. Blessing, abundant blessing, on you both now and always. Peace.

CONSIDER:
Do I really believe God has great things in store for me?
Do I actually think that He can do the impossible?

PRAY:
Lord, help me believe that You want to provide
for me. Keep me from thinking that Your blessings
are small. May I never limit You with small faith.

Courage

Fear not, for I am with you; be not dismayed, for I am
your God. I will strengthen you, yes, I will help you,
I will uphold you with My righteous right hand.
ISAIAH 41:10

I am here. Fear not. Can you really trust Me? I am a God of Power, as well as a Man of Love, so human yet so divine.

Just trust. I cannot, and I will not, fail you. All is well. Courage. Many are praying for you both.

The kind of trust God wants us to have
cannot be learned in comfort and ease.
ANNE GRAHAM LOTZ
WHY? TRUSTING GOD WHEN YOU DON'T UNDERSTAND

CONSIDER:
Do I always trust God? Do I believe that He will
never fail me? Do I have the courage to serve Him?

PRAY:
Lord, I'm being honest: You tell me, "Fear not," yet I'm not only tempted
to fear but I actually give in to that fear at times. You tell me, "Trust Me,"
but my faith sometimes falters when You take the training wheels off
and ask me to attempt something big. So please help me believe!

Help from Everywhere

*Commit your way to the LORD, trust also in Him,
and He shall bring it to pass. He shall bring forth your
righteousness as the light, and your justice as the noonday.*
PSALM 37:5–6

Your foolish little activities are valueless in themselves. Seemingly trivial or of seemingly great moment, all deeds are alike if directed by Me. Just cease to function except through Me.

I am your Lord; just obey Me as you would expect a faithful, willing secretary to carry out *your* directions. Just have no choice but Mine, no will but Mine.

I am dependent on no one agency when I am your supply. Through many channels My help and material flow can come.

CONSIDER:
*Am I making my choices based on God's will? Am I
surrendering to what He wants? Do I believe that if I act
in obedience that He will provide whatever needs come up?*

PRAY:
*Father, Your will not mine. Your provision, not mine.
Your strength, not mine. Your abundance, not mine.*

All Is Well

Direct my steps by Your word, and let no iniquity have dominion over me.
Redeem me from the oppression of man, that I may keep Your precepts.
Make Your face shine upon Your servant, and teach me Your statutes.
PSALM 119:133–135

Remember My Words to My disciples, "This kind goeth not out but by prayer and fasting." Can you tread the way I trod? Can you drink of My cup? "All is well." Say always, "All is well."

Long though the way may seem, there is not one inch too much. I, your Lord, am not only with you on the journey—I planned, and am planning, the journey.

There are Joys unspeakable in the way you go. Courage—courage—courage.

All the way my Savior leads me;
What have I to ask beside?
Can I doubt His tender mercy,
Who through life has been my guide?
Heav'nly peace, divinest comfort,
Here by faith in Him to dwell!
For I know whate'er befall me,
Jesus doeth all things well.
FRANCES JANE (FANNY) CROSBY (1820–1915)

PRAY:

Dear God, all really is well when I am following You. Thank You for the unspeakable joys You give me every day, whether I am observant enough to see them or not. Teach me to walk in Your way.

A Bud Opened

"So why do you worry about clothing? Consider the lilies of the field,
how they grow: they neither toil nor spin; and yet I say to you that even
Solomon in all his glory was not arrayed like one of these. Now if God so
clothes the grass of the field, which today is, and tomorrow is thrown into
the oven, will He not much more clothe you, O you of little faith?"
MATTHEW 6:28–30

To Me, your intimate Friend, all Power is given. It is given Me of My Father, and have not My intimate friends a right to ask it?

You cannot have a need I cannot supply. A flower or one thousand pounds, one is no more difficult than the other.

Your need is a spiritual need to carry on My work. All spiritual supply is fashioned from Love. The flower and the thousand pounds—both fashioned from Love to those who need it. Do you not see this?

I thought of you, a bud opened; you converted that into a cheer for one you love or a smile. That cheer meant increased health. Increased health means work for Me, and that means souls for Me.

And so it goes on, a constant supply, but only if the need is a spiritual one.

CONSIDER:

Do I trust God to supply my needs? Do I want my needs
supplied merely so that I will be comfortable and won't lack
anything, or is my motive so that I will then be free to serve God?

Until Your Heart Sings

*Let us draw near with a true heart in full assurance of faith,
having our hearts sprinkled from an evil conscience and our bodies
washed with pure water. Let us hold fast the confession of our hope
without wavering, for He who promised is faithful.*
HEBREWS 10:22–23

I am beside you to bless and help you. Waver not in your prayers. They shall be heard. All power is Mine. Say that to yourself often and steadily.

Say it until your heart sings with the Joy of the safety and power it means to you.

Say it until the very force of the utterance drives back and puts to nought all the evils against you.

Use it as a battle cry—"All power is given unto My Lord," "All power is given unto My Friend," "All power is given unto My Savior," and then you pass on to victory.

*Mortals, join the happy chorus
Which the morning stars began;
Father love is reigning o'er us,
Brother love binds man to man.
Ever singing, march we onward,
Victors in the midst of strife,
Joyful music leads us sunward
In the triumph song of life.*
HENRY VAN DYKE (1852–1933)

Know Me

Then I will give them a heart to know Me, that I am the LORD;
and they shall be My people, and I will be their God,
for they shall return to Me with their whole heart.
JEREMIAH 24:7

I am here. Seek not to know the future. Mercifully I veil it from you. Faith is too priceless a possession to be sacrificed in order to purchase knowledge. But Faith itself is based on a knowledge of Me.

So remember that this evening time is not to learn the future, not to receive revelation of the Unseen, but to gain an intimate knowledge of Me which will teach you all things and be the very foundation of your faith.

CONSIDER:
How often when I want to "hear from God" do I simply want
to know about future events? How many times do I merely
want God to tell me what others are thinking or planning?

PRAY:
I do want to know You, Father God. To simply know of You is not
enough. Teach me, as I sit before You, to reflect Your love and Your
character. Tomorrow is Yours to know. Today, I want to know You more.

Wonders Will Unfold

Looking unto Jesus, the author and finisher of our faith, who for
the joy that was set before Him endured the cross, despising the shame,
and has sat down at the right hand of the throne of God. For consider
Him who endured such hostility from sinners against Himself,
lest you become weary and discouraged in your souls.
HEBREWS 12:2–3

I am with you. Do not fear. Never doubt My Love and Power. Your heights of success will be won by the daily persistent doing of what I have said.

Daily, steady persistence. Like the wearing away of a stone by steady drops of water, so will your daily persistence wear away all the difficulties and gain success for you and secure your help for others.

Never falter, go forward so boldly, so unafraid. I am beside you to help and strengthen you.

Wonders have unfolded. More still will unfold, beyond your dreams, beyond your hopes.

Say "All is well" to everything. All *is* well.

CONSIDER:
Am I overcome with difficulties, or do I trust that God is slowly
winning the battle? Am I persistent daily in this journey of faith?

PRAY:
Dear Father, all is well. Even though difficulties abound, I know all is well
because You will settle whatever matter is troubling me, if I will be faithful
and surrender to Your will. Help me to endure, knowing this truth.

Follow Your Guide

Be angry, and do not sin. Meditate within your heart
on your bed, and be still. Selah. Offer the sacrifices
of righteousness, and put your trust in the LORD.
PSALM 4:4–5

I am with you to guide you and help you. Unseen forces are controlling your destiny. Your petty fears are groundless.

What of a man walking through a glorious glade who fretted because ahead there lay a river and he might not be able to cross it, when all the time, that river was spanned by a bridge? And what if that man had a friend who knew the way—had planned it—and assured him that at no part of the journey would any unforeseen contingency arise, and that all was well?

So leave your foolish fears, and follow Me, your Guide, and determinedly refuse to consider the problems of tomorrow. My message to you is trust and wait.

I feared the roaring river ahead;
I could not understand
Why I was led on a path so dread;
Not a bit as I'd have planned.
But when I neared I saw the bridge—
The river had been spanned!

PRAY:

Holy God, wisest of all, loving guide, give me the courage to follow You.
Banish my fear like an enemy; blow it away with the wind.
I will trust and I will wait for Your will to unfold.

Go Forward

Rest in the LORD, and wait patiently for Him;
do not fret because of him who prospers in his way,
because of the man who brings wicked schemes to pass.
PSALM 37:7

Rest in Me, quiet in My Love, strong in My Power. Think what it is to possess a Power greater than any earthly force. A sway greater, and more far-reaching, than that of any earthly king.

No invention, no electricity, no magnetism, no gold could achieve one-millionth part of all that you can achieve by the Power of My Spirit. Just think for one moment all that means.

Go forward. You are only beginning the new Life together. Joy, joy, joy.

Do not ask "what can I do?"
but "what can He not do?"
CORRIE TEN BOOM
AMAZING LOVE

CONSIDER:
Am I resting in God? Am I moving ahead each day believing
that I am cared for by a power greater than any other?

PRAY:
Thank You, God, for Your miracle-working power.
Thank You for Your supply. Thank You for caring for me.

Evil Mountains

*For assuredly, I say to you, whoever says to this mountain,
"Be removed and be cast into the sea," and does not doubt
in his heart, but believes that those things he says will
be done, he will have whatever he says.*

MARK 11:23

F aith and obedience will remove mountains, mountains of evil,
mountains of difficulty.

But they must go hand in hand.

*But we never can prove
The delights of His love
Until all on the altar we lay;
For the favor He shows
And the joy He bestows
Are for them who will trust and obey.*

*Trust and obey, for there's no other way
To be happy in Jesus, But to trust and obey.*
JOHN H. SAMMIS (1846–1919)

CONSIDER:

*Do I live my life with both faith and obedience? Do I see
mountains move? Do I see evil and difficulty move away from my
path? If not, what area must I obey God in first? How must I pray?*

A Life Apart

My beloved spoke, and said to me: "Rise up, my love, my fair one, and come away. For, lo, the winter is past, the rain is over and gone. The flowers appear on the earth; the time of singing has come, and the voice of the turtledove is heard in our land. The fig tree puts forth her green figs, and the vines with the tender grapes give a good smell. Rise up, my love, my fair one, and come away!"

SONG OF SONGS 2:10–13

I reward your seeking with My Presence. Rejoice and be glad. I am your God. Courage and joy will conquer all troubles. First things first.

Seek Me, love Me, joy in Me. I am your Guide. No perils can affright you, no discipline exhaust you. Persevere. Can you hold on in My strength? I need you more than you need Me. Struggle through this time for My sake. Initiation precedes all real work and success for Me.

Are you ready to live a life apart? Apart with Me? In the world and yet apart with Me? Going forth from your secret times of communion to rescue and save?

CONSIDER:
Do I believe that courage and joy will conquer all troubles?
Why is faith in Christ the foundation of courage and joy?

PRAY:
Lord, help me to put first things first. I know from experience that I can't have courage and joy unless I trust in You and seek Your face. Help me never to neglect my prayer time with You.

Deliverance

*"For you shall go out with joy, and be led out with peace;
the mountains and the hills shall break forth into singing
before you, and all the trees of the field shall clap their hands."*
ISAIAH 55:12

Be calm, be true, be quiet. I watch over you.

Rest in My Love. Joy in the very Beauty of Holiness. You are Mine. Deliverance is here for you, but Thankfulness and Joy open the gates.

Try in all things to be very glad, very happy, very thankful. It is not to quiet resignation I give My blessings, but to joyful acceptance and anticipation.

Laughter is the outward expression of joy. That is why I urge upon you Love and Laughter.

*Genuine, hearty laughter is one of the greatest gifts
imparted to us by our Father. It has the amazing power
to diminish our pain, lift our souls in joyous good cheer,
while providing bright hope for the unknown days ahead.*
W. PHILLIP KELLER
WHAT MAKES LIFE WORTH LIVING

CONSIDER:

*What a surprise that God doesn't delight in quiet resignation.
Do I sometimes think, when things are going badly and really
aggravating me, that "patient endurance" simply means sullenly
hunkering down and weathering the storm? What unpleasant
situations should I try to be very glad, very happy, about?*

Love's Offering

And He saw also a certain poor widow putting in two mites. So He said, "Truly I say to you that this poor widow has put in more than all; for all these out of their abundance have put in offerings for God, but she out of her poverty put in all the livelihood that she had."
LUKE 21:2–4

I am your Lord, gracious and loving. Rest in My Love; walk in My ways. Each week is a week of progress, steady progress upward. You may not see it, but I do.

I judge not by outward appearances, I judge the heart, and I see in both your hearts one single desire, to do My Will. The simplest offering by a child brought or done with the one desire to give you pleasure or to show you love—is it not more loved by you than the offerings of those who love you not?

So, though you may feel that your work has been spoiled and tarnished, I see it only as Love's offering. Courage, My children.

When climbing a steep hill, a man is often more conscious of the weakness of his stumbling feet than of the view, the grandeur, or even of his upward progress.

Persevere, persevere. Love and laugh. Rejoice.

PRAY:

Lord, I believe You know that I love You, despite my stumblings. I believe that my efforts to please You, actually do please You. I'm sometimes so hard on myself, but help me to see myself the way You see me.

Shut Out from God

*Let this mind be in you which was also in Christ Jesus, who, being in the
form of God, did not consider it robbery to be equal with God, but made
Himself of no reputation, taking the form of a bondservant, and coming in
the likeness of men. And being found in appearance as a man, He humbled
Himself and became obedient to the point of death, even the death of the cross.*
PHILIPPIANS 2:5–8

Do you not see, My children, that you have not yet learned all?
Soon, very soon, you will have mastered your lesson, and then you
will truly be able to do all things through Me and My Strength.

Did you not see it with My Disciples? Timid, faithless followers,
and then, so soon, themselves leaders, healers, conquerors, through Me.

All knowledge was Mine, given Me of My Father, and Mine in
manhood's years on earth. You understand this, My children, I know
you do.

Thousands of My servants have gone to their betrayal and death,
and others, who knew Me not, with no agony before it.

Had I not been Son of God, bearing man's weight of sin,
voluntarily bearing it until of My own free will—for that moment's
horror, I was shut out from His sight with man, the sinner, for one
short space—had I not been God, had not this been My suffering—
then I was but a craven mortal.

CONSIDER:
How do I live my life in light of Jesus' sacrifice?
Do I live my life in His strength?

The Priceless Blessing

You have commanded us to keep Your precepts diligently.
Oh, that my ways were directed to keep Your statutes! Then I
would not be ashamed, when I look into all Your commandments.
PSALM 119:4–6

I am here. Here as truly as I was with My Disciples of old. Here to help and bless you. Here to company with you. Do you know, even yet, My children, that this is the priceless blessing of your lives? I forgive you, as you have prayed Me to, for all neglects of My commands, but start anew from today.

Study My words and carry them out unflinchingly, unflinchingly. As you do this, you will find that you are miracle-workers, workers together with Me—for Me. Remember this, not what you *do*, but what you are—that is the miracle-working power.

Changed by My Spirit, shedding one garment of Spirit for a better; in time throwing that aside for a yet finer one, and so on from character to character, gradually transformed into My likeness.

Joy, joy, joy.

CONSIDER:
God wants to transform me spiritually.
How can I cooperate with that process?

PRAY:
Father, I am Yours. I yield my heart
to Your Spirit. Make me like You.

Greatness Is Service

And do not be called teachers; for One is your Teacher, the Christ.
But he who is greatest among you shall be your servant. And whoever exalts
himself will be humbled, and he who humbles himself will be exalted.
MATTHEW 23:10–12

My children, I am here, your waiting Lord, ready at your call. I am among you as one that serveth, Meek and Holy, ready to be used and commanded. Remember that is the finest quality of greatness— service. I, who could command a universe—I await the commands of My children. Bring Me into everything.

You will find such Joy as the time goes on in speaking to each other of Me, and together climbing higher. Always humble, meek, and lowly in heart.

Learn this—no position—just a servant.

CONSIDER:
How can I be a servant to others this week?

PRAY:
Dear Lord, show me what's in my heart. Help me see
the ways I can serve others as a way of serving You.

Divine Efficiency

Then Peter said to them, "Repent, and let every one of you be baptized in the name of Jesus Christ for the remission of sins; and you shall receive the gift of the Holy Spirit. For the promise is to you and to your children, and to all who are afar off, as many as the Lord our God will call." And with many other words he testified and exhorted them, saying, "Be saved from this perverse generation."

ACTS 2:38–40

I am all-powerful and all-knowing, and I have all your affairs in My Hands. Divine efficiency as well as Divine power is being brought to bear on them. All miracle-work is not the work of a moment as so often men imagine.

My servant Peter was not changed in a flash from a simple fisherman to a great leader and teacher, but through the very time of faithlessness—through the very time of denial—I was yet making him all that he should be. Impetuous spokesman as he always was, ready to lead the other disciples, Peter could never have been the after power he was, had he not learned his weakness. No man can save unless he understands the sinner.

The Peter who was a mighty force for Me afterwards, who, more than all others, founded My church, was not even first the Peter who said, "Thou art the Christ, the Son of the living God," but the Peter who denied Me. He who had tested My forgiveness in his moment of abject remorse, he could best speak of Me as the Savior.

The Kingdom of Heaven can only be preached by those who have learned to prize the authority of its Kingdom. A many-sided training My Apostles need. Oh! joy. Oh, rejoice. I love you. Not one test too much will I lay on you.

Heart's Interpreter

Thus says the LORD: "Stand in the ways and see, and ask for the old paths, where the good way is, and walk in it; then you will find rest for your souls. But they said, 'We will not walk in it.'"
JEREMIAH 6:16

Rest in Me. Seek this evening time just to be with Me. Do not feel you have failed if sometimes I ask you only to rest together in My Presence.

I am with you, much with you both, not only at these times, at all times. Feel conscious of My Presence. Earth has no greater joy than that.

I am the heart's great Interpreter. Even souls who are the nearest together have much in their natures that remain a sealed book to each other, and only as I enter and control their lives do I reveal to each the mysteries of the other.

Each soul is so different—I alone understand perfectly the language of each and can interpret between the two.

We shouldn't ever hesitate to invite God in on the details of our days. He already knows them, and He cares enough to want to be a part of them.
LAURIE LOVEJOY HILLIARD AND SHARON LOVEJOY AUTRY
HOLD YOU, MOMMY

CONSIDER:
What keeps me from sitting still before God's presence allowing His Spirit to search my heart? Busyness? Fear?

Easter Joy

*But the angel answered and said to the women, "Do not be afraid,
for I know that you seek Jesus who was crucified. He is not here;
for He is risen, as He said. Come, see the place where the Lord lay.
And go quickly and tell His disciples that He is risen from the dead."*
MATTHEW 28:5–7

I lay My loving Hands on you in blessing. Wait in Love and longing to feel their tender pressure and, as you wait, courage and hope will flow into your being, irradiating all your lives with the warm sun of My Presence.

Let all go this Eastertide. Loosen your hold on earth, its care, its worries, even its joys. Unclasp your hands, relax, and then the tide of Easter Joy will come. Put aside all thought of the future, of the past. Relinquish all to get the Easter Sacrament of Spiritual Life.

So often man, crying out for some blessing, has yet such tight hold on some earth-treasure that he has no hand to receive Mine, as I hold it out in Love. Easter is the wonder-time of all the year. A blessing is yours to take. Sacrifice all to that.

CONSIDER:
*Do I live a life filled with God's abundance? What earthly
treasure do I need to let go of to obtain a fuller spiritual life?*

PRAY:
*Jesus, You conquered death and offer me a part of that victory.
Thank You. Teach me to live out Easter in my everyday moments.*

Calvary

Most assuredly, I say to you, unless a grain of wheat falls
into the ground and dies, it remains alone; but if it dies,
it produces much grain. He who loves his life will lose it,
and he who hates his life in this world will keep it for eternal life.
JOHN 12:24–25

F rom the death of My Body on the Cross, as from the shedding of husks in seed-life, springs that New Life which is My Gift to every man who will accept it.

Die with Me to self—to the human life, and then you will know the rapturous Joy of Easter Resurrection.

A Risen Life so glad and free can be yours.

Mary left home and kindred, friends, all, that Easter morning in her search for Me, and not until the "Mary" had been followed by the glad triumphant rapture of her "Rabboni" was her search over.

So with each of you. Man speaks to you, too, of a buried Christ. Search until you meet Me face-to-face, and My tender uttering of your name awakes your glad "Rabboni."

CONSIDER:

In practical terms, what will it mean for me to "die to self"? What bad
habits must I crucify? What self-centered desires must be put to death?
What perfectly normal rights must I be willing to surrender? And how
will I know the rapturous joy of Easter resurrection? How do I believe
that God will reward me—in this life? In heaven?

PRAY:

Dear Lord, because of Your death and Your glorious resurrection, I have a
new life. I have been born again. May I walk in Your Spirit, triumphant.

Marks of the Kingdom

*"'Now therefore, if you will indeed obey My voice and keep My covenant,
then you shall be a special treasure to Me above all people; for all the earth
is Mine. And you shall be to Me a kingdom of priests and a holy nation.'
These are the words which you shall speak to the children of Israel."*
EXODUS 19:5–6

*Our Savior, we greet Thee. Thy Love and Sacrifice we
would return in our poor faulty measure by Love and sacrifice.*

No gift is poor if it expresses the true Love of the giver. So to
Me your heart's gifts are rich and precious. Rejoice in My glad
acceptance as you bring your Easter offerings.

My children must make a stand. "Come ye out from among them
and be ye separate" was the command. Today in life and work, in Love
and service, My children must be outstanding. I called a Peculiar People
to make known My Name. My servant Paul said that My followers
must be willing to be deemed "fools" for My Sake.

Be ready to stand aside and let the fashions and customs of the
world go by, when My Glory and My Kingdom are thereby served. Be
known by the Marks that distinguish those of My Kingdom. Be ready
to confess Me before men. To count all things as loss so that you may
gain Me in your lives.

CONSIDER:

*In what ways do I stand out because of my faith? Am I
merely a product of my culture, or does my belief in Jesus
Christ bring a depth to my life that outlasts fads and fashions?*

Risen Life

Arise, shine; for thy light is come,
and the glory of the LORD is risen upon thee.
ISAIAH 60:1 KJV

The Call comes on this My Day for all who love Me, to arise from earth-bands, from sin, and sloth and depression, distrust, fear, all that hinders the Risen Life. To arise to Beauty, to Holiness, to Joy, to Peace, to work inspired by Love and Joy, to rise from death to Life.

Remember that death was the last enemy I destroyed. So with death My Victory was complete. You have nothing then to fear. Sin, too, is conquered and forgiven, as you live and move and work with Me. All that depresses you, all that you fear, are powerless to harm you. They are but phantoms. The real forces I conquered in the wilderness, the Garden of Gethsemane, on the Cross, in the Tomb.

Let nothing hinder your Risen Life. "Risen with Christ," said My servant Paul. Seek to know more and more of that Risen Life. That is the Life of Conquest. Of that Risen Life was it truly said: "I live; yet not I, but Christ liveth in me." Fear and despair and tears come as you stand by the empty Tomb. "They have taken away my Lord, and I know not where they have laid him."

Rise from your fears and go out into the sunlight to meet Me, your Risen Lord. Each day will have much in it that you will meet either in the spirit of the tomb, or in the spirit of Ressurection. Deliberately choose the one and reject the other.

Pride Bars the Way

Blessed is the man who walks not in the counsel of the ungodly,
nor stands in the path of sinners, nor sits in the seat of the scornful;
but his delight is in the law of the LORD, and in His law
he meditates day and night.

PSALM 1:1–2

Obedience is one of the keys unlocking the door into My Kingdom, so love and obey. No man can obey Me implicitly without in time realizing My Love, in his turn responding by love to that Love, and then experiencing the joy of the beloved and the lover.

The rough stone steps of obedience lead up to the mosaic of Joy and Love that floor My Heaven. As one on earth who loves another says, "Where you are is home," so it is in relation with Me. Where I am is My Home—is Heaven.

Heaven may be in a sordid slum or a palace, and I can make My Home in the humblest heart. I can only dwell with the humble. Pride stands sentinel at the door of the heart to shut out the lowly, humble Christ.

CONSIDER:

What powerful word pictures! Obedience is a key unlocking the door; it is the rough stone steps leading up to heaven. How careful am I to obey God's commands? Do I strive to be obedient?

PRAY:

Father, remove pride from my heart—thoughts that I am so gifted and special that I don't need You, that I can accomplish great things on my own. Help me to be humble, and to admit that I need Your help.

Hold Your Fort

Come out from among them and be separate, says the Lord. Do not touch what is unclean, and I will receive you. I will be a Father to you, and you shall be my sons and daughters, says the LORD Almighty.
2 CORINTHIANS 6:17–18

Remember that My followers are to be a peculiar people, separated from among others. Different ways, a different standard of living, different customs, actuated by different motives. Pray for Love.

Pray for My Spirit of Love to be showered on all you meet. Deal with yourself severely. Learn to love discipline.

Never yield one point that you have already won. Discipline, discipline. Love it and rejoice—rejoice. Mountains can be removed by thought—by desire.

CONSIDER:
Does God's Spirit love through me?
Are the people I meet showered with His Spirit?

PRAY:
Father, it amazes me to think of the life You want to live through me. Help me to not stand in Your way. Teach me to surrender and allow Your Spirit to live through me.

Golden Opportunity

He has put a new song in my mouth—praise to our God;
many will see it and fear, and will trust in the LORD.
Blessed is that man who makes the LORD his trust,
and does not respect the proud, nor such as turn aside to lies.

PSALM 40:3–4

I am your Guide. Strength and help will come to you; just trust Me wholly.

Fear not. I am evermore ready to hear than you to ask. Walk in My ways and *know* that help will come.

Man's need is God's chance to help. I love to help and save. Man's need is God's golden opportunity for him of letting his faith find expression. That expression of faith is all that God needs to manifest His Power. Faith is the Key that unlocks the storehouse of God's resources.

My faithful servants, you long for perfection and see your bitter failures. I see faithfulness, and as a mother takes the soiled, imperfect work of her child and invests it with perfection because of the sweet love, so I take your poor faithfulness and crown it with perfection.

My need caused me to pray,
Lack drove me to my knees;
I cried, "Lord, I'm desperate!
Come to my help now, please!"

Then God came to my rescue,
And I learned a simple fact:
My need is God's opportunity,
It allows the Almighty to act.

PRAY:
Lord, please make much of my little-to-nothing. Teach me to serve You.

Gentle with All

Rejoice always, pray without ceasing, in everything give thanks;
for this is the will of God in Christ Jesus for you.
1 THESSALONIANS 5:16–18

Love and laugh. Make your world the happier for your being in it. Love and rejoice on the gray days.

There are wilderness days for My Disciples as well as Mountains of Transfiguration, but on both it is duty, persistently, faithfully done, that tells.

Be gentle with all. Try to see the heart I see, to know the pain and difficulty of the other life, that I know. Try, before you interview anyone, or speak to anyone, to ask Me to act as interpreter between you two.

Just live in the spirit of prayer. In speaking to Me, you find soul-rest. Simple tasks, faithfully done and persisted in, bring their own reward and are mosaics being laid in the pavement of success.

Welcome all who come here. I love you.

CONSIDER:
Do I treat others with the same grace I have received from God?
How can I live out my faith in a way that spreads the love of Jesus?

PRAY:
Lord Jesus, it's difficult for me to love and rejoice on days when
I feel miserable. But others are dealing with pain and difficulties
also, so with Your help I'll spread cheer, even on my gray days.

Equally Yoked

Do not be unequally yoked together with unbelievers.
For what fellowship has righteousness with lawlessness?
And what communion has light with darkness?
2 CORINTHIANS 6:14

My children, I guide you always. The walking in the way may not be always carried out, but the guiding is always so sure. God is using you both in marvelous ways. Go on gladly. You will see.

To be a perfect gymnast you must learn balance. It is balance and poise, perfect balance and poise, I am teaching you now. This will give you power in dealing with the lives of others, and that power is already being marvelously manifested.

The vision you both have is the means of clearing the obstacles away. When My disciple sees My purpose ahead, that very sight is the power that clears away every obstacle along that range of vision. You will both have mighty power to do this. Spiritual Light is in itself a miracle-worker.

People waste so much time in seeking to work out what they see. I declare to you that in the seeing My purpose all is done. Truly I said to My Disciples, "I have yet many things to say unto you, but ye cannot bear them *now*." But to you, and the twos who gather to hear Me as you do, I can declare those things now, that then I left unsaid.

Is not the message of My servant Paul now plain: "Be ye not unequally yoked together with unbelievers," because My Guidance is intensified immeasurably in power, when the two are one in desire to be with Me—but so few have understood.

Never Feel Inadequate

This Book of the Law shall not depart from your mouth,
but you shall meditate in it day and night, that you may observe
to do according to all that is written in it. For then you will make
your way prosperous, and then you will have good success.
JOSHUA 1:8

Obey My commands. They are steps in the ladder that leads to success. Above all, keep calm, unmoved.

Go back into the silence to recover this calm when it is lost even for one moment. You accomplish more by this than by all the activities of a long day. At all cost keep calm; you can help nobody when you are agitated. I, your Lord, see not as man sees.

Never feel inadequate for any task. All work here is accomplished by My Spirit, and that can flow through the most humble and lowly. It simply needs an unblocked channel. Rid yourself of self, and all is well.

Pray about all, but concentrate on a few things until those are accomplished. I am watching over you. Strength for your daily, hourly task is provided. Yours is the fault, the sin, if it is unclaimed, and you fail for lack of it.

PRAY:
Oh Father, fill me with trust in Your power, and Your willingness
to act and change situations. Teach me to accomplish much for You,
great and small things, relying on Your strength.

Love Your Servants

"And I give them eternal life, and they shall never perish; neither shall anyone snatch them out of My hand. My Father, who has given them to Me, is greater than all; and no one is able to snatch them out of My Father's hand. I and My Father are one."
JOHN 10:28–30

Love, love, love. Tender Love is the secret. Love those you are training, love those who work with you, love those who serve you.

Dwell on that thought—God is Love. Link it up with My "I and My Father are one." Dwell on My actions on earth. See in them Love in operation.

If it was God who so acted, then it was Love, Perfect Love performed those actions, those wonders. Then you, too, must put Love (God) into action in your lives. Perfect Love means perfect forgiveness. Lo, My children, you see that where God is there can be no lack of forgiveness, for that is really lack of love.

God is Love. . .no judging.
God is Love. . .no resentment.
God is Love. . .all patience.
God is Love. . .all power.
God is Love. . .all supply.

All you need to have is love to God and man. Love to God ensures obedience to every wish, every command. Love is the fulfilling of all law.

Pray much for love.

The Two Joys

Therefore my heart is glad, and my glory rejoices; my flesh also will rest in hope. For You will not leave my soul in Sheol, nor will You allow Your Holy One to see corruption. You will show me the path of life; in Your presence is fullness of joy; at Your right hand are pleasures forevermore.
PSALM 16:9–11

My children, I come. Hearts eager to do My Will, send out a call that ever I find irresistible. I know no barrier then.

Resignation to My Will keeps Me barred out from more hearts than does unbelief. Can anything be such a crime against Love as being resigned? My Will should be welcomed with a glad wonder if I am to do My Work in the heart and life.

In all true discipleship, and in the true spiritual development of each disciple, there is first the wonder and the joy of first acquaintance; then comes the long plain stretch of lesson-learning and discipline.

But the constant experience of Me, the constant persistent recognition of My Work in daily happenings, the numberless instances in which seeming chance or wonderful coincidence can be, must be, traced back to My loving forethought—all these gradually engender a feeling of wonder, certainty, and gratitude followed in time by Joy.

Joy is of two kinds. The Joy born of Love and Wonder, and the Joy born of Love and Knowledge, and between the experience of the two Joys lie discipline, disappointment, almost disillusion.

But combat these in My Strength, persevere in obeying My Will, accept My Discipline, and the second Joy will follow.

And of this second Joy it was that I said, "Your joy no man taketh from you."

Do not regret the first, the second is the greater gift.

I have found the pleasure I once craved,
It is joy and peace within;
What a wondrous blessing! I am saved
From the awful guilt of sin.

I have found that hope so bright and clear,
Living in the realm of grace;
Oh, the Savior's presence is so near,
I can see His smiling face.

It is joy unspeakable and full of glory,
Full of glory, full of glory,
It is joy unspeakable and full of glory,
Oh, the half has never yet been told.
BARNEY E. WARREN (1867–1951)

PRAY:
Father God, give me Your strength to battle the
disappointments and hardships of life. Help me to accept
Your discipline, so I might ultimately experience Your joy.

No Dark Days

And we have known and believed the love that God has for us.
God is love, and he who abides in love abides in God, and God in him.
Love has been perfected among us in this: that we may have boldness
in the day of judgment; because as He is, so are we in this world.

1 JOHN 4:16–17

Such light, such joy flows out from this house. It affects all who come here.

Do not feel that you have to try and help them. Just love them, welcome them, shower little courtesies and love-signs on them, and they must be helped.

Love is God. Give them Love, and you give them God. Then leave Him to do His Work. Love all, even the beggars. Send no one away without a word of cheer, a feeling that you care. I may have put the impulse to come here into some despairing one's heart. Think if you failed Me!

Besides, you have no choice. You told Me it was My Home. I shall use it. Remember this: There would be no dark winter days were Love in the hearts of all My children.

Oh! My children, can you not feel the joy of knowing, loving, and companying with Me?

CONSIDER:

Part of God's love is to help people in practical, tangible ways,
but I realize that I can't solve everybody's problems. Many of
them are beyond my limited ability to help. But do I show
people that I care? Do I love them and pray for them?

Life Is a Love Story

So Jesus answered and said to them, "Assuredly, I say to you, if you have faith and do not doubt, you will not only do what was done to the fig tree, but also if you say to this mountain, 'Be removed and be cast into the sea,' it will be done. And whatever things you ask in prayer, believing, you will receive."

MATTHEW 21:21–22

You need Me. I need you.

My broken world needs you. Many a weary troubled heart needs you. Many a troubled heart will be gladdened by you, drawn nearer to Me by you both.

Health—Peace—Joy—Patience—Endurance, they all come from contact with Me.

Oh! it is a glorious way, the upward way, the wonderful discoveries, the tender intimacies, the amazing, almost incomprehensible, understanding. Truly the Christian Life—Life with Me—is a Love story. Leave all to Me.

All you have missed you will find in Me, the Soul's Lover, the Soul's Friend, Father—Mother—Comrade—Brother. Try Me.

You cannot make too many demands upon Me—nor put too great a strain upon My Love and Forbearance.

Claim—claim—claim—Healing—Power—Joy—Supply—what you will.

CONSIDER:
Do I believe that God has unending love and patience with me?
Should I then hesitate to request things from Him?

PRAY:
O Lord, use me to help heal and restore the brokenness of others.

Heart's Agony

*For we do not have a High Priest who cannot sympathize with
our weaknesses, but was in all points tempted as we are, yet without
sin. Let us therefore come boldly to the throne of grace, that we
may obtain mercy and find grace to help in time of need.*
HEBREWS 4:15–16

There is a Calvary-Cross on which one hangs alone, untended by
even the nearest and dearest.

But beside that Cross, there stands another, and to My dear ones I
say little, I hang there afresh beside each one through the hours of the
heart's agony.

Have you ever thought of the Joy that the patient, gentle, loving
obedience of My disciples brings to My heart? I know no Joy such as
the Joy I feel at the loving trust of a dear one.

The wounds in the Hands and Feet hurt little compared with the
wounds in the Heart that are the wounds, not of My enemies, but of
My friends.

Little doubts, little fears, little misunderstandings. It is the tender
trifles of a day that gladden My Heart. I that speak unto you, am He—
your Master.

*Help me to not cause You pain
By little doubts and fears.
But may I make You glad today,
And through the coming years.*

PRAY:
*Father, keep me always mindful of the suffering Your Son endured on the
cross. You gave Him because of Your love, and He died because He loved me.*

You Will Conquer

And you have forgotten the exhortation which speaks to you as to sons:
"My son, do not despise the chastening of the LORD, nor be discouraged
when you are rebuked by him; for whom the LORD loves He chastens,
and scourges every son whom He receives."
HEBREWS 12:5–6

You will conquer. Do not fear changes. You can never fear changes when I, your Lord, change not. Jesus Christ, the same yesterday, today, and forever. I am beside you. Steadfastness, unchangingness, come to you, too, as you dwell with Me. Rest in Me.

As breathing rightly, from being a matter of careful practice, becomes a habit, unconsciously, yet rightly performed, so if you regularly practice this getting back into My Presence, when the slightest feeling of unrest disturbs your perfect calm and harmony, so this, too, will become a habit, and you will grow to live in that perfect consciousness of My Presence, and perfect calm and harmony will be yours.

Life is a training school. Remember, only the pupil giving great promise of future good work would be so singled out by the Master for strenuous and unwearied discipline, teaching and training.

You are asking both of you to be not as hundreds of My followers, nay as many, many thousands, but to be even as those who reflect Me in all they say and do and are. So, My dear children, take this training, not as harsh, but as the tender loving answer to your petition.

Life can never be the same again for either of you. Once you have drunk of the wine of My giving, the Life Eternal, all earth's attempts to quench your thirst will fail.

Complain Not—Laugh

I will greatly rejoice in the LORD, my soul shall be joyful in my God;
for He has clothed me with the garments of salvation, He has covered me
with the robe of righteousness, as a bridegroom decks himself
with ornaments, and as a bride adorns herself with her jewels.
ISAIAH 61:10

Trust in Me. Do as I say each moment and all indeed shall be well. Follow out My commands: Divine control, unquestioning obedience—these are the only conditions of supply being ample for your own needs and those of others.

The tasks I set you may have seemingly no connection with supply. The commands are Mine and the supply is Mine and I make My own conditions, differing in each case—but in the case of each disciple, adapted to the individual need.

Have no fear, go forward. Joy—radiant Joy must be yours. Change all disappointment, even if only momentary, into Joy. Change each complaint into laughter.

Rest—Love—Joy—Peace—Work, and the most powerful of these are Love and Joy.

CONSIDER:
Am I obedient to the Lord's commands?
Do I follow Him, or do I doubt, question, and complain?

PRAY:
O Lord, I surrender all my fears and complaints and feelings of
disappointment. Fill my heart with Your abundant joy and peace.

Too Much Talk

*"Abide in Me, and I in you. As the branch cannot bear fruit of itself,
unless it abides in the vine, neither can you, unless you abide in Me.
I am the vine, you are the branches. He who abides in Me, and
I in him, bears much fruit; for without Me you can do nothing."*
JOHN 15:4–5

Guidance you are bound to have as you live more and more with Me. It follows without doubt.

But *these* times are not times when you ask to be shown and led; they are times of feeling and realizing My Presence. Does the branch continually ask the Vine to supply it with sap, to show it in what direction to grow? No, that comes naturally from the very union with the Vine, and I said, "I am the vine, ye are the branches."

From the branches hang the choice grapes, given joy and nourishment to all, but no branch could think that the fruit, the grapes, were of *its* shaping and making.

No! the grapes are the fruit of the Vine, the Parent-Plant. The work of the branch is to provide a channel for the life-flow.

So, My children, union with Me is the one great overwhelming necessity. All else follows so naturally, and union with Me may be the result of just consciousness of My Presence. Be not too ready to speak to others.

Pray always that the need may be apparent, if you are to do this, and the guidance very plain. My Spirit has been driven out by the words of men.

Discourage too much talk. Deeds live and re-echo down the ages—words perish. As Paul: "Though I speak with the tongues of men and of angels, and have not charity, I am become as sounding brass, or a tinkling cymbal. And though I have the gift of prophecy. . .and have not charity, I am nothing. . . ."

Remember that rarely to the human heart do I speak in words. Man will see Me in My works done through you. Meet Me in the atmosphere of Love and self-effacement. Do not feel that you have to speak

When man ceased to commune with his God simply and naturally, he took refuge in words—Babel resulted. Then God wanted to do away with man from the earth. Rely less on words. Always remember that speech is of the senses. So make it your servant, never your Master.

Doing beats talking every time.
MAXIE DUNNAM
LET ME SAY THAT AGAIN

PRAY:

Lord, please help me to measure my words. Keep me from talking when I should listen. May I never talk my way out of doing good for someone else.

I Go Before

When He had stopped speaking, He said to Simon, "Launch out into the deep and let down your nets for a catch." But Simon answered and said to Him, "Master, we have toiled all night and caught nothing; nevertheless at Your word I will let down the net." And when they had done this, they caught a great number of fish, and their net was breaking.
LUKE 5:4–6

You can never perish, My children, because within you is the Life of Life. The Life that down the ages has kept My servants, in peril, in adversity, in sorrow.

Once you are born of the Spirit, *that* is your Life's breath. You must never doubt, never worry, but step by step, the way to freedom must be trodden. See that you walk it with Me.

This means no worry, no anxiety, but it does *not* mean no effort. When My Disciples told Me that they had toiled all night and taken nothing, I did not fill the boat with fishes without effort on their part. No! My command stood. "Launch out into the deep, and let down your nets for a draught."

Their lives were endangered, the ship nearly sank, the help of their fellows had to be summoned, and there were broken nets to mend. Any one of these troubles might have made them feel My help was not for them. And yet as they sat on the shore and mended those nets, they would see My Love and Care.

The man who reaches the mountain height by the help of train or car has learned no climber's lesson. But remember this does not mean no Guide—this does not mean that My Spirit is not supplying wisdom and strength. How often, when sometimes you little know it, do I go before you to prepare the way, to soften a heart here, to overrule there.

Bless Your Enemies

"A new commandment I give to you, that you love one another;
as I have loved you, that you also love one another. By this all will
know that you are My disciples, if you have love for one another."
JOHN 13:34–35

S ay often, "God bless. . ." of any whom you find in disharmony with
you, or whom you desire to help. Say it, willing that showers of
blessings and joy and success may fall upon them.

Leave to Me the necessary correcting or training; *you* must only
desire joy and blessing for them. At present your prayers are that they
should be taught and corrected.

Oh! if My children would leave My work to Me and occupy
themselves with the task I give them. Love, love, love. Love will break
down all your difficulties. Love will build up all your successes.

God the destroyer of evil, God the creator of good—is Love.
To Love one another is to use God in your life. To use God in your life
is to bring into manifestation all harmony, beauty, joy, and happiness.

Once I prayed that my enemies
Would trip and stumble and fall.
But that prayer wasn't good at all.

Then I prayed that my foes
Would be justly corrected and learn.
But God said that was not my concern.

Now, I pray for all my opponents
To receive blessings from God above,
And we both receive blessing and love.

I Make the Opportunities

Not that I speak in regard to need, for I have learned in whatever state I am, to be content: I know how to be abased, and I know how to abound. Everywhere and in all things I have learned both to be full and to be hungry, both to abound and to suffer need. I can do all things through Christ who strengthens me.
PHILIPPIANS 4:11–13

Never doubt. Have no fear. Watch the faintest tremor of fear, and stop all work, everything, and rest before Me until you are joyful and strong again.

Deal in the same way with all tired feelings. I was weary, too, when on earth, and I separated Myself from My Disciples and sat and rested on the well. Rested—and then it was that the Samaritan woman was helped.

I had to teach renewal of Spirit—force rest of body to My Disciples. Then, as your Example, I lay with My Head on a pillow, asleep in the boat. It was not, as they thought, indifference. They cried, "Master, carest thou not that we perish?" and I had to teach them that ceaseless activity was no part of My Father's plan.

When Paul said, "I can do all things through Christ which strengtheneth me," he did not mean that he was to do all things and then rely on Me to find strength. He meant that for all I told him to do, he could rely on My supplying the strength.

My Work in the world has been hindered by work, work, work. Many a tireless, nervous body has driven a spirit. The spirit should be the master always and just simply and naturally use the body as need should arise. Rest in Me.

Do not *seek* to work for Me. Never make opportunities. Live with Me and for Me. I do the work and I make the opportunities.

Seeing Christ

Jesus said to him, "Thomas, because you have seen Me, you have believed. Blessed are those who have not seen and yet have believed."

JOHN 20:29

I am beside you. Can you not feel My Presence?

Contact with Me is not gained by the senses. Spirit-consciousness replaces sight.

When man sees Me with his human sight, it does not mean of necessity that his spiritual perception is greater. *Nay, rather that for that soul I have to span the physical and the spiritual with a spiritual vision clear to human eyes.*

Remember this to cheer My disciples who have never seen Me, and yet have had a clear spiritual consciousness of Me.

CONSIDER:

Do I feel the presence of the Lord, even though I can't see Him?
When I don't sense His presence, do I still trust that He's there?

PRAY:

O God, open my heart so that I can see You in the world around me.
And Lord, let me live my life in such a way that others
can see You through my words and actions.

The Roundabout Way

But I want you to know, brethren, that the things which happened to me
have actually turned out for the furtherance of the gospel, so that it has
become evident to the whole palace guard, and to all the rest,
that my chains are in Christ.

PHILIPPIANS 1:12–13

Through briars, through waste places, through glades, up mountain heights, down into valleys, I lead. But ever with the Leadership goes the Helping Hand.

Glorious to follow where your Master goes. But remember that the varied path does not always mean that *you* need the varied training.

We are seeking lost sheep—we are bringing the Kingdom into places where it has not been known before. So realize that you are joining Me on My quest—My undying quest, tracking down souls.

I am not choosing ways that will fret and tire—just to fret and tire; we are out to save. *You* may not always see the soul we seek. I know.

CONSIDER:
Have I ever wandered aimlessly, like the children of Israel in
the desert, because of my unbelief? Have I ever run erratically
from one thing to another, anxiously seeking a solution? Have I
ever been led down confusing paths, only to see God's purpose or
lesson in the end—or to meet a person desperate for the Gospel?
Do I understand the difference between these experiences?

PRAY:
Lord, keep me on Your path, wherever it might lead. As I journey
through life, may I act in the knowledge that lost souls are all
around me, and the things I do might lead them to follow You.

Disharmony

*"Ask, and it will be given to you; seek, and you will find; knock,
and it will be opened to you. For everyone who asks receives,
and he who seeks finds, and to him who knocks it will be opened."*
MATTHEW 7:7–8

Seek and ye shall find. Shall find that inner knowledge that makes the problems of life plain.

The difficulties of life are caused by disharmony in the individual. There is no discord in My Kingdom, only a something unconquered in My disciples. The rule of My Kingdom is perfect order, perfect harmony, perfect supply, perfect love, perfect honesty, perfect obedience—all power, all conquest, all success.

But so often My servants lack power, conquest, success, supply, harmony, and think I fail in My promises because these are not manifested in their lives.

These are but the outward manifestations that result from the obedience, honesty, order, love—and they come, not in answer to urgent prayer, but naturally as light results from a lighted candle.

CONSIDER:
*Do I have a tendency to question God's power and grace because
of my own failings? Am I living in total obedience to His commands,
or do I need to make changes in my life in order to more
fully experience the results of his promises?*

PRAY:
*Lord, help me to know that power, overcoming, success,
supply, and harmony come, not so much in answer to urgent
prayer, but as a natural outgrowth of how close I am to You.*

Springtime

*Come, and let us return to the LORD; for He has torn, but He
will heal us; He has stricken, but He will bind us up. After two
days He will revive us; on the third day He will raise us up, that
we may live in His sight. Let us know, let us pursue the knowledge
of the LORD. His going forth is established as the morning; He will come
to us like the rain, like the latter and former rain to the earth.*
HOSEA 6:1–3

Rejoice in the Springtime of the year. Let there be Springtime in
your hearts. The full time of fruit is not yet, but there is the promise
of the blossom.

Know surely that your lives, too, are full of glad promise. Such
blessings are to be yours. Such joys, such wonders.

All is indeed well. Live in My Sunshine and My Love.

CONSIDER:

*Am I living my life truly believing the promises of springtime,
of rebirth and new life—or am I discouraged, thinking that
"the promise of the blossom" won't be fulfilled?*

PRAY:

*Lord, make my heart fertile ground where Your seed can take
root and blossom into a beautiful example of the change that
You make in a life. Let others see Your love and joy in me.*

Delay Is Not Denial

Cease from anger, and forsake wrath; do not fret—
it only causes harm. For evildoers shall be cut off;
but those who wait on the LORD, they shall inherit the earth.
PSALM 37:8–9

Read the lessons of Divine control in Nature's laws.

Nature is but the expression of Eternal Thought in Time. Study the outward form—grasp the Eternal Thought, and if you can read the thoughts of the Father, then indeed you know Him.

Leave Me out of nothing. Love all My ways with you. Know indeed that "All is well." Delay is but the wonderful and all-loving restraint of your Father—not reluctance, not desire to deny—but the Divine control of a Father who can scarcely brook the delay.

Delay has to be—sometimes. Your lives are so linked up with those of others, so bound by circumstances that to let your desire have instant fulfillment might in many cases cause another, as earnest prayer, to go unanswered.

But think for a moment of the Love and thoughtful care that seek to harmonize and reconcile all your desires and longings and prayers.

Delay is not denial—not even withholding. It is the opportunity for God to work out your problems and accomplish your desires in the most wonderful way possible for you.

Oh! children, trust Me. Remember that your Maker is also your Servant, quick to fulfill, quick to achieve, faithful in accomplishment. Yes. All is well.

Souls That Smile

For if you love those who love you, what reward have you? Do not even the tax collectors do the same? And if you greet your brethren only, what do you do more than others? Do not even the tax collectors do so? Therefore you shall be perfect, just as your Father in heaven is perfect.
MATTHEW 5:46–48

To conquer adverse circumstances, conquer yourselves. The answer to the desire of My Disciples to follow Me was "Be ye therefore perfect, even as your Father which is in heaven is perfect."

To accomplish much, be much. In all cases the *doing*, to be well-doing, must be the mere unconscious expression of the *being*.

Fear not, fear not, all is well. Let the day be full of little prayers to Me, little turnings toward Me. The smiles of the soul at one it loves.

Men call the Father the First Cause. Yes! See Him as the First Cause of every warm ray, every color in the sunset, every gleam on the water, every beautiful flower, every planned pleasure.

For the beauty of the earth
For the glory of the skies,
For the love which from our birth
Over and around us lies.

Lord of all, to Thee we raise,
This our hymn of grateful praise.
FOLLIOT SANDFORD PIERPOINT (1835–1917)

PRAY:

Heavenly Father, I am desperate to conquer myself—my sinful ways, my ungodly desires, my earthly shortcomings—as I strive to be like You. I can do this only by trusting and completely surrendering my life and my thoughts to You.

Kill Self Now

Fulfill my joy by being like-minded, having the same love, being of one accord, of one mind. Let nothing be done through selfish ambition or conceit, but in lowliness of mind let each esteem others better than himself. Let each of you look out not only for his own interests, but also for the interests of others.

PHILIPPIANS 2:2–4

Self dethroned—that is the lesson, but in its place put Love for Me, knowledge of Me.

Self, not only dethroned, but dead. A dead self is not an imprisoned self. An imprisoned self is more potent to harm. In all training—(in Mine of you, and in yours of others)—let self die.

But for each blow to the life of self you must at the same time embrace and hold fast the new Life, Life with Me.

And now I can make more clear to you what I would say about forgiveness of injuries. It is one of My commands that as you seek My forgiveness, so you must forgive.

But what you do not see is that you, the self in you, can never forgive injuries. The very thought of them means self in the foreground, then the injury, instead of appearing less, appears greater.

No, My children, as all true Love is *of* God, and is God, so all true forgiveness is of God and is God. The self cannot forgive. Kill self.

Cease trying to forgive those who fretted or wronged you. It is a mistake to think about it. Aim at killing the self now—in your daily life, and then, and not until then, you will find there is nothing that even remembers injury, because the only one injured, the self, is dead.

As long as it recurs to your mind, you deceive yourself if you think it forgiven.

Self must step aside, to let God work.
HANNAH WHITALL SMITH
THE CHRISTIAN'S SECRET OF A HAPPY LIFE

PRAY:

Father, sometimes I love myself, sometimes I hate myself—
but I'm almost always thinking about myself! Please replace my weak,
unforgiving selfish self with Your love, Your life, Your self. Thank You, God!

Share with Me

As a father pities his children, so the LORD pities those who fear Him.
For He knows our frame; He remembers that we are dust.
PSALM 103:13–14

Delight in My Love. Try to live in the rapture of the Kingdom. Claim big things. Claim great things. Claim Joy and Peace and freedom from care. Joy in Me.

I am your Lord, your Creator. Remember, too, that I am the same yesterday, today, and forever. Your Creator, when My thought about the world called it into being—your Creator as much, too, today, when I can, by loving thought for you, call into being all you need on the material plane.

Joy in Me, trust in Me, share all life with Me, see Me in everything, rejoice in Me. Share all with Me as a child shares its pains and cuts and griefs and newfound treasures and joys and little work with its Mother.

And give Me the joy of sharing all with you.

CONSIDER:
Am I guilty of thinking too small when I consider
how God might use me to further His kingdom?
Or do I pray for—and expect—big things?

PRAY:
Oh Father, forgive me for my small-mindedness, for my doubts and
my hesitancy to trust You. Open my heart to believe that You, the God
who created all things, can still call into being everything I need today.

Let Me Choose

But without faith it is impossible to please Him,
for he who comes to God must believe that He is,
and that He is a rewarder of those who diligently seek Him.
HEBREWS 11:6

My loved ones. Yes, with the heart, not the head, men should think of Me, and then worship would be instinctive.

Breathe in My very Spirit in pure air and fervent desire.

Keep the eye of your spirit ever upon Me, the window of your soul open toward Me. You have ever to know that all things are yours—that what is lovely I delight to give you.

Empty your mind of all that limits. Whatever is beautiful you can have. Leave more and more the choice to Me. You will have no regrets.

Lord, I throw open the window of my soul.
Let your Spirit rush in like a mighty wind!
I desire you with fervent desire, my King.
My heart is enthralled with Your love!

PRAY:

Lord, strengthen my faith so that I won't hesitate to accept the choices
that You have made for me, the purpose that You have given my life.
Let my acceptance bring glory to Your name and joy to my own soul.

Sublime Audacity

For he who sows to his flesh will of the flesh reap corruption, but he who sows to the Spirit will of the Spirit reap everlasting life. And let us not grow weary while doing good, for in due season we shall reap if we do not lose heart.
GALATIANS 6:8–9

The way is long and weary. It is a weary world. So many today are weary. "Come unto Me. . .and I will give you rest."

My children, who range yourselves under My flag, you must see that on it are inscribed those words "The Son of Man."

Whatever the world is feeling, I must feel, I—the Son of Man. You are My followers—so the weariness of man today must be shared by you—the weary and heavy-laden must come to *you* and find that rest that you found in Me.

My children, My followers must be prepared not to sit on My right hand and on My left, but to drink of the cup that I drink of.

Poor world—teach it that there is only one cure for all its ills—Union with Me. Dare to suffer, dare to conquer, be filled with My sublime audacity. Remember that. Claim the unclaimable.

Just what the world would think impossible can always be yours. Remember, My children, sublime audacity.

CONSIDER:
Am I willing to embrace "sublime audacity," to believe the impossible? Do I feel the pain of the suffering? Do I share the peace with them that I have found?

Against the Tide

*Therefore, my beloved, as you have always obeyed, not as in
my presence only, but now much more in my absence, work out
your own salvation with fear and trembling; for it is God who
works in you both to will and to do for His good pleasure.*
PHILIPPIANS 2:12–13

*What does it profit, my brethren, if someone says he
has faith but does not have works? Can faith save him?*
JAMES 2:14

The oarsman, trusting in Me, does not lean on his oars and drift
with the tide, trusting to the current.

Nay, more often—once I have shown the way—it is against the
tide you must direct all your effort. And even when difficulties come, it
is by your effort that they will be surmounted. But always strength and
the Joy in the doing you can have through Me.

My fishermen-disciples did not find the fishes ready on the shore
in their nets. I take man's effort and bless that. I need man's effort—
he needs My blessing. This partnership it is that means success.

CONSIDER:
*How can I put my faith into action, while trusting
God to guide me through difficult circumstances?*

PRAY:
*God, grant me the courage and strength to obey Your will in a world
where those who believe in You are often ignored, mocked, and ridiculed.
Give me the power to fearlessly face temptation and tribulation.*

The Rest of God

The work of righteousness will be peace, and the effect of righteousness,
quietness and assurance forever. My people will dwell in a peaceful
habitation, in secure dwellings, and in quiet resting places.
ISAIAH 32:17–18

I lead you. The way is clear. Go forward unafraid. I am beside you. Listen, listen, listen to My Voice. My Hand is controlling all.

Remember that I can work through you better when you are at rest. Go very slowly, very quietly from one duty to the next—taking time to rest and pray between.

Do not be too busy. Take all in order as I say. The Rest of God is in a realm beyond all man's activities. Venture there often, and you will indeed find Peace and Joy.

All work that results from resting with God is miracle-work. Claim the power to work miracles, both of you.

Know that you can do all things through Christ who strengthens you. Nay, more, know that you can do all things through Christ who rests you.

CONSIDER:
Do I believe that even in the midst of my busiest days,
it's beneficial to stop to rest and pray? Or do I believe that
it's time I can't really spare? What kind of miracle-working
power do I believe that I'd gain from such times?

PRAY:
O Lord, let me never become so busy that I don't take time to listen to
Your voice, to meditate on Your Word and Your will for my life. Nourish
my spirit and let me find rest in Your love that restores my soul.

Harmony Within

Repay no one evil for evil. Have regard for good things in the sight of all men. If it is possible, as much as depends on you, live peaceably with all men. Beloved, do not avenge yourselves, but rather give place to wrath; for it is written, "Vengeance is Mine, I will repay," says the Lord.
ROMANS 12:17–19

Follow My Guidance. Be afraid to venture on your own as a child fears to leave its mother's side. Doubt of your own wisdom, and reliance on Mine, will teach you humility.

Humility is not the belittling of the self. It is forgetting the self. Nay more, forgetting the self, because you are remembering Me.

You must not expect to live in a world where all is harmony. You must not expect to live where others are in unbroken accord with you. It is your task to maintain your own heart peace in adverse circumstances. Harmony is always yours when you strain your ear to catch Heaven's music.

Doubt always your power or wisdom to put things right; ask Me to right all as you leave it to Me, and go on your way loving and laughing. I am wisdom. Only My wisdom can rightly decide anything—settle any problem. So rely on Me. All is well.

CONSIDER:
Do I find myself relying on my own wisdom and power when facing challenging circumstances or difficult people—or do I forget myself and pray for God to work things out?

Calm—Not Speed

For thus saith the Lord GOD, the Holy One of Israel;
In returning and rest shall ye be saved; in quietness and
in confidence shall be your strength: and ye would not.
ISAIAH 30:15 KJV

All agitation is destructive of good. All calm is constructive of good and at the same time destructive of evil.

When man wants evil destroyed, so often he rushes to action. It is wrong. First be still and know that I am God. Then act only as I tell you. Always calm with God. Calm is trust in action. Only trust, perfect trust can keep one calm.

Never be afraid of any circumstances or difficulties that help you to cultivate this calm. As the world, to attain, has to learn speed, you, to attain, have to learn calm. All great work for Me is done first in the individual soul of the worker.

CONSIDER:
When I am offended, or when I see an injustice done to others,
am I immediately indignant? Do I often find myself responding
in anger? When I think a situation requires quick action, do I
sometimes end up making a bigger mess of things? Why is
it wise to calm myself and pray before acting?

PRAY:
Father, I ask that You still my soul and help me to trust in You, so that I make
wise decisions based on Your analysis of a situation, not mine. For only You have
the wisdom that will allow me to act constructively rather than destructively.

The Divine Third

Though one may be overpowered by another, two can withstand him.
And a threefold cord is not quickly broken.
ECCLESIASTES 4:12

When I have led you through these storms, there will be other words for you, other messages—other guidance.

So deep is your friendship and so great your desire to love and follow and serve Me that soon, when this time of difficulty is over, to be alone together will always mean to be shut in with Me.

There are few friendships in the world like that, and yet I taught, when on earth, as I have taught you both, the power of the *two together*.

And now tonight I have more to say to you. I say that the time is coming, is even now here, when those who visit you two together will know that I am the Divine Third in your friendship.

CONSIDER:
Do I feel like God is some distant force, or do
I have an intimate, personal relationship with Him?

PRAY:
Lord, do loving miracles to bring me close to You, to help me
experience the divine joy and power that come from friendship with You.

Thrill of Protection

"Offer to God thanksgiving, and pay your vows to the Most High.
Call upon Me in the day of trouble; I will deliver you,
and you shall glorify Me."
PSALM 50:14–15

Turn out all thoughts of doubt and of trouble. Never tolerate them for one second. Bar the windows and doors of your souls against them as you would bar your home against a thief who would steal in to take your treasures.

What greater treasures can you have than Peace and Rest and Joy? And these are all stolen from you by doubt and fear and despair.

Face each day with Love and Laughter. Face the storm.

Joy, Peace, Love, My great gifts. Follow Me to find all three. I want you to feel the thrill of protection and safety now. Any soul can feel this in a harbor, but real joy and victory come to those alone who sense these when they ride a storm.

Say, "All is well." Say it not as a vain repetition. Use it as you use a healing balm for cut or wound, until the poison is drawn out; *then*, until the sore is healed; *then*, until the thrill of fresh life floods your being.

All is well.

PRAY:
God, help me bar the doors and windows of my soul against
doubt and fear. Help me to believe in Your promises of
deliverance from evil, Your promises of peace and joy.

Never Judge

*"Therefore be merciful, just as your Father also is merciful.
Judge not, and you shall not be judged. Condemn not, and
you shall not be condemned. Forgive, and you will be forgiven."*
LUKE 6:36–37

What Joy follows self-conquest! You cannot conquer and control others, either of you, until you have completely conquered yourself.

Can you see yourselves absolutely unmoved? Think of Me before the mocking soldiers, being struck, spat upon, and answering never a word—*never a word.* Try to see that as Divine Power. Remember by that Power of perfect silence, perfect self-control, you can alone prove your right to govern.

Never judge. The heart of man is so delicate, so complex, only its Maker can know it. Each heart is so different, actuated by different motives, controlled by different circumstances, influenced by different sufferings.

How can one judge another? Leave to Me the unraveling of the puzzles of life. Leave to Me the teaching of understanding. Bring each heart to Me, its Maker, and leave it with Me. Secure in the certainty that all that is wrong I can set right.

CONSIDER:

*Am I quick to judge others for their words and actions,
or do I follow the Lord's command to leave the judging
to Him? Do I forgive others' offences, as He has forgiven
mine, and trust in Him to someday set things right?*

The Love of a Lover

Remember that a loving Master delights in the intimacy of demands made, as much as He desires His followers and friends to delight in the tender intimacy of *His* demands.

Only as the result of frequent converse with Me, of much prayer to Me, of listening to and obedience to My behests comes that intimacy that makes My followers dare to approach Me as friend to friend.

Yield in all things to My tender insistence but remember I yield, too, to yours. Ask not only the big things I have told you, but ask the little tender signs of Love. Remember that I came as the world's Great Lover. Never think of My Love as only a tender compassion and forgiveness. It is that, but it is also the Love of a Lover, who shows His Love by countless words and actions and by tender thought.

In each of you, too, remember there is God. It is always given to man to see in his fellow man those aspirations and qualities he himself possesses. So only I, being really God, can recognize the God in man. Remember this, too, in your relation to others.

Your motives and aspirations can only be understood by those who have attained the same spiritual level. So do not vainly, foolishly, expect from others understanding. Do not misjudge them for not giving it. Yours is a foreign language to them.

First the Spiritual

The LORD is near to those who have a broken heart, and saves such
as have a contrite spirit. Many are the afflictions of the righteous,
but the LORD delivers him out of them all.

PSALM 34:18–19

What can I say to you? Your heart is torn. Then remember "He bindeth up the broken hearts." Just feel the tenderness of My Hands as I bind up your wounds.

You are very privileged, both of you. I share My plans and secrets with you and make known to you My Purposes, while so many have to grope on.

Try to rest on these words. "Seek ye first the kingdom of God, and his righteousness; and all these things shall be added unto you." Then strive not for *them* but, untiringly, for the things of My Kingdom.

It is so strange to you mortals, you would think the material things first and then grow into the knowledge of Spiritual things. Not so in My Kingdom. It is Spiritual things first and then material. So to attain the material redouble your efforts to acquire the Spiritual.

PRAY:

Lord, I ask You: help me line up my priorities with Your heavenly will.
I don't want to have things backwards anymore. Keep me focused on the
spiritual, the eternal, and not on material things that will soon vanish.

Pray and Praise

Confess your trespasses to one another, and pray for one another, that you may be healed. The effective, fervent prayer of a righteous man avails much. Elijah was a man with a nature like ours, and he prayed earnestly that it would not rain; and it did not rain on the land for three years and six months.
JAMES 5:16–17

I will be much entreated because I know that only in that earnest supplication, and the calm trust that results, does man learn strength and gain peace. Therefore I have laid that incessant, persistent pleading as a duty upon My disciples.

Never weary in prayer. When one day man sees how marvelously his prayer has been answered, then he will deeply, so deeply, regret that he prayed so little.

Prayer changes all. Prayer re-creates. Prayer is irresistible. So pray, literally without ceasing.

Pray until you almost cease to pray, because trust has become so rocklike, and then pray on because it has become so much a habit that you cannot resist it.

And always pray until Prayer merges into Praise. That is the only note on which true prayer should end. It is the Love and Laughter of your attitude toward man interpreted in the Prayer and Praise of your attitude toward God.

PRAY:
Lord, make my entire life a prayer unto You, so that everything I think and say and do brings praise and honor to Your name.

Sorrow to Joy

Sing praise to the LORD, you saints of His, and give thanks
at the remembrance of His holy name. For His anger is but
for a moment, His favor is for life; weeping may endure
for a night, but joy comes in the morning.
PSALM 30:4–5

Weeping may endure for a night, but joy cometh in the morning."
My bravest are those who can anticipate the morning and
feel in the night of sorrow that underlying Joy that tells of confident
expectations of the morning.

I wept for a night on my pillow,
When I'd failed and wandered astray;
You saw my tears and forgave me,
And gave joy at the dawning of day.

I wept all night with deep sorrow,
Lamenting a love that had gone;
You sent me peace as I slumbered,
And I woke with new hope at the dawn.

CONSIDER:
Am I able to look beyond today's pain and sorrow
and trust the promise of joy and healing tomorrow?

PRAY:
Lord, grant me the faith and patience to believe in tomorrow's
deliverance from today's suffering, and to live my life accordingly.

New and Vital Power

*"Look to Me, and be saved, all you ends of the earth! For I am God,
and there is no other. I have sworn by Myself; the word has gone
out of My mouth in righteousness, and shall not return, that to
Me every knee shall bow, every tongue shall take an oath."*
ISAIAH 45:22–23

Look unto Me, and be ye saved, all the ends of the earth." Not for
merit was salvation; the promise was to all who looked.

To look is surely within the Power of everyone. One look suffices.
Salvation follows.

Look and you are saved from despair. Look and you are saved from
care. Look and you are saved from worry. Look, and into you there
flows a peace beyond all understanding, a Power new and vital, a Joy
wonderful indeed.

Look and keep looking. Doubt flees, Joy reigns, and Hope conquers.
Life, Eternal Life, is yours—revitalizing, renewing.

CONSIDER:
Where do I look to find joy and hope and salvation?
Do I look—and keep looking—at God?

PRAY:
Father, You are my Power, my salvation from despair and doubt.
Help me to keep my eyes on You, that I might be saved from all my problems.

Rescued and Guided

I waited patiently for the LORD; and He inclined to me,
and heard my cry. He also brought me up out of a horrible pit,
out of the miry clay, and set my feet upon a rock, and established
my steps. He has put a new song in my mouth—praise to our
God; many will see it and fear, and will trust in the LORD.
PSALM 40:1–3

Rest knowing all is so safe in My Hands. Rest is Trust. Ceaseless activity is distrust. Without the knowledge that I am working for you, you do not rest. Inaction then would be the outcome of despair.

Welcome the knowledge, delight in it. Such a truth is as a hope flung to a drowning man. Every repetition of it is one pull nearer shore and safety.

Let that illustration teach you a great truth. Lay hold of the truth, pray it, affirm it, hold on to the rope. How foolish are your attempts to save yourself, one hand on the rope and one making efforts to swim ashore! You may relinquish your hold of the rope and hinder the rescuer—who has to act with the greater caution lest he lose you.

The storms and tempests are not all of life. The Psalmist who said, "All thy waves and thy billows are gone over me," wrote also, "He brought me up also out of an horrible pit, out of the miry clay, and set my feet upon a rock, and established my goings."

Meditate upon that wonder—truth, the three steps safety, security, guidance. (1) "He brought me up also out of an horrible pit"—*Safety*. (2) "He set my feet upon a rock"—*Security*. (3) "He established my goings"—*Guidance*. No. 3 is the final stage when the saved soul trusts Me so entirely it seeks no more its own way but leaves all future plans to Me its Rescuer.

Win Me—Win All

*Oh, sing to the LORD a new song! For He has done marvelous
things; His right hand and His holy arm have gained Him
the victory. . . . Shout joyfully to the LORD, all the earth;
break forth in song, rejoice, and sing praises.*

PSALM 98:1, 4

You will conquer. The conquering spirit is never crushed. Keep a
brave and trusting heart. Face all your difficulties in the spirit of
Conquest.

Rise to greater heights than you have known before. Remember
where I am is Victory. Forces of evil, within and without you, flee at
My Presence.

Win *Me* and all is won. *All.*

---

*A mighty fortress is our God, a bulwark never failing;
Our helper He, amid the flood of mortal ills prevailing:
For still our ancient foe doth seek to work us woe;
His craft and power are great, and, armed with cruel hate,
On earth is not his equal.*

*Did we in our strength confide, our striving would be losing;
Were not the right Man on our side, the Man of God's own choosing:
Dost ask who that may be? Christ Jesus, it is He;
Lord Sabaoth, His Name, from age to age the same,
And He must win the battle.*

MARTIN LUTHER (1483–1546)

Fling It at My Feet

*"Not everyone who says to Me, 'Lord, Lord,' shall enter the kingdom
of heaven, but he who does the will of My Father in heaven."*
MATTHEW 7:21

To see Me you must bring Me your cares and show Me your heart of Trust. Then, as you leave your cares, you become conscious of My Presence.

This consciousness persisted in brings its reward of Me. Through a mist of care, no man may see My Face. Only when the burden is flung at My Feet do you pass on to consciousness and spiritual sight.

Remember obedience, obedience, obedience—the straight and narrow way into the Kingdom.

Not of you must it be said, even in lovingly tender reproach, "Why call ye me 'Lord, Lord,' and do not the things which I say?"

Character is chiseled into Beauty by the daily discipline and daily duties done. For, in many ways, My disciples must work out their own salvation, though this is not possible without My Strength and Help and without converse with Me.

Even for the Spiritual Life the training is different for different spirits. The man who would fain live a life of prayer and meditation is thrust into the busy ways of life, and the busy man is bidden to rest and wait patiently for Me. O joy, O rest, and in the busy ways be ever at peace.

Command Your Lord

For as many as are led by the Spirit of God, these are sons of God. For you did not received the spirit of bondage again to fear, but you received the Spirit of adoption by whom we cry out, "Abba, Father." The Spirit Himself bears witness with our spirit that we are children of God, and if children, then heirs—heirs of God and joint heirs with Christ, if indeed we suffer with Him, that we may also be glorified together.

ROMANS 8:14–17

Lord, I claim Thy Help.

Yes! Claim, be constantly claiming. There is a trust that waits long, and a trust that brooks no delay—that once convinced of the right of a course, once sure of God's guidance, says with all the persistence of a child, "*Now.*" "Make no long tarrying, oh, my God."

You are no longer servants but friends. A friend can command his friend—can know that all the friend, the true friend, has is his by right. That does not mean an idle living at the expense of a friend, but claiming the friend's means: name, time, all that he has, when your supply is exhausted.

Friendship—true friendship, implies the right to appropriate. And in God's service is perfect freedom. Heirs of God—you are joint heirs with Me in the inheritance. We share the Father's property. You have the same right to use and claim as I have. Use your right. A beggar supplicates. A son, a daughter, appropriates.

Small wonder when I see My children sitting before My House supplicating and waiting—that I leave them there until they realize how foolish such action, when they have only to walk into their Home and take.

This cannot be the attitude of all. There must be first a definite realization of Sonship.

Little Frets

Therefore humble yourselves under the mighty hand of God, that He may exalt you in due time, casting all your care upon Him, for He cares for you.
1 PETER 5:6–7

Your lack of control is not due to the *big* burdens, but to your permitting the *little* frets and cares and burdens to accumulate.

If anything vex you, deal with that and get that righted with Me before you allow yourself to speak to or meet anybody, or to undertake any new duty.

Look upon yourself more as performing My errands and coming back quickly to Me to tell Me that message is delivered, that task done.

Then with no feeling of responsibility as to result (your only responsibility was to see the duty done) go out again, rejoicing at still more to do for My Sake.

Little frets and little worries
Rob me of my peace of mind,
And the more I rush and hurry
Why, the more I get behind.

So I'll stop, just stop, my fretting;
I will speak with no one till
I've surrendered what upsets me,
And my heart is calm and still.

PRAY:
Lord, how easily I sometimes allow myself to get all worked up over trivial concerns and petty issues. I yield them to You right now. Give me Your perfect peace, I pray.

Abundance

Are not two sparrows sold for a copper coin? And not one of them falls to the ground apart from your Father's will. But the very hairs of your head are all numbered. Do not fear therefore; you are of more value than many sparrows.
MATTHEW 10:29–31

How unseeing the world goes on! How unknowing of your heartaches and troubles, your battles won, your conquests, your difficulties.

But be thankful, both of you, that there is One who knows, One who marks every crisis, every effort, every heartache.

For you both, who are not idle hearers, you must know that every troubled soul I tell you of is one for you to help. You must help all you can. You do not help enough. As you help, help will flow back and your circle of helpfulness will widen more and more, ever more and more.

Just feel that you are two of My disciples, present at the feeding of the five thousand, and that to you I hand out the food, and you pass it on, and ever more and more. You can always say with so few loaves and fishes "We have only enough for our own needs." It was not only My Blessing, but the Passing-on of the disciples that worked the miracle.

Get a feeling of bounteous giving into your beings. They were "all filled." There was a supply over.

I give with a large Hand and Heart. Note the draught of fishes. The net broke, the boat began to sink with the lavishness of My Gift. Lose sight of all limitations.

Abundance is God's Supply. Turn out all limited thoughts. Receive *showers* and in your turn—*shower*.

Accomplish Anything

Another parable He put forth to them, saying: "The kingdom of heaven is like a mustard seed, which a man took and sowed in his field, which indeed is the least of all the seeds; but when it is grown it is greater than the herbs and becomes a tree, so that the birds of the air come and nest in its branches."
MATTHEW 13:31–32

There will be no limit to what you can accomplish. Realize that. Never relinquish any task or give up the thought of any task because it seems beyond your power, only if you see it is not My Will for you. This I command you.

Think of the tiny snowdrop-shoot in the hard ground. No certainty even that when it has forced its weary way up, sunlight and warmth will greet it.

What a task beyond its power that must seem. But with the inner urge of Life within the seed compelling it, it carries out that task. The Kingdom of Heaven is like unto this.

CONSIDER:
What is keeping me from accomplishing great things? Is it because I feel inadequate? Can I trust that the Lord will give me the strength?

PRAY:
God, show me that my greatest strength lies in You, and that Your strength is unlimited.

Claim More

Until now you have asked nothing in My name.
Ask, and you will receive, that your joy may be full.
JOHN 16:24

Y ou are doing your claiming as I have said, and soon you will see the result. You cannot do this long without it being seen in the material. It is an undying law.

You are at present children practicing a new lesson. Practice—practice—soon you will be able to do it so readily.

You see others manifesting so easily, so readily demonstrating My Power. But you have not seen the discipline that went before. Discipline absolutely necessary before this Power is given to My disciples. It is a further initiation.

You are feeling you have learnt so much that life cannot be a failure. That is right, but others have to wait to see the outward manifestation in your lives before they realize this Spiritual Truth.

CONSIDER:
Jesus has commanded, "Ask, and you will receive," so why don't
I ask? He has told me to claim and I shall see results, so why
do I hesitate? Have past unanswered prayers discouraged me?
Do I feel myself unworthy of His blessings? How must I yield
to God before He can manifest His power in my life?

PRAY:
Lord, please give me the faith to take that first step, and then
to daily discipline myself to expect Your miracle-working power.

Roots and Fruits

That Christ may dwell in your hearts through faith; that you, being rooted and grounded in love, may be able to comprehend with all saints what is the width and length and depth and height—to know the love of Christ which passes knowledge; that you may be filled with all the fullness of God.
EPHESIANS 3:17–19

Remember the lesson of the *seed,* too, in its sending a shoot down so that it may be rooted and grounded, while at the same time it sends a shoot up to be the plant and flower that shall gladden the world.

The two growths are necessary. Without the strong root it would soon wither, as much activity fails for lack of growth in Me. The higher the growth up, the deeper must be the enrooting.

Many forget this, and thus their work ceases to be permanent for Me. Beware of the leaves and flowers without the strong root.

CONSIDER:
*Am I rooted and grounded in my faith
in Christ, and growing in His love?*

PRAY:
*God, I want to grow into an effective Christian who
bears good fruit. Help me understand clearly that all the
good I will ever do stems from a deep relationship with You.*

Test Your Love

Do not cast me away from Your presence, and do not take
Your Holy Spirit from me. Restore to me the joy of Your
salvation, and uphold me by Your generous Spirit.
PSALM 51:11–12

A great Love knows that in every difficulty, every trial, every failure, the presence of the loved one suffices. Test your Love for Me by this.

Just to be with Me, just to know I am beside you—does that bring you Joy and Peace? If not then your Love for Me, and your realization of My Love, are at fault.

Then, if this be so, pray for more Love.

CONSIDER:
Do I experience joy from just spending quiet time with Jesus?
Is my heart filled with peace just knowing that God is with me?
If not, what might be the problem? Do I not realize how great
His love for me is? Does this inadequate understanding then affect
my love for Him? If so, what should I do to resolve this issue?

PRAY:
Lord, grant me more love. Let me experience the joy and peace
of Your presence, that I might share it with those around me. Give
me a deeper knowledge of Your love, both for me and for others.

Forget

Therefore take up the whole armor of God, that you may be able to withstand in the evil day, and having done all, to stand.
EPHESIANS 6:13

Regret nothing. Not even the sins and failures. When a man views earth's wonders from some mountain height, he does not spend his time in dwelling on the stones and stumbles, the faints and failures, that marked his upward path.

So with you. Breathe in the rich blessings of each new day—forget all that lies behind you.

Man is so made that he can carry the weight of twenty-four hours, no more. Directly he weighs down with the years behind, and the days ahead, his back breaks. I have promised to help you with the burden of today only, the past I have taken from you; and if you, foolish hearts, choose to gather again that burden and bear it, then, indeed, you mock Me to expect Me to share it.

For weal or woe each day is ended. What remains to be lived, the coming twenty-four hours, you must face as you awake.

A man on a march on earth carries only what he needs for that march. Would you pity him if you saw him bearing, too, the overwhelming weight of the worn-out shoes and uniforms of past marches and years? And yet, in the mental and spiritual life, man does these things. Small wonder My poor world is heartsick and weary.

Not so must *you* act.

The Devil's Death Knell

*My soul shall be satisfied as with marrow and fatness, and my
mouth shall praise You with joyful lips. When I remember
You on my bed, I meditate on You in the night watches.*
PSALM 63:5–6

Our Lord, we praise Thee.

Praise is the devil's death knell. Resignation, acceptance of My Will,
obedience to it, have not the power to vanquish evil that praise has.

The joyful heart is My best weapon against all evil. Oh! pray and
praise.

You are learning your lesson. You are being led out into a large
place. Go with songs of rejoicing. Rejoice evermore. Happy indeed if
each day has its thrill of joy.

Talk to Me more during the day. Look up into My Face—a look
of Love, a feeling of security, a thrill of Joy at the sense of the nearness
of My Presence—these are your best prayers.

Let these smooth the day's work; then fear will vanish. And fear
is the grim figure that turns aside success.

CONSIDER:
*Do I rejoice each day, throughout the day? How could
this help to vanquish the devil and his evil influence?*

PRAY:
*O God, I look up into Your face and give You sincere praise. May my joy,
born of Your Holy Spirit, be a powerful weapon against the evil one.*

Prayer without Words

Because You have been my help, therefore in the shadow of Your wings I will rejoice. My soul follows close behind You; Your right hand upholds me.
PSALM 63:7–8

Lord, hear us, we pray.

Hear and I answer. Spend much time in prayer. Prayer is of many kinds, but of whatever kind, prayer is the linking up of the soul and mind and heart to God.

So that if it is only a glance of faith, a look or word of Love, or confidence, and no supplication is expressed, it yet follows that supply and all necessary are secured.

Because the soul, being linked to God, united to Him, receives in and through Him all things. And the soul, when in human form, needs, too, the things belonging to its habitation.

Prayer is the soul's sincere desire,
Unuttered or expressed;
The motion of a hidden fire
That trembles in the breast.

Prayer is the burden of a sigh,
The falling of a tear
The upward glancing of an eye,
When none but God is near.
JAMES MONTGOMERY (1771–1854)

PRAY:
Lord, hear my prayer, in its many forms, spoken and unspoken.
Let prayer come as naturally to me as breathing; let it permeate my every thought and action so that I am in never-ending communion with You.

Companionship

And we know that all things work together for good to those who
love God, to those who are the called according to His purpose.
For whom he foreknew, He also predestined to be conformed to the image
of His Son, that He might be the firstborn among many brethren.
ROMANS 8:28–29

The way of the soul's transformation is the Way of Divine
Companionship.

Not so much the asking Me to make you this or that but the living
with Me, thinking of Me, talking to Me—thus you grow like Me.

Love Me. Rest in Me.

Joy in Me.

My flesh is weak, my soul is dry.
Draw me near, dear Lord, I cry.
Help me give thought to You always,
And walk with You throughout my days.
I ask not, "Change me, make me new,"
I merely ask to be with You;
For when I'm near You I am changed,
My earthly thoughts are rearranged.
And as I gaze into Your face,
Your Spirit transforms me with grace.

CONSIDER:
Do I always think of God and talk to Him?

PRAY:
Lord, may I constantly seek Your
goodness, and become more like You.

My Image

Then God said, "Let Us make man in Our image, according to Our likeness; let them have dominion over the fish of the sea, over the birds of the air, and over the cattle, over all the earth and over every creeping thing that creeps on the earth." So God created man in His own image; in the image of God He created him; male and female He created them.

GENESIS 1:26–27

*My Lord and my God, we praise Thee,
we bless Thee, we worship Thee. Make us like Thee.*

You are willing to drink of the cup that I drink of—the wine of sorrow and disappointment.

You are Mine and will grow both of you more and more like Me, your Master.

True it is today as it was in the days of Moses that no man can see My Face and live.

The self, the original *Man*, shrivels up and dies, and upon the soul becomes stamped My image.

CONSIDER:
*Have I fully surrendered my self—
my flawed and sinful human ways—to God?*

PRAY:
*Perfect God, I want to be like You, not a flawed image but a complete one.
Fill me with Yourself for "God is love," and Your love is perfect.*

Eject Sin with Love

When I was a child, I spoke as a child, I understood as a child,
I thought as a child; but when I became a man, I put away childish
things. For now we see in a mirror, dimly, but then face to face.
Now I know in part, but then I shall know just as I also am known.
And now abide faith, hope, love, these three; but the greatest of these is love.
1 CORINTHIANS 13:11–13

Our Lord, we love and praise Thee.
Thou art our Joy and our exceeding great reward.

Remember that Love is the power which transforms the world. Love not only of Me, Love not only of the few dear to you, but Love of all—of the publicans, the sinners, the harlots—Love.

It is the only weapon with which sin can be driven out. Drive sin out with *Love*.

Drive fear and depression and despair and a sense of failure out with Praise.

Praise is the acknowledgment of that which I have sent you. Few men would send a further gift of payment until they had received the acknowledgment of the previous one. So praise, acknowledging, as it does, that My gift and blessing leave the way open for Me to shower yet more on the thankful heart.

Learn as a child learns to say "Thank you" as a courtesy, with perhaps no real sense of gratitude at all. Do this until at last a thrill of joy, of thankful awe, will accompany the spoken word.

Do not expect for yourselves feeling that you know others have or have had. Just go on along the arid way of obedience, and persistence will be rewarded as you come to the Spring, the glad Spring of Water.

Oh, joy in Me, and, as far as in you lies, shed Joy on all around.

Divine Patience

*And we have confidence in the Lord concerning you, both that you
do and will do the things we command you. Now may the Lord
direct your hearts into the love of God and into the patience of Christ.*
2 THESSALONIANS 3:4–5

Molding, My children, means cutting and chiseling. It means
sacrifice of the personal to conform to type. It is not only
My work but yours.

The swift recognition of the selfish in your desires and motives,
actions, words, and thoughts, and the instant appeal to Me for help to
eradicate that.

It is a work that requires cooperation—Mine and yours. It is a work
that brings much sense of failure and discouragement, too, at times,
because, as the work proceeds, you see more and more clearly
all that yet remains to be done.

Shortcomings you had hardly recognized or at least for which you
had had no sense of sorrow, now cause you trouble and dismay.

Courage. That is in itself a sign of progress.

As you see the slow progress upward made by you, in spite of your
longing and struggle, you will gain a divine patience with others whose
imperfections trouble you.

So on and up. Forward. Patience—Perseverance—Struggle.
Remember that I am beside you, your Captain and your Helper.
So tender, so patient, so strong.

Yes, we cooperate, and as I share your troubles, failures,
difficulties, heartaches, so, as My friends, you share My patience
and My strength—beloved.

That Tender Voice

When you are in distress, and all these things come upon you in the latter days,
when you turn to the LORD your God and obey his voice (for the LORD your
God is a merciful God), He will not forsake you nor destroy you, nor forget
the covenant of your fathers which He swore to them.
DEUTERONOMY 4:30–31

Very quietly I speak. Listen to My Voice. Never heed the voices of the world—only the tender Divine Voice.

Listen and you will never be disappointed. Listen, and anxious thoughts and tired nerves will become rested. The Voice Divine—not so much in strength as in tenderness. Not so much in power as in restfulness.

But the tenderness and the restfulness will heal your scars and make you strong, and then it must be your task to let all your power be My Power. Man's little power is as clay beside the granite rock of My Power.

You are My great care. Never feel at the mercy of the world. My angels guard you day and night, and nothing can harm you. You would indeed thank Me if you knew the darts of fret and evil they turn from you.

Thank Me indeed for dangers unknown—unseen—but averted.

CONSIDER:
I know that the Lord has great power and strength,
but do I also know that He has great tenderness and
restfulness? Should I be surprised then that He most often
speaks with a "still, small voice," tenderly and quietly?

PRAY:
God, I thank You that Your angels constantly stand guard over me,
shielding me from harm, from calamity, from all the fiery darts of the evil one.

How Men See Me

And my God shall supply all your need according to His riches in glory by Christ Jesus. Now to our God and Father be glory forever and ever. Amen.
PHILIPPIANS 4:19–20

I came to help a world. And according to the varying needs of each, so does each man see Me.

It is not necessary that *you* see Me as others see Me—the world, even the Church, My disciples, My followers—but it is necessary that *you* see Me, each of you, as supplying all that *you* personally need.

The weak need My Strength. The strong need My Tenderness. The tempted and fallen need My Salvation. The righteous need My Pity for sinners. The lonely need a Friend. The fighters need a Leader.

No *man* could be all these to men—only a God could be. In each of these relations of Mine to man you must see the God. The God-Friend, the God-Leader, the God-Savior.

CONSIDER:
Where do I turn for the fulfillment of my needs?
Am I looking for satisfaction from the world or from God?

PRAY:
O God, open my eyes. Don't let me forget that You are the answer to my every need: You supply me with strength and tenderness and salvation and compassion and friendship and guidance.

True Beauty

Incline your ear, and come unto me: hear, and your soul shall live.
ISAIAH 55:3 KJV

Not only live but grow in grace and power and beauty—the true Beauty, the Beauty of Holiness.

Reach ever forward after the things of My Kingdom.

In the animal world, the very form of an animal alters to enable it to reach that upon which it delights to feed.

So, reaching after the treasures of My Kingdom, your whole nature becomes changed, so that you can best enjoy and receive the wonders of that Kingdom.

Dwell on these truths.

Walk with the Lord in the beauty of holiness,
Let your life be holy, wholly without blame.
Worship the Lord in the beauty of holiness,
In whatever you do, bring praise to His name.

Grow in God's beauty, the beauty of holiness;
Let the splendor of Jesus rest fully on you.
Would you be holy? Spend time with the Holy One,
And His beautiful Spirit will fill your life too.

CONSIDER:

Do I recognize that, wherever true beauty is found,
there God resides? Do I strive most of all to lay hold on
the beautiful treasures and attributes of God's kingdom?

The Only Way

For those who live according to the flesh set their minds on the things of the flesh, but those who live according to the Spirit, the things of the Spirit. For to be carnally minded is death, but to be spiritually minded is life and peace. Because the carnal mind is enmity against God; for it is not subject to the law of God, nor indeed can be. So then, those who are in the flesh cannot please God. But you are not in the flesh but in the Spirit, if indeed the Spirit of God dwells in you. Now if anyone does not have the Spirit of Christ, he is not His.

ROMANS 8:5–9

D own through the ages, My Power alone has kept millions of souls brave and true and strong who else would have fallen by the way.

The Faith has been kept alive and handed down, not by the dwellers in ease, but by those who struggled and suffered and died for Me.

This life is not for the body, it is for the soul, and man too often chooses the way of life that best suits the body, not the way that best suits the soul. And I permit only what best suits the soul.

Accept this and a wonderful molding is the result; reject it and My Purpose is frustrated, your best prayer unanswered, progress (Spiritual progress) delayed, trouble and grief stored up.

Try, each of you, to picture your soul as a third being trained by us—by you and Me—and then you will share, and rejoice in sharing, in the discipline and training.

Stand apart from your soul with Me and welcome training—rejoice at progress.

PRAY:

Dear Lord, please help me to grasp this truth: "This life is not for the body, it is for the soul." Mold me according to Your will.

An Obstacle Race

Therefore we also, since we are surrounded by so great a cloud of witnesses,
let us lay aside every weight, and the sin which so easily ensnares us,
and let us run with endurance the race that is set before us.
HEBREWS 12:1

Rise above your fears and fancies into My Joy. It will suffice to heal all your sores and wounds. Forget all sense of failure and shortcomings, all the painful jolts and jars, and trust Me, love Me, call upon Me.

Your discipleship is an obstacle race. "So run that ye may obtain." Obtain not only your hearts' desires, but obtain Me—your souls' Joy and Haven.

What would you think of the runner who threw himself on the ground in despondency at his first hurdle?

Over, and on and up. I am your Leader and your goal.

CONSIDER:
How patient am I in dealing with the constant
obstacles that this world throws in my path? Am I
committed to running this race until the very end?

PRAY:
Lord, as I continue to run this race, grant me patience and
stamina so I won't give way to discouragement. Help me
to recognize that there will be hurdles but that with Your
grace and guidance I'll cross the finish line victorious.

The Day of Trouble

Do not lay up for yourselves treasures on earth, where moth and rust destroy and where thieves break in and steal; but lay up for yourselves treasures in heaven, where neither moth nor rust destroys and where thieves do not break in and steal. For where your treasure is, there your heart will be also.

MATTHEW 6:19–21

Offer unto Me the sacrifice of thanksgiving and pay your vows to the Most High, and then call upon Me in the day of trouble and I will deliver you.

To praise and thank and steadily fulfill your promises (vows) to Me are then, as it were, the placing of coin in My Bank, upon which, in your time of need, you can draw with confidence and certainty. Remember that.

The world wonders when it sees the man who can so unexpectedly draw large and unsuspected sums from his bank for his own need, that of a friend, or for some charity.

But what the world has not seen are the countless small sums paid into that bank, earned by faithful work in many ways.

And so in My Kingdom. The world sees the man of faith make a sudden demand upon Me, upon My stores, and lo! that demand is met.

So with you, My children. "Offer to God the sacrifice of Thanksgiving and pay your vows to the Most High and call upon Me in the day of trouble and I will deliver you."

This is a promise for the seemingly dull days of little happenings and a cheer for you, My children. When you seem not able to do big things, you can be storing your little acts and words of faithfulness in My Great Storehouse, ready for the day of your big demand.

My Mark!

Keep your tongue from evil, and your lips from speaking deceit.
Depart from evil and do good; seek peace and pursue it.
PSALM 34:13–14

O Lord, we thank Thee for Thy great gift of Peace.

That is the Peace, that only I can give in the midst of a restless world and surrounded by trouble and difficulty. To know that Peace is to have received the stamp of the Kingdom—the mark of the Lord Jesus Christ. My Mark.

When you have learned that Peace, you are fit to judge of true values, the values of the Kingdom, and the values of all the world has to offer.

That Peace is loving faith at rest.

CONSIDER:
Do I possess the peace that only Jesus Christ
can give to me? Is His mark visible in my life?

PRAY:
Father, grant me the peace that You have made available through
Your Son, Jesus Christ. And may I forever dwell in that peace!

House on a Rock

Therefore whoever hears these sayings of Mine, and does them, I will liken him
to a wise man who built his house on the rock: and the rain descended,
the floods came, and the winds blew and beat on that house; and it did not fall,
for it was founded on the rock. But everyone who hears these sayings of Mine,
and does not do them, will be like a foolish man who built his house on the sand.
MATTHEW 7:24–26

B e watchful to hear My Voice and instantly to obey. Obedience is
your great sign of faith. "Why call ye Me Lord, Lord, and do not
the things that I say?" was My word when on earth to the many who
followed and heard but did not do.

I likened the man who heard and did not do to the man who built
his house on the sand. In times of storm and trouble, he is overthrown;
his house falls.

I likened the man who obeyed Me implicitly to the man who built
his house upon a rock. In times of storm he is steadfast, immovable.

Do not feel that by this I mean only the keeping of My
Commandments, even the living of My Sermon on the Mount. I mean
more than that to those who know Me intimately. I mean the following,
in all, the Inner Guiding that I give, the little injunctions I speak to
each individual soul, the wish I express—and desire to have carried out.

The secure, steadfast, immovable life of My disciples, the Rock
Home, is not built at a wish, in a moment, but is laid, stone by stone,
foundations, walls, roof, by the acts of obedience, the daily following out
of My wishes, the loving doing of My Will.

"He that heareth these sayings of Mine and doeth them is like
unto a man who built his house upon a rock, and the rain descended
and the floods came, and the winds blew and beat upon that house and
it fell not, for it was founded upon a Rock."

Am I not giving you work, hope? Work for the gray days? Just little plain bricks of duties done and My Wishes carried out. All strengthening you and making your character that steadfast, immovable Christian Character of which My servant Paul spoke and which he urged his followers to have.

And it is in that Rock Home, man-made but divinely inspired—the House of Obedience—the truest expression of a disciple's adoration and worship—it is *there* I come to dwell with My loved one.

God-Inspired

*To speak evil of no one, to be peaceable, gentle, showing all humility
to all men. For we ourselves were also once foolish, disobedient, deceived,
serving various lusts and pleasures, living in malice and envy, hateful
and hating one another. But when the kindness and the love of God
our Saviour toward man appeared, not by works of righteousness
which we have done, but according to His mercy He saved us,
through the washing of regeneration and renewing of the Holy Spirit.*
TITUS 3:2–5

You have entered now upon a mountain climb. Steep steps lead
upward, but your power to help others will be truly marvelous.

Not alone will you arise. All toward whom you now send loving,
pitying thoughts will be helped upward by you.

Looking to Me, all your thoughts are God-inspired. Act on
them and you will be led on. They are not your own impulses but the
movement of My Spirit and, obeyed, will bring the answer to
your prayers.

Love and Trust. Let no unkind thoughts of any dwell in your
hearts, then I can act with all My Spirit-power, with nothing to hinder.

CONSIDER:
*Why would me having unloving thoughts about others
hinder God's power to answer prayer? What does Galatians
5:6 mean when it talks about "faith working by love"?*

PRAY:
*God, let all my thoughts be inspired by You, and let all my
actions be guided by these thoughts. Let me be an inspiration
to others, so that they also may put their trust in You.*

Face Today with Me

Create in me a clean heart, O God,
and renew a steadfast spirit within me.
PSALM 51:10

Our Lord and our God.
Make us all Thou wouldst have us.

It is not circumstances that need altering first, but yourselves, and then the conditions will naturally alter. Spare no effort to become all I would have you. Follow every leading. I am your only Guide.

Endeavor to put from you every thought of trouble. Take each day, and with no backward look, face the day's problem with Me, and seek My Help and guidance as to what you can do.

Never look back and never leave until the morrow that on which you can get My Guidance for today.

CONSIDER:
How do I begin my day? Do I face my troubles alone,
or head out with the assurance that God is with me,
and that He will guide me in the way that I should go?

PRAY:
God, my circumstances need changing, but I ask You
to first of all change my heart. Make me all that I should be.

"Glory, Glory Dawneth"

You prepare a table before me in the presence of my
enemies; you anoint my head with oil; my cup runs over.
Surely goodness and mercy shall follow me all the days
of my life; and I will dwell in the house of the LORD forever.
PSALM 23:5–6

I am planning for you. Wonderful are My Ways beyond your knowledge. Oh! realize My Bounty and My Goodness more and more. The wonder of being led by Me! The beauty of a guided life!

These will enter your consciousness more and more and bring you ever more and more Joy.

You are very nearly at the point when you shall ask what you will and it shall be done unto you.

You have entered upon a wonderful era—your lives are planned and blessed by Me as never before.

You are overcoming. You are counting all things but loss if you can win Me. And the promises to him that overcometh are truly wonderful, and will always be fulfilled.

May the mind of Christ, my Savior,
Live in me from day to day,
By His love and power controlling
All I do and say.

May the Word of God dwell richly
In my heart from hour to hour,
So that all may see I triumph
Only through His power.
KATE BARCLAY WILKINSON (1859–1928)

Seek Me Early

O God, You are my God; early will I seek you; my soul thirsts for you;
my flesh longs for you in a dry and thirsty land where there is no water.
So I have looked for You in the sanctuary, to see Your power and Your glory.
PSALM 63:1–2

Walk in My Way and trust Me. No evil can touch you. I am yours as truly as you are Mine. Rest in that truth.

Rest, that is, cease all struggle. Gain a calm, strong confidence in that certainty. Do not only rest in Me when the world's struggles prove too much and too many for you to bear or face alone. Rest in Me when you need perfect understanding, when you need the consciousness of tender, loving friendship and communion.

The world, my poor world, flies to Me when its difficulties are too great to be surmounted any other way, forgetting, or never realizing, that if, with the same eagerness, those hearts sought Me merely for companionship and loving communion, many of the difficulties would not arise.

The circumstances, the life, the character would be so altered—so purified, that those same difficulties would not exist.

Seek Me *early*; that is the way to find Me. *Early*, before I get crowded out by life's troubles and difficulties and pleasures.

CONSIDER:
Am I putting God first in my life—or am
I allowing other things to take precedence and
crowd out the time I would've spent with Him?

Dear Name

*That at the name of Jesus every knee should bow, of those in heaven,
and of those on earth, and of those under the earth, and that every tongue
should confess that Jesus Christ is Lord, to the glory of God the Father.*
PHILIPPIANS 2:10–11

J esus." Say My Name often. It was in My Name Peter bade the lame
man walk. "In the Name of Jesus Christ of Nazareth arise and walk."

"*Jesus.*" The very sounding of My Name, in Love and tenderness,
drives away all evil. It is the word before which all the hosts of evil flee.

"*Jesus.*" My Name is the call for a lifeline to rescue you from
temptation.

"*Jesus.*" The Name banishes loneliness—dispels gloom.

"*Jesus.*" Summons help to conquer your faults.

I will set you on high because you have known My Name.

Yes! My Name—"Jesus." Use it more. Use it tenderly. Use it
prayerfully. Use it powerfully.

*How sweet the Name of Jesus sounds
In a believer's ear!
It soothes his sorrows, heals his wounds,
And drives away his fear.*

*It makes the wounded spirit whole,
And calms the troubled breast;
'Tis manna to the hungry soul,
And to the weary, rest.*
JOHN NEWTON (1725–1807)

PRAY:
*God, keep me ever mindful of the power of Your Son's name.
Let me speak it daily with reverence, with tenderness, with love.*

Wait

Immediately Jesus made His disciples get into the boat and go before
Him to the other side, while He sent the multitudes away. And
when He had sent the multitudes away, He went up on the mountain
by Himself to pray. Now when evening came, He was alone there.
MATTHEW 14:22–23

The world has always seen service for Me to be activity. Only those near to Me have seen that a life apart, of prayer, may, and does so often, accomplish more than all the service man can offer Me.

If man lived apart with Me and only went out to serve at My direct command, My Spirit could operate more and accomplish truly mighty things.

"Lord, the day is beginning.
I must get busy," I say,
"Wait, My child," He whispers.
"Come here awhile and pray."

"But Lord," I answer now anxious,
"Things need doing right away!"
"Wait, My child," He whispers.
"Don't rush right into your day."

So though I'm eager to be busy
And deeds cry out to be done,
I set aside my "To do" list,
And kneel before God's Son.

CONSIDER:
Do I earnestly desire to hear the Lord's call?

The Success You Covet

Humble yourselves in the sight of
the Lord, and He will lift you up.
JAMES 4:10

Follow the path of obedience. It leads to the Throne of God. Your treasure, be it success necessary on the material plane, which will further the work of My Kingdom, or the hidden spiritual wonders revealed by Me to those only who diligently seek, this treasure lies at the end of the track.

From one point (a promise of Mine or a Command) to the next, you have to follow, till finally you reach the success you covet.

All *your* work for the moment is in the material plane, and the spiritual is only to help the material. When your material goal is reached, then the material will serve only to attain the spiritual.

CONSIDER:
Am I daily striving to be obedient to God?
Am I focused on the spiritual rather than the material?

PRAY:
Humble me, O Lord. Help me to realize that
true success lies not in worldly gain, but in seeking
Your will and furthering the work of Your kingdom.

Miracles Again

*By faith Sarah herself also received strength to conceive
seed, and she bore a child when she was past the age,
because she judged Him faithful who had promised.*
HEBREWS 11:11

Wait to hear My Will and then obey. At all costs obey.
Do not fear. I am a wall of protection around you. See this.
To see this with the eyes of faith is to cause it to manifest in the material.

Remember, I long to work miracles, as when on earth I wrought
them, but the same condition holds good. I cannot do many mighty
works because of unbelief.

So only in response to your belief can I do miracle-works now.

CONSIDER:
*Like Sarah, do I judge God to be faithful to keep
His promises? Do I understand what this sentence means:
"To see this with the eyes of faith is to cause it to manifest
in the material"? If I need more faith, how can I get it?*

PRAY:
*Lord, vanquish my disbelief, and open my heart and mind to believe that,
even today, You can work miracles through me if I allow You to.*

See As I See

To the Chief Musician. On stringed instruments. A Psalm. A Song.
*God be merciful to us and bless us, and cause His face to shine upon us, Selah.
That Your way may be known on earth, Your salvation among all nations.*
PSALM 67:1–2

O Lord, we praise Thee. Bless us, we beseech Thee.

I bless you. I promise you release. Joy in Me. You shall be shielded from the storm.

Wonders have unfolded. Just to come before Me and stay for a while in My Presence—this must strengthen and help you.

Learn of Me. The only way for so many in My poor world to keep calm, sane, is to have the mind which is in Jesus Christ. The mind which is in Me.

That mind you can never obtain by reasoning, or by reading, but only by living with Me and sharing My Life.

Think much of Me. Speak much of Me. See others as I see them. Let nothing less satisfy you.

CONSIDER:
*Am I looking at others with my own flawed vision,
or am I seeing them through God's eyes of love?*

PRAY:
*God, I don't want to rely on my own reasoning. Please help me
spend time with You so that I will share Your thoughts and outlook on
matters—and see people and situations the way that You see them.*

Your Red Sea

Then Moses stretched out his hand over the sea; and the Lord caused the sea to go back by a strong east wind all that night, and made the sea into dry land, and the waters were divided. So the children of Israel went into the midst of the sea on the dry ground, and the waters were a wall to them on their right hand and on their left.

EXODUS 14:21–22

G o forward fearlessly.

Do not think about the Red Sea that lies ahead.

Be very sure that when you come to it the waters will part and you will pass over to your promised land of freedom.

CONSIDER:

Am I afraid of what lies ahead of me, or do I trust God to guide me through troubled times? What "Red Sea," what uncrossable obstacle, is blocking my path right now? Is it an unreasonable deadline? Is it a financial barrier? Is it a task greater than my abilities? Do I have the faith to trust that God will do a miracle and part the water?

PRAY:

O Lord, I'm not fearless by nature. Create in me a fearless heart. Give me courage that will keep me moving on the path You have set before me. Things may seem impossible just now, but give me the faith to believe that You will make a way through this impossible situation.

Cling to Me

He makes me to lie down in green pastures;
He leads me beside the still waters. He restores my soul;
He leads me in the paths of righteousness for His name's sake.
PSALM 23:2–3

Cling to Me until the life from Me—the Divine Life, by that very contact, flows into your being and revives your fainting spirit.

Become recharged. When weary, do as I did on earth—*sit by the well. Rest.*

Rest and gain power and strength, and the work, too, will come to you as it came to Me.

Rest till every care-thought has gone, and then let the Tide of Love and Joy flow in.

CONSIDER:
Where do I seek rest and strength from? Do I look to God?
What about when I need physical rest? Am I so anxious that I
keep on pushing and risk physical, mental, and emotional burnout?
Or can I sit by the well awhile to rest, trusting that God will
take care of things while I take a much-needed time-out?

PRAY:
Grant me rest, O Lord! I'm weary with the continual
cares of this world. Let me be revived by Your power.

When Guidance Tarries

The LORD is my light and my salvation; whom shall I fear?
The LORD is the strength of my life; of whom shall I be afraid?
When the wicked came against me to eat up my flesh, my enemies
and foes, they stumbled and fell. Though an army may encamp against me,
my heart shall not fear; though war may rise against me, in this
I will be confident. One thing I have desired of the LORD, that will I seek:
that I may dwell in the house of the LORD all the days of my life,
to behold the beauty of the LORD, and to inquire in His temple.
PSALM 27:1–4

As I prompt you—act. When you have no clear guidance, then go forward quietly along the path of duty I have set before you.

No fear, no panic, quietly doing your daily duty.

This attitude of faith will receive its reward, as surely as the acting upon My direct Guidance.

Rejoice in the sense of security that is yours.

CONSIDER:
How confident am I that God is with me every moment,
even in those moments when I don't hear His voice?

PRAY:
Dear God, when You don't give me fresh guidance, help me to
quietly, faithfully continue to obey You in the things You've already
shown me to do. May I never surrender to panic when You are silent.

God's Friendship

And the Scripture was fulfilled which says, "Abraham believed God, and it was accounted to him for righteousness." And he was called the friend of God.
JAMES 2:23

I am your Friend. The Companion of the dreary ways of life.

I rob those ways of their grayness and horror. I transform them. Even in earthly friendships the common way, the weary way, the steep way may seem a way to Heaven if the presence of some loved human friend transforms them.

Let the Sabbath calm enwrap your minds and hearts. Let it be a rest from the worry and fret of life.

Have you ever realized the wonder of the friendship you can have with Me? Have you ever thought what it means to be able to summon at will the God of the World?

Even with a privileged visitor to an earthly king there is the palace antechamber, and the time must be at the pleasure of the king.

But to My subjects I have given the right to enter My Presence when they will, nay more they can summon Me to bedside, to workshop—and I am there.

When men seek to worship Me, they think of the worlds I rule over, of creation, of mighty law and order—and then they feel the awe that precedes worship.

To you I say feel awe, feel the desire to worship Me in wondering amazement. But think, too, of the mighty, tender, humble condescension of My Friendship. Think of Me in the little things of everyday life.

Do Not Rush

I wait for the LORD, my soul waits, and in His word I do hope.
PSALM 130:5

L earn in the little daily things of life to delay action until you get My Guidance....

So many lives lack poise. For in the momentous decisions and the big things of life, they ask My help, but into the small things they rush alone.

By what you do in the small things, those around you are most often antagonized or attracted.

I always pray first before big things,
But rush into small deeds all day.
Now, isn't it strange to not seek God
In small things, and do them His way?

When I rush ahead without pausing to pray
My life lacks all poise and all grace;
I antagonize people I know to no end,
And end up dead last in the race.

CONSIDER:
Do I seek God about the small
things as well as the big things?

PRAY:
God, slow me down when I'm moving too fast. Keep me from
rushing into action based on my own limited understanding.

No Self-Reproach

The eternal God is your refuge, and underneath are the everlasting arms;
he will thrust out the enemy from before you, and will say, "Destroy!"
DEUTERONOMY 33:27

The Eternal Arms shelter you. "Underneath are the Everlasting Arms." This promise is to those who rise above the earth-life and seek to soar higher, to the Kingdom of Heaven.

You must not feel the burden of your failure. Go on in faith, the clouds will clear, and the way will lighten—the path becomes less stony with every step you take. So run that you may obtain. A rigid doing of the simple duties, and success will crown your efforts.

I had no words of reproach for any I healed. The man was whole and free who had wrecked his physical being by sin—whose palsy I healed.

The woman at the well was not overwhelmed by My "Thou hast had five husbands; and he whom thou now hast is not thy husband."

The woman taken in adultery was told, "Neither do I condemn thee: go, and sin no more." She was not told to bear the burden of the consciousness of her sin. . . .

Remember now abideth these three, Faith, Hope, and Charity. Faith is your attitude toward Me. Charity is your attitude toward your fellow man but, as necessary, is Hope, which is confidence in yourself to succeed.

Table of Delights

*Make a joyful shout to the LORD, all you lands! Serve the
LORD with gladness; come before His presence with singing.
Know that the LORD, He is God; it is He who has made us,
and not we ourselves; we are His people and the sheep of His pasture.*
PSALM 100:1–3

It has not been in vain this training and teaching time. The time of
suppression, repression, depression is changed now into a time of
glorious expression.

Life is flooded through and through with Joy and Gladness. Indeed,
I have prepared a table of delights, a feast of all good things for you.

Indeed, your cup runneth over and you can feel from the very
depth of your heart. "Surely goodness and mercy shall follow me all the
days of my life: and I will dwell in the house of the LORD for ever."

CONSIDER:
*Do I constantly think about the
many blessings God has given to me?*

PRAY:
*Dear God, now that You've laid a table of delights before me,
I can see that the tough times of training were all worth it.*

My Will—Your Joy

Where can I go from Your Spirit? Or where can I flee from Your presence?
If I ascend into heaven, You are there; if I make my bed in hell, behold, You are
there. If I take the wings of the morning, and dwell in the uttermost parts of
the sea, even there Your hand shall lead me, and Your right hand shall hold me.
PSALM 139:7–10

Our Lord and our God. Lead us, we beseech Thee.
Lead us and keep us.

You can never go beyond My Love and Care. Remember that. No evil can befall you. Circumstances I bless and use must be the right ones for you.

But I know always that the first step is to lay your will before Me as an offering, ready that I shall do what is best, sure that, if you trust Me, what I do for you will be best.

Your second step is to be sure, and to tell me so, that I am Powerful enough to do everything ("The hearts of kings are in My rule and governance"), that no miracle is impossible with me ("With God all things are possible" and "I and my Father are one").

Then leave all with Me. Glad to leave all your affairs in a Master Hand. Sure of safety and protection. Remember you cannot see the future. I can.

You could not bear it. So only little by little can I reveal it to you. Accept My Will, and it will bring you joy.

Understand Them

This is My commandment, that you love one another as I have loved you.
Greater love has no one than this, than to lay down one's life for his friends.
John 15:12–13

Take joy wherever you go. You have been much blessed. You are being much blessed.

Such stores of blessing are awaiting you in the months and years that lie ahead. Pass every blessing on.

Love can and does go round the world, passed on the God-currents from one to the other.

Shed a little sunshine in the heart of one, that one is cheered to pass it on, and so My vitalizing joy-giving message goes.

Be transmitters these days. Love and Laugh. Cheer all. Love all.

Always seek to understand others and you cannot fail to love them.

See Me in the dull, the uninteresting, the sinful, the critical, the miserable.

See Me in the laughter of children and the sweetness of old age, in the courage of youth and the patience of man and womanhood.

CONSIDER:
Can others see and sense the love
of God in me? Do they feel loved?

PRAY:
O God, heighten my understanding and empathy for others—
my friends and family and neighbors and coworkers,
as well as my enemies. Let me be a transmitter of Your love.

Attack Fear

For God has not given us a spirit of fear,
but of power and of love and of a sound mind.
2 TIMOTHY 1:7

Learn daily the sublime lesson of trust and calm in the midst of storm. Whatever of sorrow or difficulty the day may bring My tender command to you is still the same—*Love and Laugh.*

Love and Laughter, not a sorrowful resignation, mark real acceptances of My Will. Leave every soul the braver and happier for having met you. For children or youth, middle or old age, for sorrow, for sin, for all you may encounter in others, this should be your attitude. *Love and Laugh.*

Do not fear. Remember how I faced the devil in the wilderness, and how I conquered with "the sword of the Spirit, which is the word of God." You, too, have your quick answer for every fear that evil may present—an answer of faith and confidence in Me. Where possible say it aloud.

The spoken word has power. Look on every fear, not as a weakness on your part due to illness or worry, but as a very real temptation to be attacked and overthrown.

CONSIDER:
How does laughter demonstrate a greater acceptance
of God's will than sorrowful resignation? Do I
see every fear as a temptation to be resisted?

The Child-Spirit

Then Jesus called a little child to Him, set him in the midst of them, and said,
"Assuredly, I say to you, unless you are converted and become as little children,
you will by no means enter the kingdom of heaven. Therefore whoever
humbles himself as this little child is the greatest in the kingdom of heaven."
MATTHEW 18:2–4

Does the way seem a stony one? Not one stone can impede your progress. Courage. Face the future, but *face* it only with a brave and happy heart. Do not seek to see it. *You* are robbing Faith of her sublime sweetness if you do this.

Just know that all is well and that Faith, not seeing, but believing, is the barque that will bear you to safety over the stormy waters. "According to your faith be it unto you" was My injunction to those who sought healing of Me.

If for wonder-working, if for healing, if for salvation faith was so necessary, then the reason is clear why I urged that all who sought entrance to My Kingdom must become as little children. Faith is the child-attitude.

Seek in every way to become childlike. Seek, seek, seek until you find, until the years have added to your nature that of the trusting child. Not only for its simple trust must you copy the child-spirit, but for its joy in life, its ready laughter, its lack of criticism, its desire to share all with all men. Ask much that you may become as little children, friendly and loving toward all—not critical, not fearful.

"Except ye. . .become as little children, ye shall not enter into the kingdom of heaven."

Spiritual Fullness

Then Jesus said to the twelve, "Do you also want to go away?"
But Simon Peter answered Him, "Lord, to whom shall we go?
You have the words of eternal life. Also we have come to believe
and know that You are the Christ, the Son of the living God."
JOHN 6:67–69

Our Lord, we love Thee and desire to live for Thee in all things.

My children, "Blessed are they which do hunger and thirst after righteousness: for they shall be filled." That is satisfaction.

Only in that fullness of spiritual things can the heartsick and faint and weary be satisfied, healed, and rested. "Lord," we cry, "to whom shall we go but to Thee." "Thou preparest a table before me." Bread of Life, Food from Heaven.

How few realize that the feeding of the four thousand and the five thousand were in each case but an illustration of the way in which I should one day be the Food of My people.

Think of the wonder of revelation still to be seen by those who live with Me. All these hundreds of years, and much of what I said and did is still mystery; much of My Life on earth is still spiritually unexplored country. Only to the simple and the loving heart that walks with Me can these things be revealed. I have carefully hidden these things from the wise and prudent and have revealed them unto babes.

Do not weigh your spirits down with the sins and sorrows of the world. Only Christ can do that and live. Look for the loving, the true, the kindly, the brave in the many all around you.

Friend of Mine

*"I delight to do Your will, O my God,
and Your law is within my heart."*
PSALM 40:8

What man calls conversion is often only the discovery of the Great Friend. What man calls religion is the knowledge of the Great Friend. What man calls holiness is the imitation of the Great Friend.

Perfection, that perfection I enjoined on all, the being perfect as your Father in Heaven is perfect, is the being like the Great Friend and in turn becoming to others a Great Friend, too.

I am your Friend. Think again of all that means—Friend and Savior. A friend is ready to help, anticipating every want, hand outstretched to help and encourage, or to ward off danger, voice of tenderness to soothe tired nerves and speak peace to restlessness and fear.

Think of what, to you, your friend is and then from that, try to see a little of what the Perfect Friend, the tireless, selfless, all-conquering, all miracle-working Friend would be. *That* Friend, and more even than your heart can imagine, that *Friend* am I.

Were I to read My Kingdom—My Kingdom of the Child Hearts—the doctrines of your churches, so often there would be no response. But the simple rules I gave My followers are known, loved, and lived by them all.

In all things seek simplicity.

You Are Invincible

Keep my soul, and deliver me; let me not be ashamed, for I put my trust in You. Let integrity and uprightness preserve me, for I wait for You.
PSALM 25:20–21

I am with you all the time controlling, blessing, and helping you. No man or woman can stand against My Will for you. A whole world of men and women cannot do this—if you trust Me and place your affairs in My Hands.

To the passenger it may seem as if each wave would overwhelm the ship or turn it aside from its course. The captain knows by experience that, in spite of wind and wave, he steers a straight course to the haven where he would be.

So trust Me, the Captain of your salvation.

CONSIDER:
Do I stay calm when I'm hit by the stormy seas of adversity?
Do my actions show that I trust the Captain of my salvation?

PRAY:
O God, calm me when I'm agitated by challenging situations and people. Help me always remember that You are with me and will keep me safe. Help me know that no one can stand against Your Will for me.

Riches

And whatever we ask we receive from Him, because we keep His
commandments and do those things that are pleasing in His sight.
1 JOHN 3:22

*N*ever let yourselves think "we cannot afford this" or "shall never be able to do that." Say "the supply for it is not here yet, but it will come if we should have it. It *will* surely come."

Persevere in saying that, and gradually a feeling of being plentifully supplied and of being surrounded by riches will possess you. That feeling is your faith claiming My Supply, and according to your faith it shall be unto you.

But it is not the faith expressed in moments of prayer and exaltation I look for but the faith that lays immediately to rest the doubts of the day as they arise, that attacks and conquers the sense of limitation.

"Ask, and ye shall receive."

CONSIDER:
Do I ask the Lord, with unwavering faith, for the
things that I truly want and need? Do I keep His
commandments and do what is pleasing to Him?

PRAY:
Dear Lord, drive away my doubts and give me the
faith to ask You without hesitation, fully believing,
for the riches that You wish to bring to me.

Painful Preparation

"For whom the LORD loves He chastens, and scourges every son whom He receives." If you endure chastening, God deals with you as with sons; for what son is there whom a father does not chasten?
HEBREWS 12:6–7

Help and peace and joy are here. Your courage will be rewarded. Painful as this time is, you will both one day see the reason of it, and see, too, that it was not cruel testing, but tender preparation for the wonderful lifework you are both to do.

Try to realize that your own prayers are being most wonderfully answered. Answered in a way that seems painful to you, but that just now is the only way.

Success in the temporal world would not satisfy you.

Great success, in both temporal and spiritual worlds, awaits you.

I know you will see this had to be.

CONSIDER:
How do I react to God's discipline? Do I treat it as only senseless, unwanted pain, or as a necessary step in my growth, to bring me closer to Him?

PRAY:
Dear God, I accept Your chastening. Grant me the strength to endure and the patience to see beyond the painful present to glorious success in the not-too-distant future.

My Secret

I will instruct you and teach you in the way
you should go; I will guide you with My eye.
PSALM 32:8

You are being guided, but remember that I said, "I will guide thee with mine eye."

And My Eye is My set purpose—My Will.

To guide with My Will is to bring all your desires into oneness with My Will, My desires.

To make My Will your only will. Then My Will guides *you*.

Guide me, O Savior, with Your Eye,
And so control my thoughts and deeds,
That I desire Your will, O Lord,
Above my own desires and needs.

Guide me with Your steadfast will,
Fulfill Your perfect work in me;
May what You wish be what I want;
And may Your truth then set me free.

CONSIDER:
Do I want only what I selfishly want in life, or do I want
what God wants for me? Am I open to being guided by His will?

PRAY:
God, never let me forget that You are in control.
Bring all my desires into line with Your will.

Why Doubt?

But I have trusted in Your mercy; my heart
shall rejoice in Your salvation. I will sing to the
LORD, because He has dealt bountifully with me.
PSALM 13:5–6

J oy in Me. Joy is infectious. Trust and pray. It is not sin for one who knows Me only as God, as Creator, to doubt Me, to question My Love and purposes.

But for one who knows Me as you do, as Friend and Savior, and who knows the world's God as Father—for that one to doubt My purpose and saving Power and tender Love is wrong indeed.

CONSIDER:
How well do I know my God? Do I have true joy in my life,
joy that others can see in me and want to experience in their
own lives? Even if I'm not a bubbly, exuberant personality
by nature, does my life exhibit a quiet, deep-settled joy?

PRAY:
God, I thank You that I know You, not only as God and Creator, but also as
Friend and Savior and Father. Help me never to doubt Your love. Help me
never to question Your purposes in my life, nor think that they're unkind.

Expect Many Miracles

*But He said, "The things which are
impossible with men are possible with God."*
LUKE 18:27

M y guardianship is so wonderful.
Expect not one miracle but many.
Each day's happenings, if of My working and under My control,
are miracle-works.

CONSIDER:
*What do I expect from God? Do I have the faith to expect
great things, large miracles? Do I have the faith to expect a
steady stream of small miracles throughout the day? How
much control do I think God has over the events in my life?*

PRAY:
*God, increase my expectations! Teach me to expect great things,
believing that they will be fulfilled. Open my eyes to the many small miracles
already happening all around me. I thank You for everything You do.*

Guardian Angels

For He shall give His angels charge over you,
to keep you in all your ways. In their hands they
shall bear you up, lest you dash your foot against a stone.
PSALM 91:11–12

You are Mine. Once I have set on you My stamp and seal of ownership, all My Hosts throng to serve and protect you. Remember that you are daughters of a King.

Try to picture a bodyguard of My servitors in the Unseen waiting, longing, efficient, to do all that is necessary for your well-being.

Feel this as you go through the day. Feel this, and all is well.

CONSIDER:
Do I believe that God is protecting me
throughout the day? Do I feel the inner peace that
comes from being wrapped in God's loving care?

PRAY:
Let me constantly remember that I am Yours,
Lord, and that You are my Protector.

Savior and Savior

Do not be afraid of sudden terror, nor of trouble from
the wicked when it comes; for the LORD will be your
confidence, and will keep your foot from being caught.
PROVERBS 3:25–26

If you believe it is My Hand that has saved you, then you must believe that I am meaning to save you yet more, and to keep you in the way that you should go.

Even a human rescuer does not save a man from drowning only to place him in other deep and dangerous waters. But rather to place him on dry land—and more—there to restore him to animation and health, and to see him to his home.

From this parable learn what I your Rescuer would do, and even more. Is the Lord's Hand shortened that it cannot perform and cannot save?

My cry on the cross of "It is finished" is My Cry of Salvation for a whole world.

I complete every task committed to Me. So trust and be not afraid.

CONSIDER:

Have I sometimes felt that yes, God has rescued me in the
past, but now He's about to give up on me and abandon me?
But hasn't God said, "I will never leave you nor forsake you"?

PRAY:

God, thank You for sending Your Son, Jesus,
to save me. I trust You to continue keeping me on
the path of righteousness, safe from Satan's grasp.

Expect the Good

My soul, wait silently for God alone, for my expectation is from Him.
He only is my rock and my salvation; He is my defense; I shall not be
moved. In God is my salvation and my glory; the rock of my strength,
and my refuge, is in God. Trust in Him at all times, you people;
pour out your heart before Him; God is a refuge for us. Selah.
PSALM 62:5–8

Can you get the expectant attitude of faith?
Not waiting for the next evil to befall you but awaiting with a child's joyful trust the next good in store?

Standing on the promises of Christ my King,
Through eternal ages let His praises ring,
Glory in the highest, I will shout and sing,
Standing on the promises of God.

Standing on the promises that cannot fail,
When the howling storms of doubt and fear assail,
By the living Word of God I shall prevail,
Standing on the promises of God.
RUSSELL KELSO CARTER (1849–1928)

CONSIDER:
Am I an optimist? Do I look forward to each day
expecting that God has good things in store for me?

PRAY:
God, restore in me a childlike trust in You, that awe and
wonder at all You have done, and will continue to do, in my life.

True Success

*Nothing is better for a man than that he should eat and
drink, and that his soul should enjoy good in his labor.
This also, I saw, was from the hand of God.*
ECCLESIASTES 2:24

Our Lord, we thank Thee that Thou hast kept us.

Rejoice indeed that you see My Hand in all the happenings and the keepings of the day. Protected, the Israelites crossed the Red Sea; so are you protected in all things.

Rely on this and go forward. You have now entered upon the stage of success. You must not doubt this. You must see this. Beyond all doubt you must know it. It is true. It is sure.

There is no age in Eternal Life. Have no pity for yourself, nothing but joy and gratitude.

These last few weeks have been the submerging before the consciousness of rescue. Go forward now and conquer. Go forward unafraid.

CONSIDER:
*What do I consider success? Are my eyes
fixed on the temporal or the eternal?*

PRAY:
*God, help me to believe Your promise of success, so that
I may go forward joyfully and without fear, to conquer.*

Songs on the Way

Who may ascend into the hill of the LORD? Or who may stand in His holy place? He who has clean hands and a pure heart, who has not lifted up his soul to an idol, nor sworn deceitfully. He shall receive blessing from the LORD, and righteousness from the God of his salvation.

PSALM 24:3–5

M any of My disciples have had to stay on in the dark, alone and friendless.

They struggled on, singing as they went.

For you, too, there must be songs on the way. Should I plant your feet on an insecure ladder? Its supports may be out of your sight, hidden in the Secret Place of the Most High, but if I have asked you to step on and up firmly—then surely have I secured your ladder.

Sing praise to God Who reigns above, the God of all creation,
The God of power, the God of love, the God of our salvation.
With healing balm my soul is filled and every faithless murmur stilled:
To God all praise and glory.
JOHANN SCHÜTZ (1640–1690)

CONSIDER:
Do I sing praise to God daily,
even through my struggles?

PRAY:
God, You have placed my feet on a secure ladder. Some of the rungs are hidden from my eyes, but I trust You that they are there.

Refuge

*He who dwells in the secret place of the Most High shall
abide under the shadow of the Almighty. I will say of the LORD,
"He is my refuge and my fortress; my God, in Him I will trust."*
PSALM 91:1–2

K now My Divine Power. Trust in Me. Dwell in My Love. Laugh
and trust. Laughter is a child's faith in God and good.

Seek safety in My Secret Place.

You cannot be touched or harmed there. That is sure.

Really feel as if you were in a strong Tower, strongly guarded,
and against which nothing can prevail.

CONSIDER:
*How much do I trust the Lord's ability to shelter me? Do I feel
safe in His care? Have past accidents or misfortunes shaken my
confidence? Have miraculous escapes increased that confidence?*

PRAY:
*Help me to know Your divine power, Lord.
Build my trust in You. Make me unafraid.*

Peace Be Still

And a great windstorm arose, and the waves beat into the boat, so that
it was already filling. But He was in the stern, asleep on a pillow.
And they awoke Him and said to Him, "Teacher, do You not care that
we are perishing?" Then He arose and rebuked the wind, and said to the sea,
"Peace, be still!" And the wind ceased and there was a great calm.
MARK 4:37–39

Rejoice, rejoice. I have much to teach you both. Think not that
I with-hold My Presence when I do not reveal more of My Truth
to you.

You are passing through a storm. Enough that I am with you to say,
"Peace, be still," to quiet both wind and waves.

It was on the quiet mountain slopes that I taught My disciples the
Truths of My Kingdom, not during the storm.

So with you, the time of the mountain slopes will come, and you
shall rest with Me and learn.

CONSIDER:

Am I quick to panic when the storms of life surround me?
Or do I trust God to quiet the wind and waves of turmoil? Have
I ever experienced the sudden, miraculous calming of a storm?
Does this encourage me to believe that God can do it again?

PRAY:

God, if I am experiencing a time of rest—or the
next time I do—let me take full advantage of the
opportunity to learn the truths of Your kingdom.

Walk Humbly

He has shown you, O man, what is good;
and what does the LORD require of you but to do justly,
to love mercy, and to walk humbly with your God?
MICAH 6:8

F ear of what others will say is want of trust in Me. This must not be. Convert all these difficulties into the purification of your characters.

See yourselves as those around you see you, not as you wish to be, and walk very humbly with your God.

I will set you on high because you have known My Name, but it must be a purified you to be so exalted.

CONSIDER:
Does my daily walk line up with my beliefs in God, or am I
overly concerned about the opinions of others? Am I afraid
of what they might say? Do I fear God enough to speak the
truth—gently and in love—to those who need to hear it?

PRAY:
Help me to walk with You daily, Lord. You promised You would exalt
me and "set me on high" if I truly know You. Help me to humble
myself under Your mighty hand that You may exalt me in due time.

Marvelous Happenings

*Ah, Lord GOD! Behold, You have made the heavens
and the earth by Your great power and outstretched
arm. There is nothing too hard for You.*
JEREMIAH 32:17

*Our Lord, with hearts full of joy we thank Thee for Thy
marvelous blessings showered on us today and every day.*

I am beside you. Follow in all things My Guiding. Marvels beyond all your imaginings are unfolding. I am your Guide. Joy in that thought. Your Guide and your Friend.

Remember that to Me a miracle is only a natural happening. To My disciples, to My chosen, a miracle is only a natural happening. But it is a natural happening operative through spiritual forces, and therefore the man who works and understands through the senses only regards it as something contrary to Nature.

My children, the children of My Kingdom are a peculiar people, set apart, with different hopes and aspirations and motives and sense of reward.

You see a marvelous happening (as that today), happening so easily, so simply, so free from all other agency, and you wonder.

My children, listen, this has not happened easily and simply. It has been achieved by hours, days, months of weariness and heartache battled against and overcome by a steadfast, unflinching desire to conquer self and to do My Will and live My teachings.

The frets and the worries and the scorn patiently borne mean spiritual Power acquired, operating marvelously.

My Standard

> *But this is what I commanded them, saying, "Obey My voice,*
> *and I will be your God, and you shall be My people. And walk in all*
> *the ways that I have commanded you, that it may be well with you."*
> JEREMIAH 7:23

Carry out My Commands and leave the result to Me. Do this as obediently and faithfully as you would expect a child to follow out a given rule in the working of a sum, with no question but that, if the working out is done according to command, the result will be right.

Remember that the commands I have given you have been already worked out by Me in the Spirit World to produce in your case, and in your circumstances, the required result. So follow My rules faithfully.

Realize that herein lies the perfection of Divine Guidance. To follow a rule, laid down, even by earth's wisest, might lead to disaster.

The knowledge of your individual life and character, capability, circumstances, and temptations must be, to some extent, lacking, but to follow My direct Guidance means to carry out instructions given with a full knowledge of you and the required result.

Each individual was meant to walk with Me in this way, to act under Divine control, strengthened by Divine Power.

Have I not taught you to love simplicity? No matter what the world may think, earth's aims and intrigues are not for you. Oh! My children, learn of Me. Simplicity brings rest. True rest and Power.

To the world foolishness, maybe, but to Me a foretaste of Divinity.

The Way of Praise

But You are holy, enthroned in the praises of Israel. Our fathers trusted in You; they trusted, and You delivered them. They cried to You, and were delivered; they trusted in You, and were not ashamed.

PSALM 22:3–5

I am teaching you both My Way of removing mountains. The way to remove mountains is the way of Praise. When a trouble comes, think of all you have to be thankful for. Praise, praise, praise.

Say "Thank you" all the time. This is the remover of mountains, your thankful hearts of praise.

Lord, You are enthroned in the praises we shout;
You are exalted in the thanks that we give.
May we trust You and rejoice in Your name
May we praise You for as long as we live.
Be enthroned, O God, in our praise! Be enthroned!

We thank You, O Lord, for mountains You move;
We praise You each day for the trouble You tame;
When we think of all Your miraculous wonders,
We offer fresh praises to Your holy name.
Be enthroned, O God, in our praise! Be enthroned!

CONSIDER:

How generous am I with my praise to God?
Do I give heartfelt thanks daily for all He has given me?

PRAY:

Lord, help me to trust You to remove mountains. In the midst of trouble, keep me aware of Your many blessings so that I will praise You continually.

Miracle of the Ages

"Most assuredly, I say to you, he who believes in Me, the works that I do he will do also; and greater works than these he will do, because I go to My Father. And whatever you ask in My name, that I will do, that the Father may be glorified in the Son. If you ask anything in My name, I will do it."
John 14:12–14

Abide in Me. "The works that I do shall ye do also; and greater works than these shall ye do; because I go unto My Father."

"Greater Works!" The blind received their sight, the lame walked, the lepers were cleansed, the poor had the Gospel preached to them. "And greater works than these shall ye do; because I go unto My Father."

Wonder of the World! Miracle of the Ages! God's Power manifest in believing man! God's Power going out to bless, through the agency of the man actuated by the Holy Spirit. Arise from the grave of sickness, poverty, doubt, despondency, limitation. "Arise, shine; for thy light is come, and the glory of the Lord is risen upon thee."

A wonderful future is before you both. A future of unlimited power to bless others. Just be channels. Be used. Ask. Ask. "Ask what ye will, and it shall be done unto you," and unto those for whom you pray.

PRAY:
Dear Lord, open my eyes to the unlimited power that is mine, power to bless my own life and others' lives.

Stop All Work Until—

*A woman, when she is in labor, has sorrow because her hour has come;
but as soon as she has given birth to the child, she no longer remembers
the anguish, for joy that a human being has been born into the world.
Therefore you now have sorrow; but I will see you again and your
heart will rejoice, and your joy no one will take from you.*

JOHN 16:21–22

Our Lord, grant us that wonderful inward Peace.

My children, that Peace does truly pass all understanding.
That peace no man taketh from you. No man has the power
to disturb that peace, but you yourselves can let the world and its
worries and distractions in.

You can give the entrance to fears and despondency. You can open
the door to the robber who breaks in upon, and destroys, your peace.

Set yourselves this task to allow nothing to disturb your peace,
your heart calm, with Me. Stop all work, stop all communion with
others—until this is restored. Do not let those about you spoil your
peace of heart and mind. Do not let anyone without, any trouble, any
irritation, any adversity disturb it for one moment.

Look on each difficulty as training to enable you to acquire this
peace. Every work, every interruption—set yourself to see that none of
it touches the harmony of the real *you* that is hid with Me in the Secret
Place of the Father.

CONSIDER:
*Am I too busy to experience the peace that God offers to me? Am I
too distracted by work, by other people, by my own worldly concerns?*

Keep Close

*Thomas said to Him, "Lord, we do not know where You are going,
and how can we know the way?" Jesus said to him, "I am the way,
the truth, and the life. No one comes to the Father except through me.
If you had known Me, you would have known My Father also;
and from now on you know Him and have seen Him."*

JOHN 14:5–7

Our Lord, guide us. Show us Thy Will and Way in everything.

Keep close to Me and you shall know the Way, because, as I said
to My disciples, I am the Way. That is the solution to all earth's
problems.

Keep close, very close to Me. Think, act, and live in My Presence.

How dare any foe touch you, protected by Me! That is the secret of
all Power, all Peace, all Purity, all influence, the keeping very near to Me.

Abide in Me. Live in My Presence. Rejoice in My Love. Thank and
Praise all the time. Wonders are unfolding.

CONSIDER:
*How is keeping close to Jesus the solution to all
earth's problems? Do I believe that if I stay very close
to Him, that all my problems will be resolved? Will they
necessarily be resolved to my liking, or according to His will?*

PRAY:
*Lord Jesus, help me to live continually in Your presence, and not
be content to follow at a distance. I want power and purity and
peace. Lord, You possess all these things, so please impart them to me.*

Wonderful Life

*Yea, though I walk through the valley of the shadow of death, I will
fear no evil; for You are with me; Your rod and Your staff, they comfort me.*
PSALM 23:4

*Because you have made the LORD, who is my refuge,
even the Most High, your dwelling place, no evil shall
befall you, nor shall any plague come near your dwelling.*
PSALM 91:9–10

I am your Lord. Lord of your lives, Controller of your days, your
present and your future. Leave all plans to Me. Only act as I bid you.

You have entered now, both of you, upon the God-guided life.
Think what that means. God-taught, God-guided.

Is anything too wonderful for such a life? Do you begin to see
how wonderful life with Me can be?

Do you see that no evil can befall you?

CONSIDER:
*Am I aware yet of just how wonderful life in
God's presence can be? Does God so control my
life that nothing happens to me except as He wills?*

PRAY:
*God, teach me and guide me daily so that I can
act and react the way that You want me to.*

Forget—Forgive

Then Peter came to Him and said, "Lord, how often shall my brother
sin against me, and I forgive him? Up to seven times?" Jesus said to him,
"I do not say to you, up to seven times, but, up to seventy times seven."
MATTHEW 18:21–22

Our Lord, we thank Thee for so much.
We bless Thee and praise Thy Glorious Name.

Fill your world with Love and laughter. Never mind what anguish
lies behind you.

Forget, forgive, love, and laugh.

Treat *all* as you would treat Me, with Love and consideration.

Let nothing that others do to you alter your treatment of them.

CONSIDER:

Do I live my daily life according to the Golden Rule?
Do I forgive others as God has forgiven me? How can
I follow the advice to never mind what anguish has happened
in the past? What past incidents still cause me pain?

PRAY:

O Father, give me a forgiving heart, one that holds no grudge
toward those who do wrong against me, loving and forgiving
even my enemies. I ask right now that You especially help me
to forgive family members and former friends who have wronged
me or offended me. Help me to sincerely forgive them.

My Consolation

I have called upon You, for You will hear me, O God; incline Your ear to me, and hear my speech. Show Your marvelous lovingkindness by Your right hand, O You who save those who trust in You from those who rise up against them. Keep me as the apple of Your eye; hide me under the shadow of Your wings.
PSALM 17:6–8

O Jesus, come and walk with us and let us feel Thy very nearness.

I walk with you. Oh! think, My children, not only to guide and comfort you and strengthen and uphold, but for solace and comfort for Myself.

When a loving child is by you, is the nearness only that you may provide protection and help for that little one?

Rather, too, that in that little child *you* may find joy and cheer and comfort in its simplicity, its Love, its trust.

So, too, is it in your power to comfort and bring joy to My Heart.

Trusting God trumps understanding God. The train will have long left the station and left us on the platform if we determine to ride only with full understanding. Life will have passed us by. I'm choosing to trust the conductor and the track he's laid down for me.
TERRY ESAU
BE THE SURPRISE

CONSIDER:
Do I bring comfort and joy to God's heart?
Do I draw near to Him, as He longs for me to?

Mistakes

Therefore you shall be perfect,
just as your Father in heaven is perfect.
MATTHEW 5:48

I am your Shield. No buffets of the world can harm you. Feel that between you and all scorn and indignity is a strong shield. Practice feeling this until nothing has the power to spoil the inward peace. Then indeed a marvelous victory shall be won.

You wonder sometimes why you are permitted to make mistakes in your choice when you sought so truly to do My Will in the matter.

To that I say it was no mistake. . . . All your lessons cannot be learned without difficulty, and this was needed to teach you a lesson. Not to him who walks on, with no obstacles in his way, but to him that *overcometh is the promise given.*

So to attain peace quickly in your surroundings, as well as in your hearts, learn your lesson quickly. And the overcoming is never the overcoming of the one who troubled you, but the overcoming of the weaknesses and wrong in your own nature, aroused by such a one.

No lower standard than My Standard shall be yours. "Be ye therefore *perfect*, even as your Father which is in heaven is perfect."

Sunlit Glades

*No temptation has overtaken you except such as is common
to man; but God is faithful, who will not allow you to be
tempted beyond what you are able, but with the temptation
will also make the way of escape, that you may be able to bear it.*
1 CORINTHIANS 10:13

Lord, bless us in this evening hour, and in Thy Mercy heal us all.

Do not think that suffering is the only path into My Kingdom. There are sunlit glades and ways amid the loveliest flowers, along which the steps and hearts of men are drawn to Me. There are birds and laughter and butterflies and warm, lifegiving summer air, and with these as tender companions and friends, the Joy-Way into the Kingdom can be taken.

Bleak, cold, and desolate, briar-beset and stony, are not all the ways. Leave all to Me. The choice of ways, the guidance in the way. But when the sunlight calls, accept it gladly.

Even in the Spirit-World appreciation results from contrary experience. Can the fireside of home be dearer than to the traveler who has forced his way over bleak moor and through blinding storm? Take to your hearts this word of cheer. He "will not suffer you to be tempted above that ye are able; but will with the temptation also make a way to escape, that ye may be able to bear it."

The world is not the Kingdom. "In the world ye shall have tribulation: but be of good cheer; I have overcome the world." Live with Me, the Conquering Christ, and the Joy and Peace of conquest shall be yours, too.

Faith Rewarded

Just as Abraham "believed God, and it was accounted to him for righteousness."
Therefore know that only those who are of faith are sons of Abraham.
GALATIANS 3:6–7

Think much of My servants of old. How Abraham believed the promise (when as yet he had no child) that in his seed all the nations of the earth should be blessed.

How Moses led the Children of Israel through the desert, sure that, at last, they would gain the Promised Land.

Down through the ages there have always been those who obeyed, not seeing but believing, and their faith was rewarded. So shall it be even with you.

CONSIDER:
Am I confident that my faith in God's promises will be
rewarded in His time? What promise has God personally made
to me that, in the natural, seems highly unlikely to ever happen?
Though I'm tempted to doubt, do I still persevere in faith?

PRAY:
Heavenly Father, help me to believe Your promises. Help me
to not only trust You to give me eternal life, but to trust that
You'll fulfill all Your other promises along the way.

Gratitude

And let the peace of God rule in your hearts,
to which also you were called in one body; and be thankful.
COLOSSIANS 3:15

G ive Me the gift of a brave and thankful heart.
Man proves his greatness by his power to see causes for thankfulness in his life.

When life seems hard, and troubles crowd, then very definitely look for causes for thankfulness.

The sacrifice, the offering of thanksgiving, is indeed a sweet incense going up to Me through the busy day.

Seek diligently for something to be glad and thankful about in every happening, and soon no search will be required.

The causes for joy and gratitude will spring to greet your loving hearts.

CONSIDER:

Do I see causes for thankfulness in my life, even in difficult times—or am I quick to grumble and complain when my plans mess up, when I'm frustrated by delays, and one thing after another goes wrong? Can I still think of reasons to be thankful?

PRAY:

Lord, give me a brave and thankful heart. Let me be always aware of my blessings—for You have truly blessed me! Thinking of them during trying frustrating times will make the difficulties seem less grievous, so remind me, O Lord!

Blessed Bond

When You said, "Seek My face," my heart said to You, "Your face, LORD,
I will seek." Do not hide your face from me; do not turn Your servant
away in anger; You have been my help; do not leave me nor forsake me,
O God of my salvation.
PSALM 27:8–9

Jesus, let Thy Beautiful Presence be always with us.

I will never leave thee, nor forsake thee."

There is no bond of union on earth to compare with the union between a soul that loves Me—and Me.

Priceless beyond all earth's imaginings is that Friendship.

In the merging of heart and mind and will a oneness results that only those who experience it can even dimly realize.

CONSIDER:
Are there times when I feel forsaken by God? Do I realize
that this is only my faulty reasoning, my guilty conscience, or my
overwhelmed emotions—and that God in fact will never leave me?

PRAY:
Let me never forget, God, that You're constantly present in my life,
that You'll never leave me nor forsake me. Help me be secure in this
fact, then go on to attain that blessed state of oneness with You.

Harvest

*So then neither he who plants is anything, nor he who waters, but God
who gives the increase. Now he who plants and he who waters are one,
and each one will receive his own reward according to his own labor.*
1 CORINTHIANS 3:7–8

My Lord, we seek Thy Blessing.

I love to pour My blessings down in rich, in choicest measure. But like
the seed-sowing—the ground must be prepared before the seed is
dropped in.

Yours to prepare the soil—Mine to drop the seed-blessing into
the prepared soil.

Together we share in, and joy in, the harvest.

Spend more time in soil-preparing. Prayer fertilizes soil. There is
much to do in preparation.

CONSIDER:
*Am I prepared to receive the Lord's blessings? If not, how can I
get the ground ready for the Lord's seed? What does Hosea 10:12
mean when it says, "Break up your fallow [unplowed] ground, for it is
time to seek the LORD, till He comes and rains righteousness on you"?*

PRAY:
*Lord, help me to do my part to prepare the soil of my heart. Help me to
plow my hard, dry ground with prayer and repentance—make it ready
for Your seed to take root in, so that it will give birth to spiritual fruit.*

Give Every Moment

Therefore whether you eat or drink,
or whatever you do, do all to the glory of God.
1 CORINTHIANS 10:31

My children, how dear to my Heart is the cry of Love that asks for all of Me, that wishes every action, thought, word, and moment to be Mine. How poor the understanding of the one who thinks that money to be used in this good work or that, is the great gift to offer. Above all I desire Love, true, warm, childlike Love, the trusting understanding Love, and then the gift I prize next is the gift of the moments, of all the moments.

I think even when Love's impetuous longing to serve Me has offered Me all Life, every day, every hour, I think even then it is a long, and not an easy lesson, to learn, what it means to give Me the moments.

The little things you planned to do, given up gladly at My suggestion, the little services joyfully rendered. See *Me* in all, and then it will be an easy task.

This is a priceless time of initiation, but remember that the path of initiation is not for all; but only for those who have felt the sorrow-cry of the world that needs a Savior and the tender plea of a Savior Who needs followers through whom He can accomplish His great work of Salvation joyfully.

Eternal Life

My sheep hear My voice, and I know them, and they follow Me. And I give them eternal life, and they shall never perish; neither shall anyone snatch them out of my hand. My Father, who has given them, Me, is greater than all; and no one is able to snatch them out of My Father's hand.
JOHN 10:27–29

O Jesus, we love Thee so and long to serve Thee.

My children, you are both to do mighty things for Me. Glories and wonders unfold. Life is one glorious whole.

Draw into your beings more and more this wonderful Eternal Life. It is the flow of the Life Eternal through spirit, mind, and body that cleanses, heals, restores, renews youth, and passes on from you to others with the same miracle-working power.

"And this is life eternal, that they might know thee. . .and Jesus Christ, whom thou hast sent." So seek by constant contact to know Me more and more.

Make Me the one abiding Presence of your day of which you are conscious all the time. Seek to *do* less and to *accomplish* more, to achieve more. Doing is action. Achievement is successful action.

Remember that Eternal Life is the only lasting life, so that all that is done without being done in the Power of My Spirit, My Life, is passing. All done in that Spirit-Life is undying.

"I give unto them eternal life; and they shall never perish, neither shall any man pluck them out of my hand." So Eternal Life means security, too, *safety*. Dwell increasingly in the consciousness of that security, that safety.

Hour of Need

*Let all those who seek You rejoice and be glad in You; let such
as love Your salvation say continually, "The LORD be magnified!"
But I am poor and needy; yet the LORD thinks upon me. You are
my help and my deliverer; do not delay, O my God.*

PSALM 40:16–17

Lord, come to us and heal us.

I am your Healer, your Joy, your Lord. You bid Me, your Lord, come.
Did you not know that I am here? With noiseless footfall I draw
near to you.

Your hour of need is the moment of My Coming.

Could you know My Love, could you measure My Longing to
help, you would know that I need no agonized pleading.

Your *need* is My Call.

---

*Sweet hour of prayer! sweet hour of prayer!
Thy wings shall my petition bear
To Him whose truth and faithfulness
Engage the waiting soul to bless.
And since He bids me seek His face,
Believe His Word and trust His grace,
I'll cast on Him my every care,
And wait for thee, sweet hour of prayer!*
WILLIAM W. WALFORD (1772–1850)

CONSIDER:
*Do I rely on the Lord for all my needs,
or is He only a last resort?*

Dwell Apart

*But you, when you pray, go into your room, and when you
have shut your door, pray to your Father who is in the secret place;
and your Father who sees in secret will reward you openly.*
MATTHEW 6:6

Rest more with Me. If I, the Son of God, needed those times of
quiet communion with My Father, away, alone, from noise, from
activity—then surely you need them, too.

Refilling with the Spirit is a need. That dwelling apart, that shutting
yourself away in the very secret place of your being—away alone with Me.
From these times you come forth in Power to bless and heal.

*When you pray, hide away in your closet,
In the deep secret place of your being;
Shut yourself away then kneel and pray
To the Father All-Wise and All-Seeing.*

*Even Christ needed times of communion,
Even Jesus needed quiet time apart;
So if you want power to bless others,
Seek the Lord in the quiet of your heart.*

CONSIDER:
*Do I make time in my daily life to get away from all the noise, activity,
and other distractions and find quiet communion with God?*

PRAY:
*O Heavenly Father, refill me with Your Spirit. Help me to
cherish my quiet times with You and to not neglect them.*

All Is Well

But my eyes are upon You, O GOD the Lord;
in You I take refuge; do not leave my soul destitute.
PSALM 141:8

Our Lord, bless us and keep us, we beseech Thee.

M y Keeping Power is never at fault, but only your realization of it. Not whether I can provide a shelter from the storm, but your failure to be sure of the security of that shelter.

Every fear, every doubt, is a crime against My Love.

Oh! children, trust. Practice daily, many times a day, saying, "All is well."

Say it until you believe it, know it.

CONSIDER:
Do I believe that "all is well"? And if I do doubt that all is
actually well, how will saying it many times a day finally cause
me to believe it? Does God honor my willingness to trust
Him, even if my trust is not perfect to start with?

PRAY:
God, help me to ignore my foolish doubts and fears, and resolve
that I will trust You. Even though I can't see Your arms sheltering
me, help me to believe that they are, in fact, doing just that.

Empty Yourself

Cause me to hear Your lovingkindness in the morning, for in You do I trust; cause me to know the way in which I should walk, for I lift up my soul to You.
PSALM 143:8

Rely on Me alone. Ask no other help. Pay all out in the Spirit of trust that more will come to meet your supply.

Empty your vessels quickly to ensure a Divine Supply.

So much retained by you, so much the less will be gained from Me. It is a Law of Divine Supply.

To hold back, to retain, implies a fear of the future, a want of trust in Me.

When you ask Me to save you from the sea of poverty and difficulty, you must trust wholly to Me. If you do not, and your prayer and faith are genuine, then I must first answer your prayer for help as a rescuer does that of a drowning man who is struggling to save himself.

He renders him still more helpless and powerless until he is wholly at the will and mercy of the rescuer. *So* understand *My* leading. Trust wholly. Trust completely.

Empty your vessel. I will fill it. You ask both of you to understand Divine Supply. It is a most difficult lesson for My children to learn. So dependent have they become on material supply they fail to understand. You must live as I tell you.

Depend on Me.

Effort and Rest

Show me Your ways, O LORD; teach me Your paths.
Lead me in Your truth and teach me, for You are
the God of my salvation; on You I wait all the day.
PSALM 25:4–5

Come to Me, talk to Me, dwell with Me, and then you will know My Way is a sure way, My Paths are safe paths.

Come very near to Me.

Dig deep down into the soil of the Kingdom. Effort and rest— a union of the two.

He leadeth me, O blessed thought!
O words with heavenly comfort fraught!
Whate'er I do, where'er I be
Still 'tis God's hand that leadeth me.

He leadeth me, He leadeth me,
By His own hand He leadeth me;
His faithful follower I would be,
For by His hand He leadeth me.
JOSEPH HENRY GILMORE (1834–1918)

CONSIDER:
How often do I come to God, talk to Him,
and consider His way? Do I dwell with Him daily?

PRAY:
Lord, draw me near to You, help me to
understand clearly how effort and rest work together.

Stray Sheep

*By this you know the Spirit of God: Every spirit that confesses that
Jesus Christ has come in the flesh is of God, and every spirit that does
not confess that Jesus Christ has come in the flesh is not of God. And this
is the spirit of the Antichrist, which you have heard was coming, and is now
already in the world. You are of God, little children, and have overcome
them, because He who is in you is greater than he who is in the world.*

1 JOHN 4:2–4

O Jesus, guide our footsteps lest we stray.

For straying, My children, there is no cure except to keep so close to
Me that nothing, no interest, no temptation, no other—can come
between us.

Sure of that you can but stay at My Side, knowing that, as I am the
very Way itself, nothing can prevent your being in the Way; nothing
can cause you to stray.

I have promised Peace but not leisure, heart-rest and comfort but
not pleasure. I have said, "In the world ye shall have tribulation"; so do
not feel, when adverse things happen, that you have failed or are not
being guided, but I have said, "In the world ye shall have tribulation:
but be of good cheer; I have overcome the world."

So learn of Me the overcoming Power of One who, though spat
upon, scourged, misunderstood, forsaken, crucified, could yet see His
Work had not been affected by these things and cry triumphantly
from His Cross, "It is finished."

Not the pain, the mocking, the agony, but His Task.

Let this thought comfort you. Amid failure, discord, contumely,
suffering, even now may friends and angels be prepared to sound the
chorus, "It is finished."

You Are Mine

"I pray for them. I do not pray for the world but for those whom You have given Me, for they are Yours. And all Mine are Yours, and Yours are Mine, and I am glorified in them. Now I am no longer in the world, but these are in the world, and I come to You. Holy Father, keep through Your name those whom You have given Me, that they may be one as We are."
JOHN 17:9–11

Jesus, Thou art watching over us to bless and care for us.

Yes! remember that always—that out of darkness I am leading you to light. Out of unrest to rest, out of disorder to order. Out of faults and failure to perfection.

So trust Me wholly. Fear nothing. Hope ever. Look ever up to Me and I will be your sure aid.

I and My Father are One. So He who made the ordered, beautiful world out of chaos, and set the stars in their courses, and made each plant to know its season, can He not bring out of your little chaos peace and order?

And He and I are One, and you are Mine. Your affairs are Mine. It is My Divine Task to order My affairs—therefore yours will be ordered by Me.

CONSIDER:
Have I turned my affairs over to God?
Have I fully surrendered to His will?

PRAY:
Dear Jesus, I am Yours. Lead me deeper
into the light, lead me to rest, order my life.

Rule the World

But by the grace of God I am what I am, and His grace
toward me was not in vain; but I labored more abundantly
than they all, yet not I, but the grace of God which was with me.
1 CORINTHIANS 15:10

Remember no prayer goes unanswered. Remember that the moment a thing seems wrong to you, or a person's actions seem not to be what you think they should be, at that moment begins your obligation and responsibility to pray for those wrongs to be righted or that person to be different.

Face your responsibilities. What is wrong in your country, its statesmen, its laws, its people? Think out quietly, and make these matters your prayer matters. You will see lives you never touch altered, laws made at your request, evils banished.

Yes! live in a large sense. Live to serve and to save. You may never go beyond one room, and yet you may become one of the most powerful forces for good in your country, in the world.

You may never see the mighty work you do, but I see it, evil sees it. Oh! it is a glorious life, the life of one who saves. Fellow-workers together with me. See this more and more.

Love with me, sharers of My life.

CONSIDER:

How seriously do I take the Bible's command to pray for my leaders?
Paul said, "I exhort, first of all, that supplications, prayers, intercessions,
and giving of thanks be made for all men, for kings and all who are in
authority" (1 Timothy 2:1–2), but how often do I do this?

Perfection

*Behold, God is my helper; the Lord
is with those who uphold my life.*
PSALM 54:4

O Jesus, help us, we beseech Thee.

Ever your Helper through dark to Light, through weakness to Power, through sin to Salvation, through danger to Security, through poverty to Plenty, through indifference to Love, through resentment to Perfect Forgiveness.

Never be satisfied with a comparison with those around you. Ever let My words ring out. "Be ye therefore perfect, even as your Father which is in heaven is perfect." Stop short at nothing less.

Make it your practice, each of you, to review your character—take it in relation to life, to your dear ones, your household, friends, acquaintances, your country, your work.

See where I, in the same relation or circumstances or situation, should act differently. Plan how best such and such a fault can be eradicated, or such and such sin, mistake, or omission be avoided.

A weekly review at least you must have.

CONSIDER:
*By whose standards do I measure myself? Who is my role model?
Am I content to meet the world's standards—or do I strive for God's?*

PRAY:
My perfect Father, help me to grow more like You every day.

My Richest Gift

I have been crucified with Christ; it is no longer I who live,
but Christ lives in me; and the life which I now live in the flesh I live
by faith in the Son of God, who loved me and gave Himself for me.
GALATIANS 2:20

Jesus, Thou didst come that we might have life, and have it more abundantly.

Life, spiritual, mental, physical, abundant Life—Joyous Life, Powerful Life. Yes! these I came to give you.

Think you not My Heart was sad that so few would accept that gracious gift!

Think! earth's richest, choicest gift held out—free to all, and no man to care to stretch out a hand to take it.

Is that possible? My Gift, the richest Heaven has to offer, that precious Gift of Life, abundant Life—man turns away from—rejects— will have none of.

Let it not be true of you. Hasten to take—to use.

CONSIDER:

Am I persuaded by the doctrine that "the abundant life" is primarily
material blessings? Or do I understand that Jesus was speaking of
the new life that He gives to my spirit—which then flows out into
all of my life? How does the knowledge that He has saved me affect
my mental attitudes and even my physical well-being?

PRAY:

God, never allow me to take Your most precious gift—Your Son,
Jesus Christ—for granted. Help me to make Him the center
of my life, and to share His love with those around me.

Not Punishment

Now as Jesus passed by, He saw a man who was blind from birth. And His disciples asked Him, saying, "Rabbi, who sinned, this man or his parents, that he was born blind?" Jesus answered, "Neither this man nor his parents sinned, but that the works of God should be revealed in him."

JOHN 9:1–3

I will guide your efforts. You are not being punished for past sins. Take My Words, revealed to you each day from the beginning, and do in all things as I say. I have been showing you the way. You have not obeyed Me in this.

I have a plan that can only in this way be revealed. So rarely do I find two souls in union who want only My Will, and only to serve Me. The union is miracle-working.

I have told you that I am longing to use you. Long ago My world would have been brought to Me had I been served by many such *two souls*.

It was always "two and two."

CONSIDER:
Am I burdened with thoughts of my past sins, and convinced that God is continuing to punish me for them? Or am I looking to what He longs to do through me today and for the rest of my life?

PRAY:
Guide my efforts, O God. Help me to forgive myself, as You have forgiven me. May I become Your obedient servant.

No Tired Work

I said, "Lord, be merciful to me;
heal my soul, for I have sinned against You."
PSALM 41:4

R est. It is wrong to force work. Rest until Life, Eternal Life,
flowing through your veins and hearts and minds, bids you bestir
yourselves, and work, glad work, will follow.

Tired work never tells.

Rest. Remember I am your Physician, Healer of mind and body.
Look to Me for cure, for rest, for Peace.

It's the rests that make the difference in the music of our lives.
STEVE AND MARY FARRAR
OVERCOMING OVERLOAD

CONSIDER:
Getting enough rest is essential for good physical and mental health.
Psalm 127:2 says, "He gives His beloved sleep." Do I trust God enough
to take sufficient rest, or do I push on even though I'm exhausted?

PRAY:
Lord, give me rest and peace in You. Recharge my batteries and renew my
spirit as I take time out to rest in You, and to remind myself that You love me.

Nature Laughs

The heavens declare the glory of God; and the firmament
shows His handiwork. Day unto day utters speech,
and night unto night reveals knowledge.
PSALM 19:1–2

I come, I come. You need Me. Live much out here. My sunshine, My glorious air, My Presence, My teaching.

Would they not make holiday anywhere for you. Sunshine helps to make glad the heart of man. It is the laughter of Nature.

Live much outside. My medicines are sun and air, trust and faith. Trust is the spirit sun, your being enwrapped by the Divine Spirit.

Faith is the soul's breathing in of the Divine Spirit. Mind, soul, and body need helping. Welcome My treatment for you both. Draw near to Me.

Nature is often My nurse for tired souls and weary bodies. Let her have her way with you both.

CONSIDER:
Do I take the time to refresh myself in
the midst of God's marvelous Creation?

PRAY:
Thank You, great God, for this mighty, awe-inspiring world You have made.
Keep my thoughts on You as I bask in Your sunshine, breathe Your air, and
explore Your forests and rivers and mountains and other wondrous creations.

All this has come upon us; but we have not forgotten You,
nor have we dealt falsely with Your covenant. Our heart has
not turned back, nor have our steps departed from Your way.
PSALM 44:17–18

I am here. No distance separates Me. In the Spirit-Kingdom we measure not by earth's miles. A false word, a fear-inspired failure, a harsh criticism, these are the distances between a soul and Me. Your training must be severe, that your work for Me be unhindered.

You seek My Presence, and they who seek shall find. It is not a question of human searching, so much as human consciousness, unconditional surrender to My Will in the small, as in the big things of life. This it is that makes My Guidance possible.

You know the difference between taking a glad, loving, joy-springing child with you along a way, when the child anticipates each direction, accepts naturally each decision as to each turning—and the child who resists, and, rebellious, has to be forced, even though in its quieter moments it may say, "Yes. I do want to go with you. I cannot be left alone, but I hate this way."

It is not the way, but the loving rejoicing in the way and the guidance, that matters with My disciples. You are ready for the guidance, but you do not rejoice as you should, both of you, in the little daily stones of the way.

A Human Temple

*The voice of the LORD is over the waters; the God of glory thunders;
the LORD is over many waters. The voice of the LORD is powerful;
the voice of the LORD is full of majesty.*
PSALM 29:3–4

Lord, we Love Thee, we worship Thee.

B ow low before Me. Worship is not supplication, though both
express man's varying needs of Me. Bow low in worship, conscious
not only of My humanity but of My Divine Majesty.

As you kneel in humble adoration, I will tell you that when I took
upon Me your humanity, it was with the desire of raising that humanity
to My Divinity.

Earth gave Me her best—a human temple to enclose My Divinity,
and I brought to her the possession of Divine Power, Divine Love, and
Divine Strength to be forever expressed in those of her children who
accepted Me, opened their hearts to Me, and sought to live My Life.

So, kneeling in a spirit of humility, turn your eyes Heaven-ward and
realize the majesty, the Power, the Beauty that may be yours. Remember
there are no limits to My giving—there may be to your accepting.

Oh! rejoice at the wonders to which you are called and, seeing them
in prayer, rise in My Strength, filled with the longing to attain them.

PRAY:
*Dear Lord, You have given us "exceedingly great and precious promises,
that through these [we] may be partakers of the divine nature" (2 Peter 1:4).
Lord, I earnestly desire to be filled with the majesty and beauty
of your Holy Spirit.*

Shame and Remorse

The troubles of my heart have enlarged; bring me out of my distresses!
Look on my affliction and my pain, and forgive all my sins.
PSALM 25:17–18

My children! Yes! "Shield from the scorn and cover from the chiding." Often I have to shield My disciples from their own scorn and chiding.

My poor Peter could never have done My work, never had the courage to live on, or the daring to live for Me, but for the tender love with which I enwrapped him. Not from the anger of My Father, who is all Love, did I need to protect him—not from the scorn of My enemies, nor from the resentment of My friends. No! but from the hatred of Peter himself.

This is a stage of development, but only a stage. What use the glad wings of a butterfly if it remain earthbound, weight down with the thought of its contemptible past? And so now today I say to you both, that you are not to dwell for one moment on your sings, and mistakes, and faults, and bad habits of the past.

And so to My followers today, as then, there come the shame and remorse and contempt of themselves, of the weak selves. They meant to be so strong and brave for Me. And then I have to protect them or never could they have the courage to fight and conquer. But this facing of the real self has to be—shame and remorse must come.

You must be as one who runs a race, stumbles and falls, rises and presses on to the goal. What avails it if he stays to examine the spot where he fell, to weep over the delay, over the shortsightedness that prevented his avoiding the obstacles?

So with you, and I lay it on you as a command—no looking back.

Give yourself and all you have ever met a fresh start from today. Remember no more their sins and failures or your own.

When I sent My Disciples out two by two—no scrip, no two coats, no money—it was an injunction to be carried out literally but figuratively, too. On Life's journey throw away all that is not important. Cast aside all the hindrances, the past imperfections of others, the failure-sense.

Travel unladen, with a light heart, and a light heart means a weight of influence.

My children, I love you.

God weeps over us when shame
and self-hatred immobilize us.
BRENNAN MANNING
THE RABBI'S HEARTBEAT

Broken Voices

Then I will give them one heart, and I will put a new spirit within them,
and take the stony heart out of their flesh, and give them a heart of flesh,
that they may walk in My statutes and keep My judgments and do them;
and they shall be My people, and I will be their God.
EZEKIEL 11:19–20

Behold, I make all things new. It is only the earthbound spirit that cannot soar. Every blessing I send you, every joy, every freedom achieved from poverty and worry will loosen a strand that ties you to earth.

It is only those strands that bind you. Therefore your freedom will mean your rising into the realm of Joy and Appreciation.

Clipped wings can grow again. Broken voices regain a strength and beauty unknown before. Your power to help other lives will soon bring its delight, even when, at first, the help to yourselves may seem too late to bring you Joy.

Worn-out and tired as you may seem, and pain-weary, I say unto you, "Behold, I make all things new." That promise shall be fulfilled. Tenderly across the years, yet tenderly close and near to your tired noise-weary ears, I speak to you, My loved ones, today.

"Come unto me, all ye that labour and are heavy laden, and I will give you rest."

PRAY:
Lord, I believe that the broken parts of my life will
regain strength and beauty, even more than they've
known before—if not in this life then in the next.

Gleams of Sunlight

For You have delivered my soul from death. Have You not kept my
feet from falling, that I may walk before God in the light of the living?
PSALM 56:13

B ecause you have both longed to save My World, I let you have that
training that shall fit you to save.

Take your pains and sufferings, difficulties and hardships—each
day, both of you, and offer them up for one troubled soul, or for some
prayer specially needed to be answered.

So the beauty of each day will live on after the trouble and distress,
difficulty and pain of the day have passed.

Learn from My Life of the suffering that saves others. So, you
will sing in your pain. Across the grayest days there are the gleams
of Sunlight.

Rain in my heart is falling,
Filling my morning with haze;
And I can't keep from thinking
It's gonna be one of those days.

But troubles give me patience,
And even the unwanted pain,
Gives me compassion for others,
So must be considered gain.

The rain outside keeps on falling,
My world still seems very gray,
But happy gleams of bright sunshine
Are driving my sorrow away!

The Summit

For we have become partakers of Christ if we hold
the beginning of our confidence steadfast to the end.
HEBREWS 3:14

S ee not the small trials and vexations of each hour of the day. See
the one purpose and plan to which all are leading. If in climbing
a mountain you keep your eyes on each stony or difficult place as you
ascend, seeing only that, how weary and profitless your climb!

But if you think of each step as leading to the summit of
achievement, from which glories and beauties will open out before you,
then your climb will be so different.

CONSIDER:
Am I focused on the small obstacles and inconveniences
along the way, or on the destination that God is leading me to?

PRAY:
God, keep my eyes on Your ultimate goal, heaven. Keep my
mind focused on Your plan and the purpose You have made me for.

Sublime Heights

The LORD is my rock and my fortress and my deliverer;
my God, my strength, in whom I will trust; my shield
and the horn of my salvation, my stronghold.
PSALM 18:2

Our Lord, we know that Thou art great and able to deliver us.

I am your deliverer. Trust in Me absolutely. Know that I will do the very best for you. Be ready and willing for My Will to be done.

Know that with Me all things are possible. Cling joyfully to that truth.

Say many times, "All things are possible with my Master, my Lord, my Friend."

This truth, accepted and firmly believed in, is the ladder up which a soul can climb from the lowest of pits to the sublimest of heights.

CONSIDER:
Do I fully believe that with God, and only with God,
all things are possible? Do I cling cheerfully to that truth?

PRAY:
All things are possible with my You, My Master. All things are possible
with You, my Lord. All things are possible with You, my Friend.
Dear God, help me not only to repeat this over and over, but to accept
and firmly believe it—for then I shall see You do miracles.

Exhaustion

My son, do not despise the chastening of the LORD,
nor detest His correction; for whom the LORD loves he
corrects, just as a father the son in whom he delights.
PROVERBS 3:11–12

We seek Thee as Thou hast told us.

And seeking you shall find. None ever sought My Presence in vain. None ever sought My Help in vain.

A breath of desire and My Spirit is there—to replenish and renew. Sometimes weariness and exhaustion are not signs of lack of spirit but of the guiding of the Spirit.

Many wonderful things would not have happened but for the physical weariness, the mind-weariness of My servants, which made the resting apart, the giving up of work, a necessity. . . .

Though My Way may seem a narrow way, it yet leads to Life, abundant Life. Follow it. It is not so narrow but that I can tread it beside you.

Never too lonely with such companionship. A comrade infinitely tender, infinitely strong will tread the way with you.

CONSIDER:
Do I praise God and delight in Him even in
my weariness, even when He corrects me?

PRAY:
Lord, thank You that You, a Friend, infinitely tender,
infinitely strong, walk through life with me.

Accept Trials

*I cried to the LORD with my voice, and He heard me
from His holy hill. Selah. I lay down and slept; I awoke,
for the LORD sustained me. I will not be afraid of ten thousands
of people who have set themselves against me all around.*

PSALM 3:4–6

Trials and troubles may seem to overwhelm you. They cannot do
more than work My Will, and that Will you have said is your Will.
Do you not see that you cannot be destroyed?

From now a new Life is opening out before you. Yours to enter into
the Kingdom I have prepared for you.

The sunlight of My Presence is on your paths. Trust and go forward
unafraid. My Grace is sufficient for all your needs.

CONSIDER:

*Do I genuinely believe that God works His purposes in my life
through the troubles that He allows me to suffer? Do I take
comfort in the fact that many men and women of God have
suffered similar things? Do I believe that I can't be destroyed?
How will such knowledge help me to go forward unafraid?*

PRAY:

*God, help me to trust in Your will for me, whatever troubles
I'm facing. Make me constantly aware that You are always
with me and will protect me through my trials.*

Tangled Skeins

In quietness and in confidence shall be your strength.
ISAIAH 30:15 KJV

Feel that. . .trust Me. Am I not leading you safely, faithfully? Will you believe Me, your Master, that all this is really to bring the answer to your prayers?

Remember that I am the Supreme Being who knows all and can control all.

Directly as you put your affairs, their confusion, and their difficulties into My Hands, I began to effect a cure of all the disharmony and disorder.

You must know that I shall cause you no more pain in the doing of it than a physician, who plans and knows he can effect a cure, would cause his patient. I will do all as tenderly as possible.

Tell Me that you trust Me in this.

CONSIDER:
*Have I put all my troubles into God's hands,
trusting them to Him, rather than trying to face them alone?*

PRAY:
*I trust You, God. Help me to always remember that You are
in control of everything, and can do absolutely anything.*

Continuous Service

*My eyes shall be on the faithful of the land, that they may
dwell with me; he who walks in a perfect way, he shall serve me.*
PSALM 101:6

Service is the Law of Heaven. My angels do always obey. "They serve
Him continually" can be said of all who love Me.

With Love there is continuous service in every action and also
even in rest.

Take this not as the end but as the beginning of a new Life
consecrated to My Service.

A Life of Power and Joy.

CONSIDER:

*Am I serving God in all that I do, in action and in rest? The Bible says,
"Therefore, whether you eat or drink, or whatever you do, do all to the
glory of God" (1 Corinthians 10:31). Do I attempt to put this verse in
practice throughout my day? What kind of attitude do I need to have
to help me constantly and consistently follow through on this?*

PRAY:

*God, make my life an unbroken act of service to You. Keep me
in continuous prayer and worship. Help everything I do to please You.*

Breathe My Name

Have I not commanded you? Be strong and of good courage;
do not be afraid, nor be dismayed, for the LORD
your God is with you wherever you go.
JOSHUA 1:9

J ust breathe My Name.
It is like the pressure of a child's hand that calls forth
an answering pressure, strengthens the child's confidence and
banishes fear.

Take the Name of Jesus with you,
Child of sorrow and of woe,
It will joy and comfort give you;
Take it then, where'er you go.

Precious Name, O how sweet!
Hope of earth and joy of heav'n.
Precious Name, O how sweet!
Hope of earth and joy of heav'n.
LYDIA BAXTER (1809–1874)

CONSIDER:
Do I sometimes forget that the Lord is with
me wherever I go? Do I act as if this is so?

PRAY:
God, may I constantly breathe Your name and the
name of Your Son. May it comfort me and banish fear.

Give, Give, Give

He who has a generous eye will be blessed,
for he gives of his bread to the poor.
PROVERBS 22:9

Give abundantly. Feel that you are rich. Have no mean thought in your heart.

Of Love, of thought, of all you have, give, give, give.

You are followers of the World's Greatest Giver. Give of time, of personal ease and comfort, of rest, of fame, of healing, of power, of sympathy, of all these and many more.

Learn this lesson, and you will become a great power to help others and to do mighty things.

Give love as if you were wealthy,
Smiles like you had them to spare;
Be generous now with your laughter,
And watch your gifts banish care.

Give of your power in the morning;
Give of your time every day.
Give up an hour of your evening;
Give healing in kind words you say.

Give as if you have plenty;
Give of your time and your cheer;
You can't lend cash if you lack it,
But friend, you can still lend an ear.

Pray and Deny

Howbeit this kind goeth not out but by prayer and fasting.
MATTHEW 17:21 KJV

You must live a life of communion and prayer if you are to save others. Take My words as a command to you. "By prayer and fasting." Pray and deny yourself, and you will be used marvelously to save and help others.

CONSIDER:

Am I allowing myself to be used to save and help others? Do I deny myself for the their good? In what ways might God ask me to deny myself? Does fasting only mean abstaining from physical food, or does it sometimes also refer to abstaining from entertainment and other normal physical activities? How can God marvelously use such self-denial to save and help others?

PRAY:

God, keep me in constant communion with You. Help me to make sacrifices so that others might be blessed. Help me not to begrudgingly surrender a meal or social media or TV show if you ask me to. Help me rather to rejoice that You're calling me to draw close to You in prayer.

How Rich You Are

I will never leave thee, nor forsake thee.
HEBREWS 13:5 KJV

My children, that word is unfailingly true. Down the centuries thousands have proved My constancy, My untiringness, My unfailing Love. "Never leave." "Never forsake." Not just a Presence is meant by this, but. . .

My Love will never leave you, My Understanding will never leave you, My Strength will never leave you. Think of all that I am:

Love—then forever you are sure of Love.

Strength—then forever, in every difficulty and danger, you are sure of strength.

Patience—then always there is One who can never tire.

Understanding—then always you will be understood.

Can you fear the future when it holds so much for you? Beloved, "set your affections on things above" (the higher, spiritual things), "and not on things on the earth" (the lower, temporal things), and you will see how rich you are.

CONSIDER:

Do I realize how rich I truly am? Do I praise God for the love, strength, patience, understanding, and other gifts He has given me, that I can use to bless others?

I Must Provide

"Thus they shall know that I, the LORD their God, am with them, and they, the house of Israel, are My people," says the Lord GOD. "You are my flock, the flock of My pasture; you are men, and I am your God," says the Lord GOD.
EZEKIEL 34:30–31

I am your Lord. Enough. Then I can command your obedient service, your loyalty. But I am bound by My Lordship to give you protection.

I am bound to fight for you, to plan for you, to secure you a sufficiency of all within My Power to provide. Think how vast that provision can be. Never doubt.

Such marvels are unfolding. Wonders beyond your dreams. They only need the watering of a grateful spirit and a loving heart to yield abundantly.

CONSIDER:
Do I fully understand what God's Lordship means? Do I think the fact that he is Lord and God simply means that He is to be obeyed— period? Or do I realize that when I accept the fact that He is Lord, I also embrace His promise to love and provide for and protect me?

PRAY:
*Lord, I trust You to provide for me and protect me.
Help me to be loyal and obedient in service to You.*

Live in the Unseen

I cried out to God with my voice—to God with my voice; and He gave ear to me. In the day of my trouble I sought the Lord; my hand was stretched out in the night without ceasing; my soul refused to be comforted. I remembered God, and was troubled; I complained, and my spirit was overwhelmed. Selah.
PSALM 77:1–3

Our Lord, the God of the troubled and the weary, come and save us.

I am your Savior. Not only from the weight of sin, but from the weight of care, from misery and depression, from want and woe, from faintness and heartache. Your Savior.

Remember that you are living really in the Unseen—that is the Real Life.

Lift up your heads from earth's troubles, and view the glories of the Kingdom. Higher and higher each day see more of Heaven. Speak to Me. Long for Me. Rest in Me. Abide in Me. No restless bringing Me your burdens, and then feverishly lifting them again and bearing them away.

No! Abide in Me. Not for one moment losing the consciousness of My Strength and Protection.

As a child in its mother's arms, stay sheltered and at rest.

CONSIDER:
Do I bring my burdens to God then carry them away again? Or am I abiding in Him?

PRAY:
Lord, thank You for saving me from sin. Thank You also for saving me from the weight of misery, heartache, and depression.

Drop Those Burdens

Cast your burden on the LORD, and He shall sustain you;
He shall never permit the righteous to be moved.
PSALM 55:22

Our God is our supply.

Look to Me for all. . . . Rely on Me for all. Drop those burdens, and then, singing and free, you can go on your way rejoicing. Encumbered with them you will fall.

Drop them at My Feet, knowing surely that I will lift them and deal with each one as is truly best.

Lord, help me hold onto the burden,
The cross You've called on me to bear;
But help me lay aside every weight
Of doubt and worry, fear and care.

Help me to lay my encumbering cares
At Your feet, and continue on free.
Your yoke is easy, Your burden is light,
For You carry them both with me.

CONSIDER:

Have I laid my burdens at God's feet, trusting Him
to deal with them? Do I know the difference between
burdens He has called me to bear, and those He has not?

PRAY:

God, forgive me for my moments of doubt and fear.
Help me to accept that You know what is best for me.

Progress

But I will hope continually, and will praise You yet more and more.
My mouth shall tell of Your righteousness and Your salvation all the day,
for I do not know their limits. I will go in the strength of the Lord GOD;
I will make mention of Your righteousness, of Yours only.
PSALM 71:14–16

Progress is the Law of Heaven. Higher, ever higher, rise to Life and Beauty, Knowledge and Power. Higher and higher.

Tomorrow be stronger, braver, more loving than you have been today. The Law of Progress gives a meaning, a purpose to life.

I'm pressing on the upward way,
New heights I'm gaining every day;
Still praying as I onward bound,
"Lord, plant my feet on higher ground."

Lord, lift me up and let me stand,
By faith, on heaven's table land,
A higher plane than I have found;
Lord, plant my feet on higher ground.
JOHNSON OATMAN, JR. (1856–1922)

CONSIDER:
What is my purpose in life? Have I accepted this purpose?
What kind of progress am I making toward fulfilling it?

PRAY:
God, lead me onward and upward, growing daily into a stronger,
braver, more loving person. Help me not to slip backwards.

Your Loved Ones

But I do not want you to be ignorant, brethren, concerning those
who have fallen asleep, lest you sorrow as others who have no hope.
For if we believe that Jesus died and rose again, even so God
will bring with Him those who sleep in Jesus.
1 THESSALONIANS 4:13–14

Your loved ones are very safe in My Keeping. Learning and loving and working, theirs is a life of happiness and progress. They live to serve, and serve they truly do. They serve Me and those they love. Ceaselessly they serve.

But their ministrations, so many, so diverse, you see no more than those in My time on earth in human form could have seen the angels who ministered unto Me in the wilderness.

How often mortals rush to earthly friends who can serve them in so limited a way, when the friends who are freed from the limitations of humanity can serve them so much better, understand better, protect better, plan better, and even plead better their cause with Me.

You do well to remember your friends in the Unseen. Companying with them the more you live in this Unseen World, the gentler will be your passing when it comes. Earth's troubles and difficulties will seem, even now, less overwhelming as you look, not at the things that are seen, but at the real, the Eternal Life.

"And this is Life Eternal that we may know Thee, the Only True God, and Jesus Christ whom Thou hast sent."

Learning to know Me draws that Kingdom very near, and in Me, and through Knowledge of Me, the dear ones there become very near and dear.

Everlasting Arms

The eternal God is thy refuge, and underneath are the everlasting arms.
DEUTERONOMY 33:27 KJV

Arms, sheltering Arms, express the loving tenderness of your Father (My Father) in Heaven. Man, in his trouble and difficulty, needs nothing so much as a refuge. A place to hide in. A place where none and nothing can touch him.

Say to yourself, "He is our Refuge." Say it until its truth sinks into your very soul. Say it until you know it—are so sure of it, that nothing can make you afraid.

Feel this not only until fear goes, but until Joy ripples through in its place. Refuge. Everlasting Arms so untiring, so safe—so sure.

What a fellowship, what a joy divine,
Leaning on the everlasting arms;
What a blessedness, what a peace is mine,
Leaning on the everlasting arms.

Leaning, leaning, safe and secure from all alarms;
Leaning, leaning, leaning on the everlasting arms.
ELISHA ALBRIGHT HOFFMAN (1839–1929)

PRAY:
Lord, I need a refuge from the cares and worries of this world, a place of safety where I can hide. Only You are such a refuge. Take me in Your loving arms, O Lord.

Walk in My Love

*Therefore be imitators of God as dear children. And walk in
love, as Christ also has loved us and given Himself for us,
an offering and a sacrifice to God for a sweet-smelling aroma.*
EPHESIANS 5:1–2

When supply seems to have failed, you must know it has not done so. But you must, at the same time, look around to see what you can give away. Give away something.

There is always a stagnation, a blockage, when supply seems short. Your giving clears that away and lets the Spirit of My Supply flow clear.

A consciousness of My Presence as Love makes all Life different. The consciousness of Me means the opening of your whole nature to Me, and that brings relief. Relief brings Peace. Peace brings Joy. The "Peace that passeth all understanding" and the "Joy no man taketh from you."

Beyond all words are My Love and Care for you. Be sure of it. Rejoice in it. Walk in My Love. These words mean much. There is a joy, a spring, a gladness in the walk of those who walk in My Love. That walk becomes a glad conquering and triumphant march. So walk.

PRAY:
*Lord, let me walk daily in Your generous love,
giving freely so that I may receive even more of Your blessings.*

Cultivate—Yourself

But as for me, I will come into Your house in the multitude of Your mercy; in fear of You I will worship toward Your holy temple. Lead me, O LORD, in Your righteousness because of my enemies; make Your way straight before my face.
PSALM 5:7–8

In Thy Strength we conquer.

Yes! Your conquering Power you gain from Me. There can be no failure with me. The secret of success then is Life with Me.

Do you want to make the best of life? Then live very near to Me, the Master and Giver of all Life.

Your reward will be sure. It will be perfect success, but My success.

Sometimes the success of souls won, sometimes the success of disease cured or devils cast out. Sometimes the success of a finished sacrifice as on Calvary. Sometimes the success of one who answered never a word in the face of the scorn and torture and jeering cries of His enemies, or the success of a Risen Savior as He walked through the Garden of Joseph of Arimathea on that first Easter morning.

But My success. The world may deem you failures. The world judges not as I judge.

Bend your knees in wonder before My revelation. The joy of seeing Spiritual Truths is a great Joy. When the Heavens are opened and the Voice speaks, not to all hearts, but to the faithful loving hearts.

Remember your great field of labor is yourself. That is your first task, the weeding, the planting, digging, pruning, bearing fruit. When that is done, I lead you out into other fields.

God or Mammon?

*"No one can serve two masters; for either he will hate
the one and love the other, or else he will be loyal to the one
and despise the other. You cannot serve God and mammon."*
MATTHEW 6:24

Y̶ou must be ready to stand apart from the world. Do you want
the full and complete satisfaction that you find in Me, and the
satisfaction of the world, too? Then you are trying to serve God and
Mammon, or if not trying to serve, then claiming the wages of both God
and Mammon.

If you work for Me, you have your reward. But then you turn to the
world, to human beings, and expect that reward, too. This is not right.

Do not expect love or gratitude or acknowledgment from any.
All reward necessary I will give you.

CONSIDER:
*Am I ready to stand apart from the world, serving God?
Am I willing to sacrifice the reward and recognition
from human beings for a heavenly reward?*

PRAY:
*Lord, free me of my desire to please human beings and
earn their gratitude. Make me desire only the satisfaction
I find in You, for that is the best reward I could have.*

A Generous Giver

*I am come that they might have life,
and that they might have it more abundantly.*
JOHN 10:10 KJV

Yes, I, your Master, am a generous Giver. Abundant Life, in overflowing measure, I give to you. For that I came. Life for souls. The Life, Eternal Life, that pulses through your whole being, that animates your mind and body, too.

A generous Giver. A Kingly Giver. For this I came that man might live in Me. Life it was of which I spoke when I said, "I am the Vine and ye are the branches." The life flow of the Vine is in the branches.

Our lives are one—yours and Mine. All that is in My Nature must therefore pass into yours, where the contact is so close a one.

I am Love and Joy and Peace and Strength and Power and Healing and Humility and Patience, and all else you see in Me your Lord. Then these, too, you must have as My Life flows through you. So courage.

You do not make yourselves loving and strong and patient and humble. You live with Me, and then My Life accomplishes the miracle-change.

CONSIDER:

Am I trying to change myself? Or am I allowing God's life to flow through me, so that I can be loving and strong and patient and humble?

Money Values

But seek ye first the kingdom of God, and his righteousness;
and all these things shall be added unto you.
MATTHEW 6:33 KJV

If therefore thine eye be single,
thy whole body shall be full of light.
MATTHEW 6:22 KJV

The eye of the soul is the will. If your one desire is My Kingdom, to find that Kingdom, to serve that Kingdom, then truly shall your whole body be full of light.

When you are told to seek first the Kingdom of God, the first step is to secure that your will is for that Kingdom. A single eye to God's glory. Desiring nothing less than that His Kingdom come. Seeking in all things the advance of His Kingdom.

Know no values but Spiritual values. No profit but that of Spiritual gain. Seek in all things His Kingdom *first*.

Only seek material gain when that gain will mean a gain for My Kingdom. Get away from money values altogether. Walk with Me. Learn of Me. Talk to Me. Here lies your true happiness.

Do you want your whole body to be full of light?
Then seek God's Kingdom with all of your might.
Keep the good of His Kingdom always in sight,

Pray, "Thy Kingdom come." Desire nothing less!
And seek in all things His Kingdom to bless.
Make gaining His Kingdom your true happiness.

No Other Name

*And whatever you do in word or deed, do all in the name of
the Lord Jesus, giving thanks to God the Father through him.*
COLOSSIANS 3:17

My Name is the Power that turns evil aside, that summons all good
to your aid. Spirits of evil flee at the sound of "Jesus." Spoken in
fear, in weakness, in sorrow, in pain, it is an appeal I never fail to answer.
"Jesus."

Use My Name often. Think of the unending call of "Mother" made
by her children. To help, to care, to decide, to appeal, "Mother." Use
My Name in that same way—simply, naturally, forcefully. "Jesus."

Use it not only when you need help but to express Love. Uttered
aloud, or in the silence of your hearts, it will alter an atmosphere from
one of discord to one of Love. It will raise the standard of talk and
thought. "Jesus."

"There is none other Name under Heaven whereby you can be
saved."

CONSIDER:
How often do I use the name of Jesus?
Do I call on Him expecting an answer?

PRAY:
*Jesus, I call on You to drive evil away from me, to bring
Your good power to help me. Answer my prayer and save me.*

When Faith Fails

Lord, I believe; help thou mine unbelief.
MARK 9:24 KJV

This cry of the human heart is as expressive of human need as it was when uttered to Me while I was on earth. It expresses the soul's progress.

As a soul realizes Me and My Power, and knows Me as Helper and Savior, that soul believes in Me more and more. At the same time it is more conscious than before of its falling short of absolute trust in Me.

"Lord, I believe. Help Thou mine unbelief." The soul's progress, an increased belief—then a cry for more faith—a plea to conquer all unbelief, all lack of trust.

That cry heard. That prayer answered. More faith, and at the same time more power to see where trust is lacking.

My children seek to go up this path, leading by each stage, nearer to Me.

CONSIDER:
How much faith do I have? How conscious am I of the limitations of my faith? How much do I wish that I had greater faith, and how often I pray God to increase my faith? What miracles, large or small, has God done for me recently, and how have they helped overcome my unbelief?

PRAY:
Lord, I'm only human. I confess that there are times when my faith fails me, or that I just don't have enough faith to believe You for a needed miracle. Please, dear God, answer my cry for more faith.

Quiet Strength

The LORD will give strength to His people;
the LORD will bless His people with peace.
PSALM 29:11

Rest in Me. When tired nature rebels, it is her call for rest. Rest then until My Life-Power flows through you.

Have no fear for the future. Be quiet, be still, and in that very stillness your strength will come and will be maintained.

The world sees strength in action. In My Kingdom it is known that strength lies in quiet. "In quietness and in confidence shall be your strength."

Such a promise! Such glorious fulfillment! The strength of Peace and the Peace of strength. Rest in Me. Joy in Me.

CONSIDER:
Do I find renewed strength and
peace when I'm quiet and restful?

PRAY:
Quiet me, Lord, so that I can find rest in You.
Still my soul until Your Life-Power flows through me.

Assurance

And the work of righteousness shall be peace;
and the effect of righteousness quietness and assurance for ever.
ISAIAH 32:17 KJV

My Peace it is which gives quietness and assurance forever. My Peace that flows as some calm river through the dry land of life. That causes the trees and flowers of life to spring forth and to yield abundantly.

Success is the result of work done in peace. Only so can work yield its increase. Let there be no hurry in your plans. You live not in time but in Eternity. It is in the Unseen that your life-future is being planned.

Abide in Me, and I in you, so shall you bring forth much fruit. Be calm, assured, at rest. Love, not rush. Peace, not unrest. Nothing fitful. All effectual. Sown in Prayer, watered by Trust, bearing flower and fruit in Joy. I love you.

CONSIDER:
Am I rushed by the demands of time and the world,
or am I making an effort to live in eternity?

PRAY:
God, let me partake of Your quiet assurance and find peace
during times when I feel the world's pressure bearing down on me.

Faltering Steps

You have also given me the shield of Your salvation;
Your right hand has held me up, Your gentleness has made me
great. You enlarged my path under me, so my feet did not slip.
PSALM 18:35–36

Show us Thy way, O Lord, and let us walk in Thy paths.

You are doing so. This is the way. The way of uncertain future and faltering steps. It is My Way....

Put all fear of the future aside. *Know* that you will be led. *Know* that you will be shown. I have promised.

He leads us on by paths we did not know;
Upward He leads us, tho' our steps be slow;
Tho' oft we faint and falter on the way,
Tho' storms and darkness oft obscure the day,
Yet when the clouds are gone,
We know He leads us on.

He leads us on thro' all th'unquiet years;
Past all our dreamland hopes, and doubts, and fears
He guides our steps; thro' all the tangled maze
Of losses, sorrows, and o'er clouded days
We know His will is done,
And still He leads us on.
HIRAM O. WILEY (19TH CENTURY)

CONSIDER:
How confident am I that God will lead me in the way I should go?

Dwell There

He that dwelleth in the secret place of the most
High shall abide under the shadow of the Almighty.
PSALM 91:1 KJV

Hidden in a sure place, known only to God and you. So secret that no power on earth can even find it.

But, My beloved children, you must dwell therein. No fitful visit, a real abiding. Make it your home. Your dwelling place.

Over that home shall My Shadow rest, to make it doubly safe, doubly secret. Like brooding mother-bird wings that Shadow rests. How safe, how sure, you must feel there.

When fears assail you and cares trouble you, it is because you have ventured out of that protecting Shadow. Then the one, the only thing to do is to creep back into shelter again. So rest.

CONSIDER:
Do I dwell in the Secret Place, under the Shadow of the Almighty—
or do I just duck in for a quick visit then quickly leave?

PRAY:
God, keep me in Your care, restful and
secure under Your protective shadow.

Full Joy

These things have I spoken unto you. . .that your joy might be full.
JOHN 15:11 KJV

Remember that the Truths I teach you have all been given to you, too, (as to My disciples of old) with the idea of giving you that overflowing Joy. . . .

Search for the Joy in life. Hunt for it as for hidden treasure. Love and Laugh. *Delight* yourselves in the Lord.

Joy in Me. Full Joy it was I wished My disciples to have. I intended them to have it. Had they lived My Teachings out in their daily lives, they would have had Fullness of Joy.

You promised to fill us with peace,
You said You'd provide every need;
These things You have spoken to us
That our joy might be full indeed.

You told us to live lives of love,
To forgive as we've been forgiven;
May we obey all that You've taught,
And rejoice in the Kingdom of Heaven.

May Your joy overflow in our spirits,
As we live Your commandments each day;
May we search for joy in each moment,
And find it on life's weary way.

CONSIDER:
Do I delight in the Lord? What is the connection between obeying Jesus' commandments and finding true joy and contentment?

Taste and Trust

O taste and see that the LORD is good.
PSALM 34:8 KJV

He is good. Trust in Him. Know that all is well. Say "God is good. God is good." Just leave in His Hands the present and the future, knowing only that He is good. He can bring order out of chaos, good out of evil, peace out of turmoil. God is good.

I and My Father are one. One in desire to do good. For God to do good to His children is for Him to share His goodness with them. God is good, anxious to share His goodness, and good things, with you, and He will do this.

Trust and be not afraid.

CONSIDER:
Do I trust God, or am I afraid?
Do I trust that He is eager to share good things?

PRAY:
You are good, God. Thank You so much for Your goodness to me.
Help me to trust You and leave both my present and my future in Your hands.

See the Father

Lord, show us the Father, and it sufficeth us.
JOHN 14:8 KJV

My children, have I been so long time with you, coming to you, speaking to you, and yet have you not known the Father?

Your Father is the God and Controller of a mighty Universe. But He is as I am. All the Love and the Strength and Beauty you have seen in Me are in My Father.

If you see that, and know Him and Me as we really are, then that sufficeth you—is really sufficient for you—completes your life—satisfies you—is all you need.

See the Father, see Me, and it sufficeth you. This is Love in abundance. Joy in abundance. All you need.

CONSIDER:
Do I truly know God the Father? Can I see His handiwork all around me in the universe He created?

PRAY:
God, I want to know You like never before. I want to experience more of Your love and strength and beauty.

Joy—Tribute

*You shall increase my greatness, and comfort me on every side. Also with
the lute I will praise You—and Your faithfulness, O my God! To You
I will sing with the harp, O Holy One of Israel. My lips shall greatly
rejoice when I sing to You, and my soul, which You have redeemed.*
PSALM 71:21–23

Jesus, our Lord, we Thee adore.

Sing unto Me from a glad heart. Sing and praise My Holy Name.
Praise is man's joy-tribute to Me, and as you praise, thrills of joy
surge through your being, and you learn something of the joy of the
Heavenly Host.

I will ever sing Thy praises,
Mighty God and gracious King;
Loud my heart its tribute raises,
And to Thee my psalms I sing;
Thou art King of all creation,
Every land and every nation;
"Thousand, thousand thanks to Thee,
Mighty God," my song shall be!
RUDOLPH A. JOHN (20TH CENTURY)

CONSIDER:
*Am I uninhibited in my praise of God? Why should I hold back
my praise, or restrain my joy because of the opinions of others?*

PRAY:
I praise Your name, Lord! I am thrilled to sing and adore Your name!

Turn Again

Draw nigh to God, and he will draw nigh to you.
JAMES 4:8 KJV

This is a law in the Spiritual Life. You must turn to Me before you are conscious of My nearness. It is that turning to Me you must cultivate in every circumstance. A glad turning of thankfulness, or a turning of weak appeal.

It is so wonderful that naught is needed but that mute appeal. You have no need to voice your longing. No need to plead, no need to bring gifts. How wonderful to feel you can so simply claim help, and so promptly, so lovingly, it is there.

Not only Help but the comfort and joy of Divine Nearness and Companionship. A nearness that brings sweetness into life, and confidence, and peace.

Never fear, never lose heart. Draw nigh to Me, and in that nearness is all you need. My Presence alone can transform conditions and lives—bring Harmony and Beauty, Peace and Love.

CONSIDER:
How conscious am I of God's nearness? How often do I turn to Him, even silently, without a word?

PRAY:
God, I want to draw nearer to You, to feel Your constant presence in my life.

Learn of Me

Lord, to whom shall we go? thou hast the words of eternal life.
JOHN 6:68 KJV

Learn of no one but Me. Teachers are to point the way to Me. After that you must accept Me, the Great Teacher.

The words of Eternal Life are all the words controlling your being, even controlling your temporal life. Take these, too, from Me. Have no fear. Abide in Me and accept My ruling.

Be full of gratitude. Wing up your prayers on Praise to Heaven. Take all that happens as My planning. All is well. I have all prepared in My Love. Let your heart sing.

Wing your way in prayer to Heaven,
Come with praise before the Throne;
Let Christ teach you precious wisdom,
Let Him teach you, and Him alone.

You may learn wise things from teachers,
Things you truly need to know,
But the deep truths, lasting life truths,
Are the ones just Christ can show.

Abide in Him, accept His ruling.
Have no fear, for all is planned;
For those who recognize His Spirit,
Know these things are from His hand.

Come and Stay

Come unto me, all ye that labour and
are heavy laden, and I will give you rest.
MATTHEW 11:28 KJV

Yes, come for rest. But stay for rest, too. Stop all feverish haste and be calm and untroubled. Come unto Me, not only for petitions to be granted but for nearness to Me.

Be sure of My Help, be conscious of My Presence, and wait until My Rest fills your soul.

Rest knows no fear. Rest knows no want. Rest is strong, sure. The rest of soft glades and peacefully flowing rivers, of strong, immovable hills. Rest, and all you need to gain this rest is to come to Me. So come.

CONSIDER:
Am I weary and burdened by cares, by pressures,
by deadlines—the many responsibilities of this world?

PRAY:
God, grant me rest amid the frustrations and troubles that
I face in this life. May I find rest and peace in Your presence.

Serve All

For you, brethren, have been called to liberty; only do not use liberty as an opportunity for the flesh, but through love serve one another.
GALATIANS 5:13

I am among you as one that serveth.

Yes! remember to serve all. Be ready to prove your Sonship by service. Look on all you meet as guests in your Father's House, to be treated with Love, with all consideration, with gentleness.

As a servant of all, think no work beneath you. Be ever ready to do all you can for others. Serve. Serve. Serve.

There is a gladness in service, a Joy in doing My Will for others, in being My expression of all good for them.

Remember that, when you serve others, you are acting for your Master and Lord who washed His disciples' feet. So, in service for others, express your Love for Me.

CONSIDER:
What am I doing to serve all? Am I hospitable to others? Do I treat my fellow humans with love, consideration, and gentleness? And do I do so with gladness and joy? Am I able to strike a proper balance between doing acts of service for others, and getting enough rest, so that I don't overtax my strength and burn out?

PRAY:
Dear Lord, help me to express my love for You by showing love to others—both with thoughtful, considerate acts of kindness, and practical help to meet pressing needs. May I reach out to others gladly and joyfully, not grudgingly.

Divine Restraint

And He sat down, called the twelve, and said to them, "If anyone desires to be first, he shall be last of all and servant of all."
MARK 9:35

Is My Hand shortened that it cannot save? No! My power to save increases as your power to understand My Salvation increases. So from Strength to Strength, from Power to Power, we go in Union.

Limitless is My Miracle-working Power in the Universe, though it has limitations in each individual life, but only to the extent of the lack of vision of that individual. There is no limit to My Power to save. Also there is no limit to My desire and longing to save. My Hand is not shortened, and it is "stretched out still," longing and waiting to be allowed to bless and help and save.

Think how tenderly I respect the right of each individual soul. Never forcing upon it My Help, My Salvation. Perhaps in all My suffering for humanity, that is the hardest, the restraint of the Divine Impatience and longing to help, until the call of the soul gives Me My right to act.

Think of Love shown in this. Comfort My waiting, loving, longing Heart by claiming My Help, Guidance, and Miracle-working Power.

The Secret Path

Suffer it to be so now: for thus it
becometh us to fulfil all righteousness.
MATTHEW 3:15 KJV

Upon this I founded My three years' Mission on earth on the acceptance of the difficulty and discipline of life so as to share that human life with My followers in all the ages.

Much that you both must accept in life is not to be accepted as being necessary for you personally, but accepted, as I accepted it, to set an example, to share in the sufferings and difficulties of mankind.

In this "to share" means "to save." And there, too, for you both. . . the same must be true as was so true of Me. "He saved others. Himself He cannot save."

Beloved, you are called to save and share in a very special way. The way of sorrows if walked with Me, the Man of Sorrows, is a path kept sacred and secret for My nearest and dearest, those whose one desire is to do all for Me, to sacrifice all for Me, to count, as My servant Paul did, "all things but loss so that they might gain Me."

But, dreary as that Path must look to those who view it only from afar, it has tender lights and restful shades that no other walk in life can give.

I Touch Your Arm

The steps of a good man are ordered by the Lord, and He delights in his way.
Though he fall, he shall not be utterly cast down; for the Lord upholds him
with His hand. I have been young, and now am old; yet I have not seen
the righteous forsaken, nor his descendants begging bread.

Psalm 37:23–25

Thy touch has still its ancient Power.

Yes! when you are quiet before Me I lay My Hand upon each head, and Divine Spirit flows through that healing, powerful Touch into your very beings. Wait in silence before Me to feel that.

When you look to Me for guidance My Hand is laid upon your arm, a gentle Touch to point the way. When in mental, physical, or spiritual weakness you cry to Me for healing, My Touch brings Strength and Healing, the renewal of your youth, the power to climb and strive.

When you faint by the way, and stumbling footsteps show human strength is waning, My Touch of the Strong and Helping Hand supports you on your Way.

Yes! My children, My touch has still its ancient Power, and that Power is promised to you. So go forward into the future bravely and unafraid.

CONSIDER:
Throughout the Gospels, Jesus laid His hands on people to
heal their bodies or to bless them, so is it surprising that
He would still do the same now? Do I believe that when I
come before Jesus in spirit, that He literally touches me?

PRAY:
Lord, I ask for Your Spirit's touch now.

Wisdom

*Then he said to them, "Go your way, eat the fat, and drink the sweet,
and send portions to those for whom nothing is prepared; for this day is
holy to our Lord. Do not sorrow, for the joy of the LORD is your strength."*
NEHEMIAH 8:10

As thy days so shall thy strength be.

I have promised that for every day you live, the strength shall be given
you. Do not fear.

Face each difficulty sure that the wisdom and strength will be given
you for it. Claim it.

Rely on Me to keep My Promise about this. In My Universe,
for every task I give one of My children, there is set aside all that is
necessary for its performance. So why fear? So why doubt?

*God has promised you strength for each day;
For each task He gives strength to do it.
When trouble comes along, pause a moment to pray,
And God will give wisdom to get through it.*

CONSIDER:
*Have I claimed the wisdom and
strength that God has promised me?*

PRAY:
*Banish my fears and doubts, O Lord. Allow me to rest assured in
Your promise of wisdom and strength, for I desperately need them.*

Secret of Prosperity

Look unto me, and be ye saved, all the ends of the earth.
ISAIAH 45:22 KJV

Look to no other source for Salvation. Only look unto Me. See no other supply. Look unto Me, and you shall be saved. Regard Me as your only supply. That is the secret of prosperity for you, and you in your turn shall save many from poverty and distress.

Whatever danger threatens look unto Me. . . . Whatever you desire or need, or desire or need for others, look unto Me. Claim all from My Storehouse. Claim, claim, claim.

Remember that I fed the Children of Israel with Heaven-sent manna. I made a way through the Red Sea for them. I led them through the wilderness of privation, difficulty, discipline. I led them into a land flowing with milk and honey. So trust. So be led.

Rejoice. These are your wilderness days. But surely and safely, you are being led to your Canaan of Plenty.

CONSIDER:
Do I feel as if I'm wandering aimlessly through a barren wilderness?
If so, have I called on God to lead me through these difficult times?

PRAY:
Help me to rejoice even in my trials and tribulations, Lord.
Help me to trust You for my salvation and prosperity.

True Meekness

Seek the LORD, all you meek of the earth, who have upheld
His justice. Seek righteousness, seek humility. It may be
that you will be hidden in the day of the LORD's anger.
ZEPHANIAH 2:3

How easy it is to lead and guide when you are responsive to My wish! The hurts of life come only when you, or those about whom you care, endeavor to go your, or their, own way and resist the pressure of My Hand.

But in willing My Will there must be a gladness. Delight to do that Will.

"The meek shall inherit the earth," I said. That is, control others, and the material forces of the earth.

But this exalted state of possession is the result of a yielded will. That was My meaning of the word meek.

So live. So yield. So conquer.

All to Jesus, I surrender;
Make me, Savior, wholly Thine;
Let me feel the Holy Spirit,
Truly know that Thou art mine.
I surrender all, I surrender all,
All to Thee, my blessed Savior, I surrender all.
JUDSON WHEELER VAN DEVENTER (1855–1939)

CONSIDER:
Do I tend to go my own way, resisting God's guidance,
and then complain about the hurts that come my way?

Blessed Assurance

And the work of righteousness shall be peace;
and the effect of righteousness quietness and assurance for ever.
ISAIAH 32:17 KJV

Be still and know that I am God. Only when the soul attains this calm can there be true work done, and mind and soul and body be strong to conquer and to bear.

The Peace is the work of righteousness living the right life, living with Me. Quietness and assurance follow.

Assurance is the calm born of a deep certainty in Me, in My Promises, in My Power to save and keep. Gain this calm, and at all costs keep this calm. Rest in Me. Live in Me. Calm, quiet, assured—at Peace.

CONSIDER:

Do I have assurance, the calm born of a deep certainty
in God and His promises? Is this something that only
very spiritual people can know, or is it available to all
Christians? I'm told to "gain this calm," but how do I gain it?
Do I make an effort to quiet my spirit and to draw close to God?

PRAY:

God, please give me this calm, this "peace of God, which surpasses
all understanding." Help me to be still and know that You are God.

All You Desire

> *He hath no form nor comeliness; and when we shall see him,*
> *there is no beauty that we should desire him.*
> ISAIAH 53:2 KJV

My children, in this verse My servant Isaiah spoke of the wonderful illumination given to those who were Spirit-guided.

To those who know Me not, there is in Me nothing to appeal to them or to attract them.

To those who know Me there is nothing more to be desired. "No beauty they could desire of Him."

Oh! My children, draw very near to Me. See Me as I really am, that ever you may have the Joy of finding in Me all you could desire. The fulfillment of all you could desire in Master, Lord, or Friend.

CONSIDER:
What do I find attractive about Jesus? Is there anything
I have difficulty with? Do I truly see Him as He is?

PRAY:
Oh God, illuminate me with Your Spirit. Draw me near to
You so that I can experience the joy of truly knowing You.

No Chance Meetings

*The LORD shall preserve thy going out and thy coming
in from this time forth, and even for evermore.*
PSALM 121:8 KJV

All your movements, your goings and comings, controlled by Me.
Every visit, all blessed by Me. Every walk arranged by Me.
A blessing on all you do, on every interview.

Every meeting not a chance meeting, but planned by Me.
All blessed.

Not only now, in the hour of your difficulty, but from this time
forth and for evermore.

Led by the Spirit, a proof of Sonship. "As many as are led by the
Spirit of God, they are the Sons of God," and if children then heirs—
heirs of God.

What a heritage! Heirs—no prospect of being disinherited.
"Heirs of God and joint heirs with Christ: if so be that you suffer
with Him that you may be also glorified together."

So your suffering has its purpose. It is a proof of Sonship. It leads
to perfection of character (the being glorified), and to Union with Me,
God, too. Think of, and dwell upon, the rapture of this.

PRAY:
*God, help me to trust You despite my suffering.
I know that You're still in my life, leading me every day.*

A Child's Hand

Be strong and of good courage, do not fear nor be afraid
of them; for the LORD your God, He is the One who goes
with you. He will not leave you nor forsake you.
DEUTERONOMY 31:6

Dear Lord, we cling to Thee.

Yes, cling. Your faith shall be rewarded. Do you not know what it means to feel a little trusting hand in yours, to know a child's confidence?

Does that not draw out your Love and desire to protect, to care? Think what My Heart feels, when in your helplessness you turn to Me, clinging, desiring My Love and Protection.

Would you fail that child, faulty and weak as you are? Could I fail you? Just know it is not possible. Know all is well. You must not doubt. You must be sure. There is no miracle I cannot perform, nothing I cannot do. No eleventh-hour rescue I cannot accomplish.

CONSIDER:
God has planted in parents the instinctive, unconscious desire to love,
protect, and care for their children. Why did He think that these were
good and necessary attributes to have? Is this not then evidence that this
is the way God feels toward us, His children on earth? In fact, how strong
does Isaiah 49:15 say that God's protective thoughts toward us are?

PRAY:
Heavenly Father, I cling to You, childlike and trusting,
confident that my faith will in good time be rewarded.
In all my weakness, I trust myself to Your loving protection.

Rejoice at Weakness

And he said to me, "My grace is sufficient for you, for My strength is made perfect in weakness." Therefore most gladly I will rather boast in my infirmities, that the power of Christ may rest upon me.
2 CORINTHIANS 12:9

Savior, breathe forgiveness o'er us.
All our weakness Thou dost know.

Yes! I know all. Every cry for mercy. Every sigh of weariness. Every plea for help. Every sorrow over failure. Every weakness. I am with you through all. My tender sympathy is yours. My strength is yours.

Rejoice at your weakness, My children. My strength is made perfect in weakness. When you are weak then am I strong. Strong to help, to cure, to protect.

Trust Me, My children. I know *all*. I am beside you. Strong, strong, strong to save. Lean on My Love, and know that all is well.

CONSIDER:
Am I able to actually be glad for my weaknesses?
Do I trust God to help and protect me despite them?

PRAY:
Give me the faith to depend on Your strength, Lord,
and to trust that all is well when I am in Your care.

The Dark Places

If I take the wings of the morning, and dwell in the uttermost parts of the sea, even there Your hand shall lead me, and Your right hand shall hold me. If I say, "Surely the darkness shall fall on me," even the night shall be light about me; indeed, the darkness shall not hide from You, but the night shines as the day; the darkness and the light are both alike to You.

PSALM 139:9–12

Jesus, the very thought of Thee with Sweetness fills us.

Yes. Love Me until just to think of Me means Joy and rapture. Gladness at the thought of One very near and dear.

It is the balm for all sorrows, the thought of Me. Healing for all physical, mental, and spiritual ills you can always find in thinking of Me and speaking to Me.

Are doubts and fears in your hearts? Then think of Me, speak to Me. Instead of those fears and doubts there will flow into your hearts and beings such sweet Joy as is beyond any joy of earth.

This is unfailing. Never doubt it. Courage. Courage. Courage. Fear nothing. Rejoice even in the darkest places. Rejoice.

Are doubts and fears in your heart? Think of Me.
Is sorrow now filling your heart? Speak to Me.
Are you spiritually or mentally unwell? Think of Me.
Are you disabled or physically ill? Speak to Me.

Instead of those fears that you're feeling inside,
Shall flow the sweetness of joy's healing tide;
And My Spirit shall rise as a wonderful light,
Lighting your darkness and making things right.

Love Me More

*Give to the LORD the glory due His name; bring an offering,
and come into His courts. Oh, worship the LORD in the
beauty of holiness! Tremble before Him, all the earth.*
PSALM 96:8–9

*Jesus, our Lord, we Thee adore.
Oh, make us love Thee more and more.*

Yes! I would draw you closer and closer to Me by bonds of Love. The Love of the sinner for the Savior, of the rescued for the Rescuer, of the sheep for the Loving Shepherd, of the child for its Father.

So many ties of Love there are to bind you to Me.

Each experience in your life of Joy, and sorrow, of difficulty or success, of hardship or ease, of danger or safety, each makes its own particular demand upon Me. Each serves to answer the prayer: "Make me love Thee more and more."

CONSIDER:
*How often do I pray that God would
help me love and appreciate Jesus more?*

PRAY:
*Continue to draw me closer to You, Lord Jesus, through all my sorrows,
difficulties, hardships, and dangers, as well as through my successes
and times of ease and safety. Let my love for You never stop growing.*

Extra Work

*"If you are willing and obedient, you shall eat the good of the land;
but if you refuse and rebel, you shall be devoured by the sword";
for the mouth of the LORD has spoken.*

ISAIAH 1:19–20

---

*Our Lord and our God. Help us through poverty to plenty.
Through unrest to rest, through sorrow to Joy, through weakness to Power.*

I am your Helper. At the end of your present path lie all these
blessings. So trust and know that I am leading you.

Step with a firm step of confidence in Me into each unknown day.
Take every duty and every interruption as of My appointment.

You are My servant. Serve Me as simply, cheerfully, and readily
as you expect others to serve you.

Do you blame the servant who avoids extra work, who complains
about being called from one task to do one less liked? Do you feel you
are ill served by such a one?

Then what of Me? Is not that how you so often serve Me?
Think of this. Lay it to heart and view your day's work in this light.

Be strong!

*We are not here to play, to dream, to drift;
We have hard work to do and loads to lift;
Shun not the struggle, face it, 'tis God's gift.
Be strong, be strong, be strong!*

*Say not the days are evil—who's to blame?
And fold the hands and acquiesce—O shame!
Stand up, speak out, and bravely, in God's Name.
Be strong, be strong, be strong!*

MALTBIE DAVENPORT BABCOCK (1858–1901)

Shame and Distress

I will bless the LORD at all times: his praise shall continually
be in my mouth. . . . I sought the LORD, and he heard me,
and delivered me from all my fears. They looked unto him,
and were lightened: and their faces were not ashamed.
PSALM 34:1, 4–5 KJV

See, My children, that even in distress, the first step is *Praise*. Before you cry in your distress, bless the Lord; even when troubles seem to overwhelm you.

That is My Divine order of approach. Observe this always. In the greatest distress, search until you find cause for thankfulness. Then bless and thank.

You have thus established a line of communication between yourself and Me. Along that line let your cry of distress follow.

Thus you will find I do My part, and deliverance will be sure. Oh! the gladness of heart. Lightened you will be, the burden rolled away, as the result of looking to Me.

The shame and distress will be lifted, too. That is always the second step. First right with Me, and then you will be righted, too, in the eyes of men.

CONSIDER:
Do I praise the Lord in all my circumstances,
even in my distress and shame?

PRAY:
God, help me to make praising You my first step,
even in times of stress and trouble and shame. I have
reasons to be thankful, whatever I'm going through.

You Are My Joy

Thine they were, and thou gavest them me;
and they have kept thy word.
JOHN 17:6 KJV

Remember, that just as you thank God for Me, so I thank God for His Gift to Me of you. In that hour of My agony on earth, one note of Joy thrilled through the pain: the thought of the souls, given Me by My Father, who had kept My Word.

They had not then done great deeds, as they did later, for and in My Name. They were simple doers of My Word, not hearers only. Just in their daily tasks and ways they kept My Word.

You, too, can bring Joy to My Heart by faithful service. Faithful service in the little things. Be faithful.

Do your simple tasks for Me.

CONSIDER:
If Jesus could give thanks to His Father in His hour of
pain and agony, how can I not thank Him for all that He
does—and show my gratitude through my faithful service?

PRAY:
Thank You, God, for sending Your Son to die for me.
Thank You, Jesus, for giving Your life to atone for my sins. I commit
myself to keep and obey Your word, that I might bring You joy.

The Sculptor's Skill

And the apostles said to the Lord,
"Increase our faith."
LUKE 17:5

Lord, we believe, help Thou our unbelief.
Lord, hear our prayers and let our cries come unto Thee.

Along the road of praise, as I told you. Yes! I will indeed help your unbelief, and in answer to your prayers grant you so great a faith, such an increasingly great faith, that each day you may look back, from the place of your larger vision, and see the faith of the day before as almost unbelief.

The Beauty of My Kingdom is its growth. In that Kingdom there is always progress, a going on from strength to strength, from glory to glory. Be in My Kingdom and of My Kingdom, and there can be no stagnation. Eternal Life, abundant Life is promised to all in it and of it.

No misspent time over failures and shortcomings. Count the lessons learnt from them but as rungs in the ladder. Step up, and then cast away all thought of the manner of the making of the rung. Fashioned of joy or sorrow, of failure or success, of wounds or healing balm, what matter, My children, so long as it served its purpose?

Learn another lesson. The Sculptor who finds a faulty marble casts it aside. Because it has no fashioning, it may regard itself as perfect; and it may look with scorn upon the marble the Sculptor is cutting and shaping into perfection. From this, My children, learn a lesson for your lives.

The Sacrifice

Behold the Lamb of God, which taketh away the sin of the world.
JOHN 1:29 KJV

C hrist our Passover is sacrificed for us." I am the Lamb of God. Lay upon Me your sins, your failures, your shortcomings. My sacrifice has atoned for all. I am the mediator between God and Man, the man Christ Jesus.

Do not dwell upon the past. You make My Sacrifice of no effect.

No! realize that in Me you have all, complete forgiveness, complete companionship, complete healing.

CONSIDER:
Do I understand the full meaning of Christ's sacrifice for me?
Do I realize that His death on the cross means that I am
completely forgiven of my sins, that I have full communion
with Him, that I can be completely healed?

PRAY:
Dear Jesus, thank You for Your loving rebuke—telling me that
if I dwell upon my past sins, if I continue to wallow in guilt and
remorse and regret, that I'm acting as if Your death for my sins
wasn't enough. I'm acting like I still need to do something to earn
Your forgiveness. Help me to truly grasp that I have complete forgiveness,
and have been already restored to full fellowship with the Father.

Feel Plenty

Consider the ravens, for they neither sow nor reap,
which have neither storehouse nor barn; and God feeds
them. Of how much more value are you than the birds?
LUKE 12:24

Live in My Secret Place, and there the feeling is one of full satisfaction. You are to feel plenty. The storehouses of God are full to overflowing, but you must see this in your mind.

Be sure of this before you can realize it in material form.

Think thoughts of plenty. See yourselves as Daughters of a King. I have told you this. Wish plenty for yourselves and all you care for and long to help.

My Maker and my King,
To Thee my all I owe;
Thy sovereign bounty is the spring
Whence all my blessings flow;
Thy sovereign bounty is the spring
Whence all my blessings flow.
ANNE STEELE (1716–1778)

PRAY:
God, help me to trust that You have good things in
store for me. I believe that Your storehouses are full to
overflowing, and You're ready to overflow on my life.

The Imprisoned God

But You are holy, enthroned in the praises of Israel.
Our fathers trusted in You; they trusted, and You delivered them.
PSALM 22:3–4

Our Lord, we praise Thee and bless Thy Name forever.

Yes! Praise. That moment, in the most difficult place, your sorrow is turned to Joy, your fret to praise, the outward circumstances change from those of disorder to order, of chaos to calm.

The beginning of all reform must be in yourselves. However restricted your circumstances, however little you may be able to remedy financial affairs, you can always turn to yourselves, and seeing something not in order there, seek to right that.

As all reform is from within out, you will always find the outward has improved, too. To do this is to release the imprisoned God-Power within you.

That Power, once operative, will immediately perform miracles. Then indeed shall your mourning be turned into Joy.

PRAY:
God, Your Spirit dwells within me, and if I have done
anything to offend You, show me so I can set things right—
so that Your miraculous power may be released in my life again.

Faith-Vision

*"As the Father loved Me, I also have loved you; abide in My love.
If you keep My commandments, you will abide in My love, just as
I have kept My Father's commandments and abide in His love."*
JOHN 15:9–10

Turn your eyes to behold Me. Look away from sordid surroundings, from lack of beauty, from the imperfections in yourselves and those around you. Then you who have the Faith-Vision will see all you could and do desire in Me.

In your unrest behold My calm, My rest. In your impatience, My unfailing patience. In your lack and limitation, My Perfection.

Looking at Me you will grow like Me, until men say to you, too, that you have been with Jesus.

As you grow like Me, you will be enabled to do the things I do, and greater works than these shall ye do because I go unto My Father.

From that place of abiding, limited by none of humanity's limitations, I can endue you with the all-conquering, all miracle-working Power of your Divine Brother and Ally.

*O soul, are you weary and troubled?
No light in the darkness you see?
There's light for a look at the Savior,
And life more abundant and free!*

*Turn your eyes upon Jesus,
Look full in His wonderful face,
And the things of earth will grow strangely dim,
In the light of His glory and grace.*
HELEN HOWARTH LEMMEL (1863–1961)

Loneliness

And they all forsook him, and fled.
MARK 14:50 KJV

Down through the ages all the simple acts of steadfast devotion, of obedience in difficulty, of loving service, have been taken by Me as an atonement for the loneliness My humanity suffered by that desertion.

Yet I, who had realized to the full the longing of the Father to save, and His rejection by men, the misunderstanding of His mind and purpose, how could I think that I should not know that desertion, too?

Learn, My children, from these words two lessons. Learn first that I know what loneliness, desertion, and solitude mean. Learn that every act of yours of faithfulness is a comfort to My Heart. Learn, too, that it was to those deserters I gave the task of bringing My Message to mankind. To those deserters, those fearful ones, I gave My Power to heal, to raise to life.

Earth's successes are not the ones I use for the great work of My Kingdom. "They all forsook Him and fled." Learn My tender understanding and pardon of human frailty. Not until man has failed has he learnt true humility. And it is only the humble who can inherit the earth.

Hear My Answer

Lord, hear our prayer, and let our cry come unto Thee.

The cry of the human soul is never unheard. It is never that God does not hear the cry, but that man fails to hear the response.

Like parts of a machine, made to fit each into the other, and to work in perfect harmony, so is the human cry and the God-response.

But man treats this cry as if it were a thing alone, to be heard, or not, as it pleased God, not realizing that the response was there in all eternity, awaiting the cry, and only man's failing to heed, or to listen, kept him unaware of the response, and unsaved, unhelped by it.

CONSIDER:
Am I aware of God's response to the
cry of my soul? Or do I fail to heed it?

PRAY:
Lord, quiet my soul so I can hear Your
answer to my prayer, and be helped.

No Burden Irks

Teach me to do Your will, for You are my God;
Your Spirit is good. Lead me in the land of uprightness.
PSALM 143:10

Our Lord and our God.
Be it done unto us according to Thy Word.

Simple acceptance of My Will is the Key to Divine Revelation. It will result in both Holiness and Happiness. The way to the Cross may be a way of sorrow, but at its foot the burdens of sin and earth-desire are rolled away.

The yoke of My acceptance of My Father's Will in all things is adjusted to My servants' shoulders, and from that moment no burden irks or presses.

But not only in the great decisions of life accept and welcome My Will. Try to see in each interruption, each task, however small, the same fulfillment of Divine intent.

Accept it; say your thanks for it. Do so until this becomes a habit, and the resulting Joy will transfigure and transform your lives.

CONSIDER:
Have I accepted God's will—in the great decisions of life,
as well as the small ones that I face throughout each day?

A Love Feast

*Behold, I stand at the door, and knock: if any man hear my voice, and open
the door, I will come in to him, and will sup with him, and he with me.*
REVELATION 3:20 KJV

See, My children, the knocking rests upon no merit of yours though
it is in response to the longing of your heart for Me.

Keep, keep that listening ear. "If any man will hear My Voice."
Again no merit of yours. Only the ear bent to catch My tones, and to
hear the sound of My gentle knocking.

Then listen: "If any man hear My Voice, and open the door, I will
come in to him, and will sup with him, and he with Me."

What a feast! You think it would have been Joy to have been
present at the Marriage Feast of Cana of Galilee, or to have been one of
My disciples in the Upper Room, seated with Me at the Last Supper or
one of the two at Emmaus, or one of the few for whom I prepared that
lakeside feast!

But oh! at each of these feasts, God-provided and God-
companioned as they were, you could not have known the rapture
you may know as you hear the knocking and the Voice, and,
opening, bid Me welcome to My Feast.

A Feast of tenderest companionship, of Divine Sustenance, truly
a Love Feast.

Home-Building

Jesus answered and said to him, "If anyone loves Me,
he will keep My word; and My Father will love him,
and We will come to him and make Our home with him."
JOHN 14:23

You are building up an unshakable faith. Be furnishing the quiet places of your souls now.

Fill them with all that is harmonious and good, beautiful, and enduring.

Home-build in the Spirit now, and the waiting time will be well spent.

Lord, I have built a solid faith
To withstand the tempest's blast;
With You as my foundation,
My home will surely last.

Now may Your Spirit's beauty
Fill each and every space,
With treasures pure and lasting
Created by Your grace.

CONSIDER:

Jesus, is my life built upon You, the one, true foundation?
Are my spiritual walls strong? What are the furnishings in my soul?
Am I filled with harmony, goodness, and beauty?

PRAY:

God, may I labor in Your Spirit to build an
unshakable faith that will endure for all time.

Hill of Sacrifice

*For in it the righteousness of God is revealed from
faith to faith; as it is written, "The just shall live by faith."*
ROMANS 1:17

You must trust to the end. You must be ready to go on trusting to the last hour.

You must know even when you cannot see. . . . You must be ready, like My servant Abraham, to climb the very Hill of Sacrifice, to go to the very last moment, before you see My Deliverance.

This final test has to come to all who walk by Faith. You must rely on Me alone.

Look to no other arm, look for no other help. Trust in the Spirit Forces of the Unseen, not in those you see. Trust and fear not.

CONSIDER:

*Am I living by faith, trusting to the end, even when
I cannot see? Have I turned my fears over to God?*

PRAY:

*Dear Lord, strengthen my resolve to love and obey You,
even if it looks like I must sacrifice the thing I hold most dear.*

Salt of the Earth

*"You are the salt of the earth; but if the salt loses its flavor,
how shall it be seasoned? It is then good for nothing but
to be thrown out and trampled underfoot by men."*
MATTHEW 5:13

Our Lord, we bless Thee and thank Thee for Thy Keeping Power.

Yes! "Kept by the Power of God" is a promise and an assurance
that holds Joy and Beauty for the believing soul.

The keeping that means security, safety, is wonderful. There is,
too, the keeping that implies Life, freshness, purity, the being "kept
unspotted from the world."

Then there is the keeping that I ensure to those of whom I speak
as the salt of the earth.

"Ye are the salt of the earth: but if the salt have lost his savour it
is henceforth good for nothing, but to be cast out, and to be trodden
under foot of men."

Only in very close contact with Me is the keeping Power realized.
That keeping Power which maintains the salt at its freshest and best,
and also preserves from corruption that portion of the world in which
I place it.

What a work! Not by activity in this case, but simply by its existing,
by its quality.

CONSIDER:

*Am I truly the salt of the earth? Do I live close to God and go
out from His presence to flavor the world with His love and power?*

No Unemployment

Whoever has no rule over his own spirit is
like a city broken down, without walls.
PROVERBS 25:28

The way of conquest over the material, the temporal, which all My disciples should know, is learned by the conquest of the physical, the self-life, in each of you.

So seek, in all things, to conquer. Take this as a very definite Guidance. Circumstances are adverse. Temporal power, as money, needs to be forthcoming.

Then seek daily more and more to obtain this self-conquest, and you are gaining surely, though you may not see it, conquest over the temporal forces and powers.

Unemployment would cease if man realized this.

If he has not the work, let him make himself a conquering force, beginning with the conquest of all evil in himself, then in his home, then in all round him. He will have become a force that will be needed and must be employed.

There are no idle hours in My Kingdom. Waiting may seem a time of inactivity, as far as the outer world is concerned, but it can, and should, be a time of great activity in the inner life and the surrounding material plane.

Deserters

*Now Peter sat outside in the courtyard. And a servant girl came
to him, saying, "You also were with Jesus of Galilee." But he denied
it before them all, saying, "I do not know what you are saying."
And when he had gone out to the gateway, another girl saw him and said
to those who were there, "This fellow also was with Jesus of Nazareth."
But again he denied with an oath, "I do not know the Man!"*
MATTHEW 26:69–72

You must believe utterly. My Love can bear nothing less. I am so
often "wounded in the house of My friends." Do you think the
spitting and scorn of My enemies, the mocking and reviling hurt me? No!

"They all forsook Him and fled." "I know not the man." These left
their scars.

So now, it is not the unbelief of My enemies that hurts, but that
My friends, who love and know Me, cannot walk all the way with Me
and doubt My Power to do all that I have said.

*Lord, may I not doubt Your power,
May I walk with You right to the end.
And in temptation's final hour
May I still stand with You, my Friend.*

CONSIDER:
*Have I caused pain to my Savior by my doubt? Do I
believe that He has the power to do what He has said?*

PRAY:
*God, forgive me for those times when my belief has wavered, when I held
back, doubting Your power. May I walk all the way with You in full faith.*

Days of Conquest

Evening and morning and at noon I will pray, and cry aloud,
and He shall hear my voice. He has redeemed my soul in peace from
the battle that was against me, for there were many against me.
PSALM 55:17–18

I see the loving, striving, not the defects. I see the conquest of your particular battle. I count it victory, a glad victory.

I do not compare it with the strenuous campaigns of My great Saints.

For you it is victory, and the angels rejoice, and your dear ones rejoice, as much as at any conquest noted, and rejoiced over, by Heaven.

My children, count the days of conquest as very blessed days.

CONSIDER:
Do I rejoice in the conquests God has given me, even though they may
seem to be small victories compared to what others have accomplished?
Why does the Bible say, "but they. . .comparing themselves among
themselves, are not wise" (2 Corinthians 10:12)? Am I thankful
for what God has allowed me to accomplish?

PRAY:
God, I'm truly grateful for the part You allow me to play in Your plans.
I rejoice in the victories You have given me over sin and difficulties.
You don't see things the way that we see them, and small things are
large in Your eyes. Help me to continue to be faithful in all things.

Glad Surprises

But Jesus called them to Him and said, "Let the little children
come to Me, and do not forbid them; for of such is the kingdom
of God. Assuredly, I say to you, Whoever does not receive the
kingdom of God as a little child will by no means enter it."
LUKE 18:16–17

Our Lord, we know that all is well. We trust Thee for all.
We love Thee increasingly. We bow to Thy Will.

Bow not as one who is resigned to some heavy blow about to fall
or to the acceptance of some inevitable decision.

Bow as a child bows, in anticipation of a glad surprise being
prepared for it by one who loves it.

Bow in such a way, just waiting to hear the loving word to raise
your head, and see the glory and Joy and wonder of your surprise.

CONSIDER:
Do I anticipate that the Lord has prepared glad surprises
for me? Or am I plagued by constant feelings of anxiety
or dread, thinking that God keeps a record of all my sins,
and is just waiting to punish me? Where do such feelings
originate? How can I grow out of such an attitude?

PRAY:
God, grant me again that wonder, awe, and anticipation that I once
felt as a child. I want to fully experience Your joy and love again.

Discount Money

*Then Jesus said to His disciples, "Assuredly, I say to you that
it is hard for a rich man to enter the kingdom of heaven.
And again I say to you, it is easier for a camel to go through the
eye of a needle than for a rich man to enter the kingdom of God."*
MATTHEW 19:23–24

Never count success by money gained. That is not the mind of My
Kingdom. Your success is the measure of My Will and Mind that
you have revealed to those around you.

Your success is the measure of My Will that those around you have
seen worked out in your lives.

CONSIDER:

*How do I count success? Is it in money, earthly power, the acclaim
of others, or the fulfillment of my personal dreams and goals? Or do
I measure success by how much God's will is fulfilled in my life?
For me, is true success the lasting riches that come from faith in God?*

PRAY:

*God, impress the true meaning of success upon my soul. Lead me to
seek Your mind and follow Your will in all matters, great and small.*

The Hardest Lesson

"And now, Lord, what do I wait for? My hope is in You. Deliver me from all my transgressions; do not make me the reproach of the foolish."
<small>PSALM 39:7–8</small>

Wait and you shall realize the Joy of the one who can be calm and wait, knowing that all is well. The last, and hardest lesson, is that of waiting. So wait.

I would almost say tonight, "Forgive Me, children, that I allow this extra burden to rest upon you even for so short a time."

I would have you know this, that from the moment you placed all in My Hands, and sought no other aid, from that moment I have taken the quickest way possible to work out your salvation, and to free you.

There is so much you have had to be taught—to avoid future disaster. But the Friend with whom you stand by the grave of failure, of dead ambitions, of relinquished desires, that Friend is a Friend for all time.

Use this waiting time to cement the Friendship with Me and to increase your Knowledge of Me.

CONSIDER:
Does God allow me to suffer failure to teach me to avoid future disasters? Why is it sometimes good to die to my ambitions and relinquish my desires? Does deepening my friendship with Jesus compensate for the loss I suffer?

PRAY:
Lord, help me to believe that from the first hour that I placed my needs in Your hands, that You heard me, and started to answer. Help me to continue to trust You even if it takes a while to bring the answer to full fruition.

The Voice Again

Thy word is a lamp unto my feet, and a light unto my path.
PSALM 119:105 KJV

Yes! My Word, the Scriptures. Read them, study them; store them in your hearts, use them as you use a lamp to guide your footsteps.

But remember, My children, My Word is more even than that. It is the Voice that speaks to your hearts, that inner consciousness that tells of Me.

It is the Voice that speaks to you intimately, personally, in this sacred evening time. It is even more than that. It is I your Lord and Friend.

"And the Word was made flesh and dwelt among us." Truly a lamp to your feet and a light to your path.

CONSIDER:
Do I regularly read, study, and learn from God's Word?
Am I listening to His voice?

PRAY:
Lord, You are the lamp to my feet and the light to my path.
Help me to heed Your Word and to be obedient to Your voice.

Prayer of Joy

LORD, I cry out to You; make haste to me! Give ear to my voice
when I cry out to You. Let my prayer be set before You as
incense, the lifting up of my hands as the evening sacrifice.
PSALM 141:1–2

Joy is the messenger, dear Lord, that bears our prayers to Thee.

Prayer can be like incense, rising ever higher and higher, or it can be like a low earth-mist clinging to the ground, never once soaring.

The Eye that sees all, the Ear that hears all, knows every cry.

But the prayer of real faith is the prayer of Joy, that sees and knows the heart of Love it rises to greet and that is so sure of a glad response.

Break forth, break forth, O joyful heart,
And make His goodness known,
Who all thy life, though undeserved,
Such love to thee has shown.

Break forth, break forth, O joyful heart,
Break forth, no longer silent be;
Break forth, break forth in grateful praise
To Him Who came to ransom Thee.
FRANCES JANE (FANNY) CROSBY (1820–1915)

CONSIDER:
Are my prayers carried up by joy? Do they show
real faith in God and all that He can do in my life?

PRAY:
God, give me strong faith and real joy. Let my prayers rise
to You like fragrant incense, sure of Your happy response.

Spend

*The rich man's wealth is his strong city, and like
a high wall in his own esteem. Before destruction the
heart of a man is haughty, and before honor is humility.*
PROVERBS 18:11–12

Give, give, give. Keep ever an empty vessel for Me to fill. In future use all for Me, and give all *you* cannot use.

How poor die those who leave wealth! Wealth is to use, to spend, for Me.

Use as you go. Delight to use.

God gives His mercies to be spent;
Your hoard will do your soul no good.
Gold is a blessing only lent,
Repaid by giving others food.
WILLIAM COWPER (1731–1800)

CONSIDER:

*Am I hoarding my wealth—whether money
or talents or time—or am I using it for God?*

PRAY:

*God, let me not doubt the fact that I am wealthy,
blessed with many gifts from You. Then let me freely give
of this wealth to bring glory to You, and to meet others' needs.*

No Limit

And whatever you ask in My name, that I will do,
that the Father may be glorified in the Son.
JOHN 14:13

Unlimited supply, that is My Law. Oh! the unlimited Supply, and oh! the poor, blocked channels! Will you feel this, that there is no limit to My Power?

But man asks, and blasphemes in asking, such poor, mean things. Do you not see how you wrong Me? I desire to give you a gift, and if you are content with the poor and the mean and the sordid, then you are insulting Me, the Giver.

"Ask what ye will and it shall be done unto you." How I can fulfill the promise is My Work, not yours, to consider. . . . Have a big Faith, and expect big things, and you will get big things.

CONSIDER:
How big is my faith? Am I insulting God
by only believing He can give me petty things?

PRAY:
God, increase my faith so that I will not hesitate to
ask for the great things that You wish to give me.

I Am beside You

In thy presence is fulness of joy;
at thy right hand there are pleasures for evermore.
PSALM 16:11 KJV

Do not seek to realize this fullness of Joy as the result of effort. This cannot be, any more than Joy in a human friend's presence would come as the result of trying to force yourself to like to have that friend with you.

Call often My Name, "Jesus."

The calling of My Name does not really summon Me. I am beside you. But it removes, as it were, the scales from your eyes, and you see Me.

It is, as it were, the pressure of a loved one's hand, that brings an answering pressure, and a thrill of Joy follows, a real, and a joyful sense of nearness.

Lord, often will I call out Your name,
And trust that You're already near;
Help me to see You with eyes of faith
And rejoice that You're always here.

PRAY:
Let me become more aware of Your presence beside me, Lord. You are not only my Savior but also by dearest, closest, most trustworthy Friend.

Second Advent

And now, little children, abide in Him, that when He appears,
we may have confidence and not be ashamed before Him at His coming.
1 JOHN 2:28

Jesus, Comforter of all the sorrowing,
help us to bring Thy comfort into every heart
and life to which Thou art longing
to express that comfort through us. Use us, Lord.
The years may be many or few.
Place us where we can best serve Thee,
and influence most for Thee.

The world would be brought to Me so soon, so soon, if only all who acknowledge Me as Lord, as Christ, gave themselves unreservedly to be used by Me.

I could use *each* human body as mightily as I used My own human body as a channel for Divine Love and Power.

I do not delay My second coming. My *followers* delay it.

If each lived for Me, by Me, in Me, allowing Me to live in him, to use him to express the Divine through him, as I expressed it when on earth, then long ago the world would have been drawn to Me, and I should have come to claim My own.

So seek, My children, to live, knowing no other desire but to express Me, and to show My Love to your world.

God in Action

*Now may the God of hope fill you with all joy and peace in believing,
that you may abound in hope by the power of the Holy Spirit.*
ROMANS 15:13

Power is not such an overwhelming force as it sounds, a something
you call to your aid, to intervene in crises. No! *Power is just God
in action.*

Therefore, whenever a servant of Mine, however weak he humanly
may be, allows God to work through him, then all he does is *powerful.*

Carry this thought with you through the days in which you seem
to accomplish little. Try to see it is not you, but the Divine Spirit in you.
All you have to do, as I have told you before, is to turn self out. A very
powerful ax in a Master Hand accomplishes much. The same in the
hand of a weak child, nothing. So see that it is not the instrument,
but the Master Hand that wields the instrument, that tells.

Remember no day is lost on which some Spiritual Truth becomes
clearer. No day is lost which you have given to Me to use. My use of it
may not have been apparent to you. Leave that to Me. Dwell in Me,
and I in you; so shall ye bear much fruit. The fruit is not the work of
the branches, though proudly the branches may bear it. It is the work
of the Vine that sends its life-giving sap through those branches.
I am the Vine and ye are the branches.

Self Kills Power

For though He was crucified in weakness,
yet He lives by the power of God. For we also are weak in Him,
but we shall live with Him by the power of God toward you.
2 CORINTHIANS 13:4

Dwelling with Me, desiring only My Will and to do My work, My Spirit cannot fail to pass through the channel of your life into the lives of others.

Many think it is humility to say they do little and are of little value to My world. To think that is pride.

What if the pipe were to say, "I do so little; I wish I could be more use." The reply would be, "It is not you, but the water that passes through you, that saves and blesses. All you have to do is to see there is nothing to block the way so that the water cannot flow through."

The only block there can be in your channel is self. Keep that out, and know that My Spirit is flowing through. Therefore all must be the better for coming in contact with both of you, because you are channels. See this, and you will think it natural to know they are being helped, not by you, but by My Spirit flowing through you as a channel.

Wipe the Slate

But this one thing I do, forgetting those things which are behind,
and reaching forth unto those things which are before,
I press toward the mark.
PHILIPPIANS 3:13–14 KJV

Forget the past. Remember only its glad days. Wipe the slate of your remembrance with Love, which will erase all that is not confirmed in Love. You must forget your failures, your failures and those of others. Wipe them out of the book of your remembrance.

I did not die upon the Cross for man to bear the burdens of his sins himself. "Who His own self bare our sins in His own body on the tree."

If you forget not the sins of others, and I bear them, then you add to My sorrows.

CONSIDER:
What painful memories, grudges, regrets, and other burdens
am I holding on to from the past? Why is it important to not
only forgive the failures of others, but to forgive my own failures?

PRAY:
Lord, help me to wipe clean the slate of my memory, just as You wiped
clean the slate of my sins when You died on the cross for me. I know I
can't pretend that bad things have never happened, but may love
and forgiveness take the sting out of those memories so that they
don't keep resurfacing in my consciousness to trouble me.

Wonderful Friendship

> *"But you, Israel, are My servant, Jacob whom I*
> *have chosen, the descendants of Abraham My friend."*
> ISAIAH 41:8

Think of Me as a Friend, but realize, too, the wonder of the Friendship. As soon as man gives Me not only worship and honor, obedience, allegiance, but loving understanding, then he becomes My Friend, even as I am his.

What I can do for you. Yes! but also what we can do for each other. What you can do for Me.

Your service becomes so different when you feel I count on your great friendship to do this or that for Me. . . .

Dwell more, dwell much, on this thought of you as My friends, and of the sweetness of My knowing where I can turn for Love, for understanding, for help.

CONSIDER:
What kind of friend am I to God?
Do I look at our friendship as a two-way street?

PRAY:
God, thank You for Your friendship. You are unfailing in Your loving
relationship with me. I humbly ask that You bear with me as I strive
to be a worthy friend to You. May You find joy in me as I worship,
honor, obey, and pledge my eternal allegiance to You.

New Forces

Now to Him who is able to keep you from stumbling,
and to present you faultless before the presence of His glory with
exceeding joy, to God our Savior, who alone is wise, be glory and
majesty, dominion and power, both now and forever. Amen.
JUDE 24–25

Remember that life's difficulties and troubles are not intended to arrest your progress, but to increase your speed. You must call new forces, new powers into action.

Whatever it is must be surmounted, overcome. Remember this.

It is as a race. Nothing must daunt you. Do not let a difficulty conquer you. You must conquer it.

My strength will be there awaiting you. Bring all your thought, all your power, into action. Nothing is too *small* to be faced and overcome. To push small difficulties aside is to be preparing big troubles.

Rise to conquer. It is the path of victory I would have you tread. There can be no failure with Me.

"Now unto him that is able to keep you from falling, and to present you faultless before the presence of his glory with exceeding joy. . ."

CONSIDER:
Am I intimidated and daunted by life's difficulties
and troubles? Or have I risen to the challenge,
calling forth the power of God that I have at my disposal?

Heaven's Colors

But He knows the way that I take; when He has tested me,
I shall come forth as gold. My foot has held fast to His steps;
I have kept His way and not turned aside.
JOB 23:10–11

Looking back you will see that every step was planned. Leave all to Me. Each stone in the mosaic fits into the perfect pattern, designed by the Master Artist.

It is all so wonderful!

But the colors are of Heaven's hues, so that your eyes could not bear to gaze on the whole until you are beyond the veil.

So, stone by stone, you see and trust the pattern to the Designer.

I stumble over stones half blind,
I cannot see God's grand design;
But one day I'll have a higher view
Of all His mosaic's radiant hue.

CONSIDER:
Am I able to trust the Lord, knowing that
everything in life fits into His perfect pattern?

PRAY:
Forgive me, O God, for I often complain about the
obstacles in my way. I trust that You will fit each of
these stumbling stones into Your grand, final mosaic.

The Voiceless Cry

And if anyone thinks that he knows anything, he knows nothing yet as he
ought to know. But if anyone loves God, this one is known by Him.
1 CORINTHIANS 8:2–3

Jesus, hear us, and let our cry come unto Thee.

That voiceless cry that comes from anguished hearts is heard above all the music of Heaven.

It is not the arguments of theologians that solve the problems of a questioning heart, but the cry of that heart to Me, and the certainty that I have heard.

CONSIDER:
Do I believe that God hears my anguished cry more
than all the music of heaven—that He truly hears and
cares when I'm so troubled that I can't even speak?

PRAY:
God, there's so much I don't understand—about Christian doctrine
and about the sufferings and troubles of life. Help me not to trust in my
own wisdom. I know that when I cry out to You that You will answer
me with power, not with mere scholarly arguments and reasonings.

Every Problem Solved

On the last day, that great day of the feast, Jesus stood and cried out,
saying, "If anyone thirsts, let him come to Me and drink."
JOHN 7:37

Man has such strange ideas of the meaning of My invitation "Come unto Me." Too often has it been interpreted as an urge to pay a duty owed to a Creator or a debt owed to a Savior.

The "Come unto Me" holds in it a wealth of meaning far surpassing even that. "Come unto Me" for the solution of every problem, for the calming of every fear, for all you need—physical, mental, spiritual.

Sick, come to Me for health. Homeless, ask Me for a home. Friendless, claim a friend. Hopeless, a refuge.

"Come unto Me" for everything.

CONSIDER:
Where do I look first for the
solutions to the problems I face in life?

PRAY:
God, help me to understand what "Come unto Me" really means.
Let me never forget that You are the answer to my every prayer.

Devious Ways

L ife is not easy, My children. Man has made of it not what My Father meant it to be.

Ways that were meant to be straight paths have been made by man into ways devious and evil, filled with obstacles and stones of difficulty.

*This world is one great battlefield
With forces all arrayed,
If in my heart I do not yield
I'll overcome some day.
I'll overcome some day,
I'll overcome some day,
If in my heart I do not yield,
I'll overcome some day.*

*A thousand snares are set for me,
And mountains in my way,
If Jesus will my leader be,
I'll overcome some day.
I'll overcome some day,
I'll overcome some day,
If Jesus will my leader be,
I'll overcome some day.*

CHARLES ALBERT TINDLEY (1851–1933)

By My Spirit

Therefore He who supplies the Spirit to you and works miracles among you, does He do it by the works of the law, or by the hearing of faith?
GALATIANS 3:5

Man is apt to think that once in time only was My Miracle-working Power in action. That is not so. Wherever man trusts wholly in Me, and leaves to Me the choosing of the very day and hour, then there is My miracle-working Power as manifest, as marvelously manifest today, as ever it was when I was on earth, as ever it was to set My Apostles free or to work miracles of wonder and healing through them.

Trust in Me. Have a boundless faith in Me, and you will see, and, seeing, will give Me all the glory. Remember, and say often to yourselves, "Not by might, nor by power, but by My spirit, saith the LORD."

Dwell much in thought upon all I accomplished on earth, and then say to yourselves, "He, our Lord, our Friend, could accomplish this now in our lives."

Apply these miracles to your present-day need, and know that your Help and Salvation are sure.

CONSIDER:
Do I see miracles as phenomenas that existed only in biblical times?
Or do I believe in—and have I experienced—God's miracles in my life today?

Union Is Power

For where two or three are gathered together
in my name, there am I in the midst of them.
MATTHEW 18:20 KJV

Claim that promise always. Know it true that when two of My lovers meet, I am the Third. Never limit that promise.

When you two are together in My Name, united by one bond in My Spirit, I am there. Not only when you meet to greet Me and to hear My Voice.

Think what this means in Power. It is again the lesson of the Power that follows *two united to serve Me.*

CONSIDER:
How often do I get together with another believer,
not merely for recreation and entertainment, but to
claim God's promise of the power of two united?

PRAY:
God, may I continually gather with other believers, united in
Your Spirit, fully believing that Your power is available to us.

Quiet Lives

Well done, thou good and faithful servant. . .
enter thou into the joy of thy lord.
MATTHEW 25:21 KJV

These words are whispered in the ears of many whom the world would pass by unrecognizing. Not to the great, and the world-famed, are these words said so often, but to the quiet followers who serve Me unobtrusively, yet faithfully, who bear their cross bravely, with a smiling face to the world. Thank Me for the quiet lives.

These words speak not only of the passing into that fuller Spirit Life. Duty faithfully done for Me does mean entrance into a Life of Joy—My Joy, the Joy of your Lord. The world may never see it, the humble, patient, quiet service, but I see it, and My reward is not earth's fame, earth's wealth, earth's pleasures, but the Joy Divine.

Whether here or there, in the earth-world or in the spirit-world, this is My reward. Joy. The Joy that carries an exquisite thrill in the midst of pain and poverty and suffering. That Joy of which I said no man could take it from you. Earth has no pleasure, no reward, that can give man that Joy. It is known only to My lovers and My friends.

This Joy may come, not as the reward of activity in My service. It may be the reward of patient suffering, bravely borne.

Suffering, borne with Me, must in time bring Joy, as does all real contact with Me. So live with Me in that Kingdom of Joy, My Kingdom, the Gateway into which may be service, it may be suffering.

Dazzling Glory

Arise, shine; for thy light is come,
and the glory of the LORD is risen upon thee.
Isaiah 60:1 KJV

The glory of the Lord is the Beauty of His Character. It is risen upon you when you realize it, even though on earth you can do so only in part.

The Beauty of the Purity and Love of God is too dazzling for mortals to see in full.

The Glory of the Lord is also risen upon you when you reflect that Glory in your lives, when in Love, Patience, Service, Purity, whatever it may be, you reveal to the world something of the Father, an assurance that you have been with Me, your Lord and Savior.

CONSIDER:
Have I revealed the Father's character to the world?
Can others see Him in me?

PRAY:
Lord, it's refreshing to catch even rare glimpses of Your glory. I look
forward to the day when the veil will be drawn aside and I'll see Your
full beauty. Until then, may I reflect a measure of Your glory in my life.

Hills of the Lord

I will lift up mine eyes unto the hills, from whence cometh my help.
My help cometh from the LORD, which made heaven and earth.
PSALM 121:1–2 KJV

Yes! always raise your eyes, from earth's sordid and mean and false, to the Hills of the Lord. From poverty, lift your eyes to the Help of the Lord.

In moments of weakness, lift your eyes to the Hills of the Lord.

Train your sight by constantly getting this long view. Train it to see more and more, farther and farther, until distant peaks seem familiar.

The Hills of the Lord. The Hills whence comes your help.
A parched earth looks to the Hills for its rivers, its streams, its life.
So look you to the Hills. From those Hills comes Help. Help from the Lord—who made Heaven and earth.

So, for all your spiritual needs, look to the Lord, who made Heaven, and for all your temporal needs, look to Me, owner of all this, the Lord who made the earth.

PRAY:
Lord, I lift my eyes to Heaven's hills. I lift up my
prayers to You. Please help me and provide what I need.

Mysteries

But we speak the wisdom of God in a mystery, the hidden wisdom which God ordained before the ages for our glory, which none of the rulers of this age knew; for had they known, they would not have crucified the Lord of glory. But as it is written, "Eye has not seen, nor ear heard, nor have entered into the heart of man the things which God has prepared for those who love Him."
1 CORINTHIANS 2:7–9

Your Hope is in the Lord. More and more set your hopes on Me. Know that whatever the future may hold it will hold more and more of Me. It cannot but be glad and full of Joy. So in Heaven, or on earth, wherever you may be, your way must be truly one of delight.

Do not try to find answers to the mysteries of the world. Learn to know Me more and more, and in that Knowledge you will have all the answers you need here, and when you see Me face-to-face, in that purely Spiritual world, you will find no need to ask. There again all your answers will be in Me.

Remember, I was the answer in time to all man's questions about My Father and His Laws. Know no theology. Know Me. I was the Word of God. All you need to know about God you know in Me. If a man knows Me not, all your explanations will fall on an unresponsive heart.

CONSIDER:

How well do I know Jesus—truly know Him? How much do I long to know Him better? Is that longing stronger than my desire to learn about life's mysteries and understand why certain things happened to me?

PRAY:

Dear Lord, help me to know You better. Jesus, You are the way, the truth, and the life. Help me, when I read my Bible, not to merely understand doctrine, but to love You and know You.

Radiate Joy

Nor do they light a lamp and put it under a basket, but on a lampstand, and it gives light to all who are in the house. Let your light so shine before men, that they may see your good works and glorify your Father in heaven.
MATTHEW 5:15–16

Not only must you rejoice, but your Joy must be made manifest. "Known unto all men." A candle must not be set under a bushel, but on a candlestick, that it may give light to all who are in the house.

Men must see and know your Joy, and seeing it, know, without any doubt, that it springs from trust in Me, from living with Me.

The hard, dull way of resignation is not My Way. When I entered Jerusalem, knowing well that scorn and reviling and death awaited Me, it was with cries of Hosanna and with a triumphal procession. Not just a few "Lost Cause" followers creeping with Me into the city. There was no note of sadness in My Last Supper talk with My disciples, and "when we had sung an hymn" we went out unto the Mount of Olives.

So trust, so conquer, so joy. Love colors the way. Love takes the sting out of the wind of adversity.

Love. Love. Love of Me. The consciousness of My Presence, and that of My Father, we are one, and He—God—is Love.

Only Love Lasts

*Though I speak with the tongues of men and
of angels, and have not charity, I am become
as sounding brass, or a tinkling cymbal.*
1 CORINTHIANS 13:1 KJV

See that only Love tells. Only what is done in Love lasts, for God is Love, and only the work of God remains.

The fame of the world, the applause given to the one who speaks with the tongues of men and of angels, who attracts admiration and compels attention, it is all given to what is passing, is really worthless, if it lacks that God-quality, Love.

Think how a smile or word of Love goes winged on its way, a God-Power, simple though it may seem, while the mighty words of an orator can fall fruitless to the ground. The test of all true work and words is— are they inspired by Love?

If man only saw how vain is so much of his activity! So much work done in My Name is not acknowledged by Me. As for Love: Turn out from your hearts and lives all that is not loving, so shall ye bear much fruit, and by this shall all men know ye are My disciples, because ye have Love one toward another.

Earth's Furies

In the world ye shall have tribulation:
but be of good cheer; I have overcome the world.
JOHN 16:33 KJV

Then you may ask why have you, My children, to have tribulation if I have overcome the world.

My overcoming was never, you know, for Myself, but for you, for My children. Each temptation, each difficulty, I overcame as it presented itself.

The powers of evil were strained to their utmost to devise means to break Me. They failed, but how they failed was known only to Me, and to My Father, who could read My undaunted spirit. The world, even My own followers, would see a Lost Cause. Reviled, spat upon, scourged, they would deem Me conquered. How could they know My Spirit was free, unbroken, unharmed?

And so, as I had come to show man God, I must show him God unconquered, unharmed, untouched by evil and its power. Man could not see My Spirit untouched, risen above these earth furies and hates, into the Secret Place of the Father. But man could see My Risen Body and learn by that, that even the last attempt of man had been powerless to touch Me.

Take heart from that, for you must share My tribulations.

And in My conquering Power you walk unharmed today.

Suffer to Save

*But rejoice to the extent that you partake of Christ's sufferings, that when
His glory is revealed, you may also be glad with exceeding joy. If you are
reproached for the name of Christ, blessed are you, for the Spirit of glory and
of God rests upon you. On their part He is blasphemed, but on your part He
is glorified. But let none of you suffer as a murderer, a thief, an evildoer,
or as a busybody in other people's matters. Yet if anyone suffers as a Christian,
let him not be ashamed, but let him glorify God in this matter.*
1 PETER 4:13–16

Take each day's happenings as work you can do for Me. In that
Spirit a blessing will attend all you do. Offering your day's
service thus to Me, you are sharing in My Life-work and therefore
helping Me to save My world.

You may not see it, but the power of vicarious sacrifice is
redemptive beyond man's power of understanding here on earth.

CONSIDER:
*How do I react when adversities enter my day? Do I look
at them as opportunities to patiently endure and to serve God?*

PRAY:
*God, help me to cheerfully make sacrifices. May I be
unafraid and unashamed to experience suffering
in Your name, to help You to save the world.*

The Heavenly Beggar

Behold, I stand at the door, and knock.
REVELATION 3:20 KJV

Oh, ponder again these words and learn from them My great humility.

There is that gracious invitation, too, for those who yearn to realize a happiness, a rest, a satisfaction they have never found in the world and its pursuits. To them the pleading answer to their quest is "Come to Me and I will give you rest."

But to those who do not feel their need of Me, who obstinately reject Me, who shut the doors of their hearts so that I may not enter, to these I go, in tender, humble longing. Even when I find all closed, all barred, I stand a Beggar, knocking, knocking. The Heavenly Beggar in His Great Humility.

Never think of those who have shut you out or forgotten you that now they must wait, you have no need of them. No! remember that, the Heavenly Beggar, and learn of Me, humility.

Learn, too, the value of each man's happiness and peace and rest, to Me, his God; and learn, and learning pray to copy the Divine Unrest until a soul finds rest and peace in Me.

My Beauty

Give to the LORD the glory due His name; bring an offering, and come before Him. Oh, worship the LORD in the beauty of holiness!
I CHRONICLES 16:29

The prophet realized the Truth of My later saying, "He that hath ears to hear let him hear," which might be rendered, "He that hath eyes to see let him see."

The God who was to be born upon earth was not to be housed in a body so beautiful that men would follow and adore for the beauty of His Countenance.

No! He was to be as one whom the world would despise, but to the seeing eye, the Spirit that dwelt in that body should be so beautiful as to lack nothing. "Yet when we shall see Him, there is no Beauty that we should desire Him."

Pray for the seeing eye, to see the Beauty of My Character, of My Spirit. Nay, more, as faith saw the Beauty of the Godhead in One who had no form nor comeliness, so pray to have that faith to see the Beauty of My Love in My dealings with you, in My actions. Till, in what the world will distort into cruelty and harshness, you, with the eyes of faith, will see all that you could desire.

Know Me. Talk to Me. Let Me talk to you, so that I may make clear to your loving hearts what seems mysterious now and purposeless ("having no form nor comeliness").

Not Thwarted

And He was withdrawn from them about a stone's throw,
and He knelt down and prayed, saying, "Father, if it is Your will,
take this cup away from Me; nevertheless not My will, but Yours, be done."
LUKE 22:41–42

Not our wills but Thine, O Lord.

Man has so misunderstood Me in this. I want no will laid grudgingly upon My Altar. I want you to desire and love My Will, because therein lies your happiness and Spirit-rest.

Whenever you feel that you cannot leave the choice to Me, then pray, not to be able to accept My Will, but to know and love Me more. With that knowledge, and the Love, will come the certainty that I know best, and that I want only the best for you and yours.

How little those know Me who think I wish to thwart them. How often I am answering their own prayers in the best and quickest way.

PRAY:
God, You know and want what's best for me. You're not some killjoy
simply out to spoil my fun. I pray that I'll come to know and love
You more, and gain a greater understanding of Your will for me.

The Way of the Spirit

If we live in the Spirit, let us also walk in the Spirit.
GALATIANS 5:25

Jesus, we come to Thee with Joy.

The Joy of meeting Me should more and more fill your lives. It will. Your lives must first of all be narrowed down, more and more, into an inner circle life with Me (the three of us), and then, as that friendship becomes more and more engrossing, more and more binding, then, gradually, the circle of your interests will widen.

For the present do not think of it as a narrow life. I have My Purpose, My Loving Purpose, in cutting you away from other work and interests, for the time.

To work from large interests and a desire for great activities and world movements, to the inner circle life with Me, is really the wrong way. That is why so often, when, through all these activities and interests, a soul finds Me, I have to begin our Friendship by cutting away the ties that bind it to the outer and wider circle. When it has gained strength and learned its lesson in the inner circle, it can then widen its life, working this time from within out, taking then to each contact, each friendship, the inner circle influence.

And this is to be your way of life.

This is the way of the Spirit. Man so often misunderstands this.

When Two Agree

"Again I say to you that if two of you agree on earth concerning anything that they ask, it will be done for them by My Father in heaven. For where two or three are gathered together in My name, I am there in the midst of them."
MATTHEW 18:19–20

If two of you shall agree.

I am the Truth. Every word of Mine is true. Every promise of Mine shall be fulfilled.

First, "gathered together in My Name," bound by a common loyalty to Me, desirous only of doing My Will.

Then, when this is so, I am present, too, a self-invited guest, and when I am there and one with you, voicing the same petition, making your demands Mine, then it follows the request is granted.

But what man has failed perhaps to realize is *all* that lies behind the words. For two to agree about the wisdom of a request, to be certain it *should* be granted, and will be granted (if it should be), is not the same as two agreeing to pray that request.

The devil often laughs when we work,
but he trembles when we pray.
CORRIE TEN BOOM
AMAZING LOVE

PRAY:
God, help me—and those who pray with me—
to make the leap from intellectual understanding and
agreement to deep-seated belief in the power of prayer.

From Self to God

The eternal God is thy refuge.
DEUTERONOMY 33:27 KJV

A place to flee to, a sanctuary. An escape from misunderstanding, from yourself. You can get away from others into the quiet of your own being, but from yourself, from the sense of your failure, your weakness, your sins and shortcomings, whither can you flee?

To the Eternal God your refuge. Till in His Immensity you forget your smallness, meanness, limitations.

Till the relief of safety merges into Joy of appreciation of your refuge, and you absorb the Divine, and absorbing gain strength to conquer.

CONSIDER:
Where do I find a refuge—not only from others but also from myself, from the sense of my own failures and shortcomings?

PRAY:
God, You are my sanctuary. May I rest fully in You, my secret refuge, where I can gain strength to be victorious.

Responsibility

When the day began to wear away, the twelve came and said to Him,
"Send the multitude away, that they may go into the surrounding towns
and country, and lodge and get provisions; for we are in a deserted place
here." But He said to them, "You give them something to eat." And they
said, "We have no more than five loaves and two fish, unless
we go and buy food for all these people."
LUKE 9:12–13

I am beside you. A very human Jesus, who understands all your weaknesses, and sees, too, your struggles and conquests.

Remember, I was the Companion of the Weak. Ready to supply their hunger. Teaching My followers their responsibility toward all, not only those near and dear to them, but to the multitude.

"Lord, send them away that they may go into the villages and buy themselves victuals," said My disciples, with no sympathy for the fainting, exhausted men, women, and children.

But I taught that Divine Sympathy includes responsibility. "Give ye them to eat" was My reply. I taught that pity, without a remedy for the evil, or the need, is worthless.

"Give ye them to eat." Wherever your sympathy goes, you must go, too, if possible. Remember that in thinking of your own needs. Claim from Me the same attitude now.

The servant is not above his Master, certainly not in Spiritual attainments, and what I taught My disciples, I do.

So fainting and needy, by the lakeside of life, know that I will supply your need, not grudgingly, but in full measure.

The Ideal Man

So when the LORD saw that he turned aside to look, God called to him from the midst of the bush and said, "Moses, Moses!" And he said, "Here I am." Then He said, "Do not draw near this place. Take your sandals off your feet, for the place where you stand is holy ground." Moreover He said, "I am the God of your father—the God of Abraham, the God of Isaac, and the God of Jacob." And Moses hid his face, for he was afraid to look upon God.
EXODUS 3:4–6

Draw nigh, shoes off thy feet, in silent awe and adoration. Draw nigh, as Moses drew near to the burning bush.

I give you the loving intimacy of a friend, but I am God, too, and the wonder of our communion, the miracle of your intimacy with Me, will mean the more to you if sometimes you see the Majestic Figure of the Son of God.

Draw nigh in the utter confidence that is the sublimest prayer. Draw nigh. No far-off pleading, even to a God clothed with majesty of fire. Draw nigh. Draw nigh, not as a suppliant, but as a listener. I am the Suppliant, as I make known to you My wishes. For this Majestic God is Brother, too, longing so intensely that you should serve your brother-man, and longing even more intensely that you should be true to that Vision He has of you.

You speak of your fellow man as disappointing you, as falling short of the ideal you had of him. But what of Me? For every man there is the ideal man I see in him. The man he could be, the man I would have him be.

Judge of My Heart when he fails to fulfill that promise. The disappointments of man may be great and many, but they are nothing as compared with My disappointments. Remember this, and strive to be the friend I see in My vision of you.

A Journey with Me

*"I still have many things to say to you, but you cannot bear them now.
However, when He, the Spirit of truth, has come, He will guide you
into all truth; for He will not speak on his own authority, but whatever
He hears He will speak; and He will tell you things to come."*
JOHN 16:12–13

Fret not your souls with puzzles that you cannot solve. The solution
may never be shown you until you have left this flesh-life.

Remember what I have so often told you, "I have yet many things
to say unto you, but ye cannot bear them now." Only step by step and
stage by stage can you proceed in your journey upward.

The one thing to be sure of is that it is a journey with Me. There
does come a Joy known to those who suffer with Me. But that is not
the result of the suffering, but the result of the close intimacy with Me,
to which suffering drove you.

CONSIDER:
*Am I willing and eager to continue
in my journey to know Jesus better?*

PRAY:
*God, don't let me worry about puzzles I can't solve, or questions
I can't answer. Instead, make me willing to suffer with Jesus,
knowing that joy will be the ultimate result.*

Man of Sorrows

He is despised and rejected of men; a man of sorrows,
and acquainted with grief: and we hid as it were our faces
from him; he was despised, and we esteemed him not.
ISAIAH 53:3 KJV

That these words strike a note of Beauty in the hearts of those attuned to hear the Beautiful shows truly that the heart recognizes the need for the Man of Sorrows. That it sees nothing contemptible in One despised by the world.

One of the things My disciples must ever seek to do is to set aside the valuation of the world and judge only according to the values of Heaven. Do not seek the praise and the notice of men. You follow a despised Christ. See, the mob is hooting, throwing stones, jeering, and yet in that quiet little throng, there is a happiness and Joy the reviling crowds could never know.

In your dark hours, when human help fails, keep very close to the Man of Sorrows. Feel My Hand of Love press yours in silent but complete understanding. I, too, was acquainted with grief. No heart can ache without My heart aching, too. "He was despised, and we esteemed Him not."

CONSIDER:
Am I a true disciple? Do I value what the world values,
or do I value the things of heaven more? Am I
willing to suffer with the Man of Sorrows?

But I say to you, love your enemies, bless those who curse you, do good to those
who hate you, and pray for those who spitefully use you and persecute you,
that you may be sons of your Father in heaven; for He makes His sun rise
on the evil and on the good, and sends rain on the just and on the unjust.
MATTHEW 5:44–45

The first law of giving is of the spirit world. Give to all you meet, or whose lives touch yours, of your prayers, your time, yourselves, your love, your thought. You must practice this giving first.

Then give of this world's goods and money, as you have them given to you. To give money and material things, without having first made the habit daily, hourly, ever increasingly, of giving on the higher plane, is wrong.

Give, give, give all your best to all who need it.

Be great givers—great givers. Give as I said My Father in Heaven gives. He who makes His sun to shine on the evil and on the good, and sendeth rain on the just and on the unjust. Remember, as I have told you before, give according to need, never according to desert. In giving, with the thought of supplying a real need you most closely resemble that Father in Heaven, the Great Giver.

As you receive, you must supply the needs of those I bring to you. Not questioning, not limiting. Their nearness to you, their relationship, must never count. Only their need is to guide you. Pray to become great givers.

Expect Temptation

Let no one say when he is tempted, "I am tempted by God"; for God cannot be tempted by evil, nor does He Himself tempt anyone. But each one is tempted when he is drawn away by his own desires and enticed.
JAMES 1:13–14

Lord, give us Power to conquer temptation as Thou didst in the wilderness.

The very first step toward conquering temptation is to see it as temptation. To dissociate yourself from it.

Not to think of it as something resulting from your tiredness, or illness, or poverty, or nerve-strain, when you feel you might well excuse yourself for yielding, but first to realize very fully that when you have heard My voice ("the Heavens opened," as it were) and are going to fulfill your mission to work for me and to draw souls to me, you must expect a mighty onslaught from the evil one, who will endeavor with all his might to frustrate you and to prevent your good work. Expect that.

Then when these little temptations, or big ones, come, you will recognize them as planned by evil to thwart Me. Then for very love of Me you will conquer.

CONSIDER:
Do I see temptation for what it is—an onslaught from Satan, the evil one, designed to thwart me and prevent me from doing good work for the Lord?

Food of Life

> *But He said to them, "I have food to eat of which you do not know."*
> *Therefore the disciples said to one another, "Has anyone brought*
> *Him anything to eat?" Jesus said to them, "My food is to do the*
> *will of Him who sent Me, and to finish His work."*
> JOHN 4:32–34

Those were My words to My Disciples in the early days of My Ministry. Later I was to lead them on to a fuller understanding of that Majestic Union of a soul with God in which strength, life, and food pass from One to the other.

Meat is to sustain the body. To do the Will of God is the very strength and support of Life. Feed on that Food.

Soul-starvation comes from the failing to do, and to delight in doing, My Will. How busy the world is in talking of bodies that are undernourished! What of the souls that are undernourished?

Make it indeed your meat to do My Will. Strength and Power will indeed come to you from that.

CONSIDER:
How faithful am I to eat to sustain my body?
Do I nourish my soul by doing God's will, or do I
disobey God then wonder why I lack spiritual power?

PRAY:
Dear God, constantly remind me that I must
sustain my soul with the food of spiritual life.

My Kingdom

*"Most assuredly, I say to you, he who believes
in Me, the works that I do he will do also; and greater
works than these he will do, because I go to My Father."*
JOHN 14:12

---

*And greater works than these shall ye do,
because I go unto My Father.*

While I was on the earth, to those with whom I came in contact, Mine was a lost cause. Even My disciples only believed, half-doubting, half-wondering. When they all forsook Me and fled, it was not so much fear of My enemies as the certainty that My Mission, however beautiful they thought it, had failed.

In spite of all I had taught them, in spite of the revelation of the Last Supper, they had secretly felt sure that when the final moment came and the hatred of the Pharisees was declared against Me, I should sound some call to action, and that I should lead My many followers and found My earthly kingdom. Even the disciples who had eyes to see My Spiritual Kingdom had thought material forces had proved too strong for Me.

But with My Resurrection came hope. Faith revived. They would remind each other of all I had said. They would have the assurance of My Divinity, Messiahship. And they would have all My Power in the Unseen—the Holy Spirit—to help them.

Those who lived in the Kingdom were to do the work—greater works than I was able to do. Not a greater Power shown, not a greater Life lived, but, as men recognized My Godhead, opportunities for works in My Name would increase. My work on earth was to gather around Me the nucleus of My Kingdom, and to teach the Truths of My Kingdom to them. In those Truths they were to live and work.

Your Search Rewarded

But from there you will seek the LORD your God, and you will find
Him if you seek Him with all your heart and with all your soul.
DEUTERONOMY 4:29

Lord, all men seek for Thee.

All men seek for Me, but all men do not know what they want.
They are seeking because they are dissatisfied without realizing
that I am the object of their quest.

Count it your greatest joy to be the means, by your lives,
sufferings, words, and love, to prove to the questing ones you know that
their search would end when they saw Me.

Profit by My Example. I left My work—seemingly the greatest
work—that of saving souls, to seek communion with My Father. Did
I know perhaps that with many it was idle curiosity? Did I know that
there must be no rush into the Kingdom, that the still small voice, not the
shoutings of a mob, would alone persuade men I was the Son of God?

Why be surrounded by multitudes if the multitudes were not really
desiring to learn from, and to follow, Me? Follow the Christ into the
quiet places of prayer.

CONSIDER:
In my desire to serve and please God, do I neglect time
alone with Him? Do I trust in my works to convince people
of the truth, or do I realize that God alone can do this?

The Quiet Time

I will praise You forever, because You have done it; and in the
presence of Your saints I will wait on Your name, for it is good.
PSALM 52:9

There may be many times when I reveal nothing, command nothing, give no guidance. But your path is clear, and your task, to grow daily more and more into the knowledge of Me. That this quiet time with Me will enable you to do.

I may ask you to sit silent before Me, and I may speak no word that you could *write*. All the same that waiting *with* Me will bring comfort and Peace. Only friends who understand and love each other can wait silent in each other's presence.

And it may be that I shall prove our friendship by asking you to wait in silence while I rest with you, assured of your Love and understanding. So wait, so love, so joy.

PRAY:
God, grant me the patience to wait in silence, resting in Your Presence,
allowing You to bring me comfort and peace. I wait for You to speak to me,
whether in a "still, small voice," or by assuring me of Your love,

A Sunrise Gift

The hope of the righteous will be gladness,
but the expectation of the wicked will perish.
PROVERBS 10:28

To those whose lives have been full of struggle and care, who have felt as you both have, the tragedy of living, the pity of an agonized heart for My poor world—to those of My followers I give that Peace and Joy that bring to age its second Spring, the youth they sacrificed for Me and for My world. . . .

Take each day now as a joyous sunrise gift from Me. Your simple daily tasks done in My strength and Love will bring the consciousness of all your highest hopes. Expect great things. Expect great things.

Still, still with Thee, when purple morning breaketh,
When the bird waketh, and the shadows flee;
Fairer than morning, lovelier than daylight,
Dawns the sweet consciousness, I am with Thee.

Alone with Thee, amid the mystic shadows,
The solemn hush of nature newly born;
Alone with Thee in breathless adoration,
In the calm dew and freshness of the morn.
HARRIET BEECHER STOWE (1811–1896)

PRAY:
God, allow me to see each day as a gift from You.
Let me find the peace and joy that You offer to me daily.
Help me to never give up on expecting great things.

Carefree

*Peace I leave with you, My peace I give to you; not as the world gives
do I give to you. Let not your heart be troubled, neither let it be afraid.*
JOHN 14:27

Perfect love casteth out fear.

L ove and fear cannot dwell together. By their very natures they
cannot exist side by side. Evil is powerful, and fear is one of evil's
most potent forces.

Therefore a weak, vacillating love can be soon routed by fear,
whereas a perfect Love, a trusting Love, is immediately the Conqueror,
and fear, vanquished, flees in confusion.

But I am Love because God is Love, and I and the Father are one.
So the only way to obtain this perfect Love, that dispels fear, is to have
Me more and more in your lives. You can only banish fear by My
Presence and My Name.

Fear of the future—Jesus will be with us.

Fear of poverty—Jesus will provide. (And so to all the temptations
of fear.)

You must not allow fear to enter. Talk to Me. Think of Me. Talk of
Me. Love Me. And that sense of My Power will so possess you that no
fear can possess your mind. Be strong in this My Love.

Perpetual Guidance

*You in Your mercy have led forth the people whom You have redeemed;
You have guided them in Your strength to Your holy habitation.*
Exodus 15:13

Fullness of Joy. The Joy of Perpetual Guidance. The Joy of knowing that every detail of your lives is planned by Me, but planned with a wealth of tenderness and Love.

Wait for Guidance in every step. Wait to be shown My way. The thought of this loving leading should give you great Joy. All the responsibility of Life taken off your shoulders. All its business worry taken off your shoulders. It is indeed a Joy for you to feel so free and yet so planned for.

Oh! the wonder of this God-guided life. To think anything impossible in such circumstances is to say it cannot be done by Me. To say that is surely a denial of Me.

CONSIDER:
*Do I think things are impossible? Am I weighted down
by responsibility and worry, or do I feel God's tender care?*

PRAY:
*God, You are my perpetual Guide. Slow me down, and let me wait
for Your guidance. Allow me to see that, with You, nothing is impossible.*

Storms

Then they cry out to the LORD in their trouble, and He brings them out of their distresses. He calms the storm, so that its waves are still.
PSALM 107:28–29

Our loving Lord, we thank Thee for Thy marvelous keeping power.

There is no miracle so wonderful as the miracle of a soul being kept by My Power. Forces of evil batter and storm but are powerless. Tempests rage unavailingly.

It is like a cool garden with sweet flowers and bees and butterflies and trees and playing fountains set in the midst of a mighty roaring city. Try to see your lives as that.

Not only as calm and unmoved, but as breathing fragrance, expressing beauty. Expect storms. Know this—you cannot be united in your great friendship and bond to do My work, and in your great Love for Me, and not excite the envy, hatred, and malice of all whom you meet who are not on My side.

Where does the enemy attack? The fortress, the stronghold, not the desert waste.

CONSIDER:
Is my life like a serene garden in the midst of a bustling city?
Do I trust that the Lord will keep me safe and in perfect
peace in His fortress as the storms of life rage around me?

My Shadow

You have hedged me behind and before, and laid Your hand upon me.
Such knowledge is too wonderful for me; it is high, I cannot attain it.
Where can I go from Your Spirit? Or where can I flee from Your presence?
PSALM 139:5–7

Learn that each day must be lived in My Power, and in the consciousness of My Presence, even if the thrill of Joy seems to be absent. Remember that if sometimes there seems a shadow on your lives, it is not the withdrawal of My Presence. It is My shadow as I stand between you and your foes.

Even with your nearest and dearest there are the quiet days. You do not doubt *their* Love because you do not hear their laughter, and feel thrill of joy at their nearness.

The quiet gray days are the days for duty. Work in the calm certainty that I am with you.

CONSIDER:
Do I feel anxious during my silent, gray days,
or do I trust that God is still with me?

PRAY:
God, I know You're always present, even when it seems there is a shadow
over me. Thank You for standing between me and my enemies.

What Joy Is

*My little children, let us not love in word or in tongue, but in deed
and in truth. And by this we know that we are of the truth,
and shall assure our hearts before Him. For if our heart condemns us,
God is greater than our heart, and knows all things.*
1 JOHN 3:18–20

*Lord, give us Thy Joy, that Joy that no man, no poverty,
no circumstances, no conditions can take from us.*

You shall have My Joy. But Life just now for you both is a march—
a toilsome march. . . . The Joy will come, but for the moment
do not think of that, think simply of the march. Joy is the reward. . . .

Between My Promise of the Gift of Joy to My disciples and their
realization of that Joy came sense of failure, disappointment, denial,
desertion, hopelessness, then hope, waiting, and courage in the face
of danger.

Joy is the reward of patiently seeing Me in the dull dark days,
of trusting when you cannot see. . . . Joy is as it were your heart's
response to My smile of recognition of your faithfulness. . . .

Stop thinking your lives are all wrong if you do not feel it. . . .
Remember you may not yet be joyous, but you are brave, and courage and
unselfish thought for others are as sure signs of true discipleship as Joy.

Conditions of Blessing

*You who fear the LORD, trust in the LORD; He is their help and
their shield. The LORD has been mindful of us; He will bless us;
He will bless the house of Israel; He will bless the house of Aaron.
He will bless those who fear the LORD, both small and great.*
PSALM 115:11–13

*Jesus, we love Thee. We see that all things are planned
by Thee. We rejoice in that vision.*

Rejoice in the fact that you are Mine. The privileges of the members
of My Kingdom are many. When I said of My Father, "He maketh
His Sun to rise on the evil and on the good, and sendeth rain on the
just and on the unjust," you will notice it was of temporal and material
blessings I spoke.

I did not mean that believer and unbeliever could be treated alike.
That is not possible; I can send rain and sunshine and money and
worldly blessings equally to both, but of the blessing of the Kingdom
that would be impossible.

There are conditions that control the bestowal of these. My
followers do not always understand this, and it is necessary they
should do so if they are remembering My injunction which followed—
"Be ye therefore perfect even as your Father in Heaven is perfect."

To attempt to bestow on all alike your Love and Understanding
and interchange of thought would be impossible. But temporal
blessings you, too, bestow, as does My Father. All must be done in
Love and in the spirit of true forgiveness.

See Wonders

*Your way, O God, is in the sanctuary; who is so great
a God as our God? You are the God who does wonders;
You have declared Your strength among the peoples.*
PSALM 77:13–14

Think your thought-way into the very heart of My Kingdom.
See there the abundance of delights in my storehouse, and lay
eager hands on them.

See wonders, ask wonders, bear wonders away with you. Remember
this beautiful earth on which you are was once only a thought of Divine
Mind. Think how from your thought one corner of it could grow and
become a Garden of the Lord, a Bethany-Home for your Master,
a place to which I have a right to bring My friends, My needy ones,
for talk and rest with Me.

CONSIDER:
*Like Mary and Martha of Bethany, have I opened my home
to the Lord? Do I also welcome the people He brings my way?*

PRAY:
*God, let me delight in Your abundant storehouse. Thank You for inviting me
to enter, to lay my hands on Your treasures, and to bear them away.*

Perfect Love

For I hear the slander of many; fear is on every side; while they take counsel together against me, they scheme to take away my life. But as for me, I trust in You, O LORD; I say, "You are my God."

PSALM 31:13–14

Our Lord, give us that Perfect Love of Thee that casts out all fear.

Never let yourselves fear anybody or anything. No fear of My failing you. No fear that your faith will fail you. No fear of poverty or loneliness. No fear of not knowing the way. No fear of others. No fear of their misunderstanding.

But, My children, this absolute casting out of fear is the result of a Perfect Love, a perfect Love of Me and My Father. Speak to Me about everything. Listen to Me at all times. Feel My tender nearness, substituting at once some thought of Me for the fear.

The powers of evil watch you as a besieging force would watch a guarded city—the object being always to find some weak spot, attack that, and so gain an entrance. So evil lurks around you, and seeks to surprise you in some fear.

The fear may have been but a small one, but it affords evil a weak spot of attack and entrance, and then in come rushing despondency, doubt of Me, and so many other sins. Pray, My beloved children, for that Perfect Love of Me that indeed casts out all fear.

Depression

I pour out my complaint before Him; I declare before Him my trouble. When my spirit was overwhelmed within me, then You knew my path. In the way in which I walk they have secretly set a snare for me. Look on my right hand and see, for there is no one who acknowledges me; refuge has failed me; no one cares for my soul. I cried out to You, O LORD: I said, "You are my refuge, my portion in the land of the living."
PSALM 142:2–5

Fight fear as you would fight a plague. Fight it in My Name. . . . Fear, even the smallest fear, is the hacking at the cords of Love that bind you to Me.

However small the impression, in time those cords will wear thin, and then one disappointment or shock and they snap. But for the little fears the cords of Love would have held.

Fight fear.

Depression is a state of fear. Fight that, too. Fight. Fight. Depression is the impression left by fear. Fight and conquer, and oh! for Love of Me, for the sake of My tender, never-failing Love of you, fight and love and win.

PRAY:
God, thank You for warning me about small fears. In Your name I fight the fears and the depression that would wear away the cords of love that bind me to You. With Your help, I'll conquer these forces.

Smile Indulgently

But I have trusted in Your mercy; my heart shall rejoice in Your salvation.
I will sing to the LORD, because He has dealt bountifully with me.
PSALM 13:5–6

Children, take every moment as of My Planning and ordering.
Remember your Master is the Lord of the day's little happenings.
In all the small things yield to My gentle pressure on your arm.
Stay or go, as that pressure, Love's pressure, indicates.

The Lord of the moments, Creator of the snowdrop and the
mighty oak. More tender with the snowdrop than the oak.

And when things do not fall out according to your plan, then smile
at Me indulgently, a smile of Love, and say, as you would to a human
loved one, "Have Your way then"—knowing that My loving response
will be to make that way as easy for your feet as it can be.

Have Thine own way, Lord! Have Thine own way!
Hold o'er my being absolute sway!
Fill with Thy Spirit till all shall see
Christ only, always, living in me.
ADELAIDE A. POLLARD (1862–1934)

PRAY:
Have Your way, Lord. For You have planned and ordered
my days, even when my own plans are interrupted or go
completely offtrack. Lord, You are Master of the day's happenings.

Practice Protection

> *"But whoever listens to me will dwell safely,*
> *and will be secure, without fear of evil."*
> PROVERBS 1:33

Fear no evil because I have conquered evil. It has power to hurt only those who do not place themselves under My Protection. This is not a question of feeling; it is an assured fact.

All you have to do is to say with assurance that whatever it is cannot harm you, as I have conquered it. Children, in not only the big, but the little things of life, be sure of My conquering Power. Know that all is well. Be sure of it. Practice this. Learn it until it is unfailing and instinctive with you.

But practice it in the quite small things, and then you will find you will do it easily, naturally, lovingly, trustingly in the big things of life.

CONSIDER:

How sure am I of God's power over evil?
Have I placed myself under His protection?

PRAY:

God, help me as I declare—and believe—that You are protecting me
and that evil cannot harm me. Strengthen my belief in these truths.

The World's Song

*Bless us, O Lord, we beseech Thee and show us
the way in which Thou wouldst have us walk.*

Walk with Me in the way of Peace. Shed Peace, not discord, wherever you go. But it must be My Peace.

Never a Peace that is a truce with the power of evil. Never harmony if that means your life-music being adapted to the mood and music of the world.

My disciples so often make the mistake of thinking all must be harmonious. No! Not when it means singing the song of the world.

I, the Prince of Peace, said that I came "not to bring Peace but a sword."

CONSIDER:
*Do I "sing God's song" by living my faith and following
Christ's commands? Or do I compromise and sometimes
"sing the world's song"? Can I let people know what I stand
for and still live peaceably with all men?*

PRAY:
*Lord, not everyone will like the tunes, but help my life's music to be
consistent. Show me ways to live in peace with others without compromising.
Help me to know when I should be bold, and when I should be agreeable.*

He Is Coming

*Behold, the virgin shall be with child, and bear a Son, and they
shall call His name Immanuel, which is translated, "God with us."*
MATTHEW 1:23

Our Lord, Thou art here. Let us feel Thy nearness.

Yes! but remember the first Hail must be that of the Magi in the
Bethlehem stable. Not as King and Lord in Heavenly triumph
must you first hail Me. But as amongst the lowliest, bereft of earth's
pomp like the Magi.

So to the humble the worship of humility—the Bethlehem
Babe—must be the first Hail.

Then the worship of repentance. As earth's sinner, you stand
by Me in the Jordan, baptized of John, worshiping Me, the Friend
and Servant of sinners.

Dwell much on My Life. Step out beside Me. Share it with Me.
Humility, Service, Worship, Sacrifice, Sanctification—Steps in the
Christian Life.

CONSIDER:
*On this Christmas Eve, do I feel the nearness of the Lord?
Have I stilled my Spirit before Him in worship?*

PRAY:
*God, thank You so much for sending Your Son to be with us. I repent of my
sins of complacency and selfishness. I worship You and seek to serve You.*

*And when they had come into the house, they saw the young
Child with Mary His mother, and fell down and worshiped
Him. And when they had opened their treasures, they presented
gifts to Him: gold, frankincense, and myrrh.*
MATTHEW 2:11

Kneel before the Babe of Bethlehem. Accept the truth that the
Kingdom of Heaven is for the lowly, the simple.

Bring to Me, the Christ-child, your gifts, truly the gifts of
earth's wisest.

The Gold—your money.

Frankincense—the adoration of a consecrated life.

Myrrh—your sharing in My sorrows and those of the world.

"And they presented unto Him gifts: gold, frankincense, and myrrh."

CONSIDER:
*What do I have to offer the Babe of Bethlehem?
Am I aware that even someone as ordinary as
me has very precious gifts to give to Him?*

PRAY:
*God, please accept my gifts—my talents, my time,
and my money—which all come from You in the
first place. On this special day, I offer myself to You.*

Health and Wealth

B e not afraid; health and wealth are coming to you both. My wealth
which is sufficiency for your needs, and for My work you long to do.

Money, as some call wealth, to hoard, to display, you know is not
for My Disciples.

Journey through this world simply seeking the means to do My
Will and work. Never keep anything you are not using. Remember all
I give you will be Mine, only given to you to use. Could you think
of Me hoarding My Treasures? You must never do it. Rely on Me.

To store for the future is to fear and to doubt Me. Check every
doubt of Me at once. Live in the Joy of My constant Presence. Yield
every moment to Me. Perform every task, however humble, as at My
gentle bidding, and for Me, for love of Me. So live, so love, so work.

You are the Apostles of the Little Services.

CONSIDER:

*Am I hoarding my money, or am I using as much as I can
spare for God's work? Do I rely on Him to provide for me?*

Glorious Work

Truly my soul silently waits for God; from Him comes
my salvation. He only is my rock and my salvation;
He is my defense; I shall not be greatly moved.
PSALM 62:1–2

I have stripped you of much, that it should be truly a life of well-being.
Build up stone by stone upon a firm foundation, and that Rock is
your Master—that Rock is Christ.

A life of discipline and of joyous fulfillment is to be yours. . . .
Never lose sight of the glorious work to which you have been called.

Let no riches, no ease entice you from the path of miracle-working
with Me upon which your feet are set. Love and Laugh. Trust and pray.
Ride on now in a loving humility to victory.

CONSIDER:
Are my eyes firmly focused on my life's
mission that God has called me to?

PRAY:
God, let me not be enticed by riches, ease, or other distractions.
Keep me on the path of expecting miracles, which can
come only when I pray, trust, and follow You.

Signs and Feelings

Jesus Christ is the same yesterday, today, and forever. Do not be carried about with various and strange doctrines. For it is good that the heart be established by grace, not with foods which have not profited those who have been occupied with them.
HEBREWS 13:8–9

Our Lord, Thou art here. Let us feel Thy nearness.

I am here. Do not need feeling too much. To ask for feeling too much is to ask for a sign, and then the answer is the same as that I gave when on earth. "There shall no sign be given but the sign of the prophet Jonas. . . . For as Jonas was three days and three nights. . .so shall the Son of Man be three days and three nights in the heart of the earth."

Veiled from sight to the unbeliever. To the believer the veiling is only temporary, to be followed by a glorious Resurrection. . . .

What does it matter what you feel? What matters is what I am, was, and ever shall be to you—A Risen Lord. . . . The feeling that I am with you may depend upon any passing mood of yours—upon a change of circumstances, upon a mere trifle.

I am uninfluenced by circumstances. . . . My Promise given is kept. I am here, one with you in tender loving friendship.

Work and Prayer

But Jesus looked at them and said to them,
"With men this is impossible, but with God all things are possible."
MATTHEW 19:26

Work and prayer represent the two forces that will ensure you success. Your work and My work.

For prayer, believing prayer, is based on the certainty that I am working for you and with you and in you.

Go forward gladly and unafraid. I am with you. With men your task may be impossible, but with God all things are possible.

CONSIDER:
Am I working and praying faithfully? Do I believe that
God will help me and that, with God, all things are possible?

PRAY:
God, keep me praying as I go forward gladly and without fear.
Allow me to see the possibilities that await me when I do these things.

Fishers of Men

*And as He walked by the Sea of Galilee, He saw Simon and Andrew
his brother casting a net into the sea; for they were fishermen. Then Jesus
said to them, "Follow Me, and I will make you become fishers of men."*
MARK 1:16–17

When you think of those of whom you read who are in anguish,
do you ever think how My Heart must ache with the woe of it,
with the anguish of it?

If I beheld the city and wept over it, how much more should I
weep over the agony of these troubled hearts, over lives that seek
to live without My sustaining Power.

"They will not come unto Me that they might have Life."

Live to bring others to *Me*, the only Source of Happiness
and Heart-Peace.

CONSIDER:
*Do I feel sorrow, as Jesus does, for those who don't
know Him and who are living without His power?*

PRAY:
*Lord, strengthen and inspire me as I seek to live in
a way that brings others to You. May they experience
the happiness and peace that come from knowing You.*

Jesus the Conqueror

"And behold, you will conceive in your womb and bring forth
a Son, and shall call His name JESUS. He will be great, and will
be called the Son of the Highest; and the Lord God will give Him
the throne of His father David. And He will reign over the house
of Jacob forever, and of His kingdom there will be no end."
LUKE 1:31–33

Jesus. That is the Name by which you conquer. Jesus. Not as cringing suppliants but as those recognizing a friend, say My Name—Jesus. "Thou shall call His Name Jesus, for He shall save His people from their sins."

And in that word "sins" read not only vice and degradation, but doubts, fears, tempers, despondencies, impatience, lack of Love in big and little things. Jesus. "He shall save His people from their sins." The very uttering of the Name lifts the soul away from petty valley-irritations to mountain heights.

"He shall save His people from their sins." Savior and Friend, Joy-bringer and Rescuer, Leader and Guide—Jesus. Do you need delivering from cowardice, from adverse circumstances, from poverty, from failure, from weakness?

"There is none other Name. . .whereby you can be saved"—Jesus. Say it often. Claim the Power it brings.

PRAY:

God, deliver me from my sins—not only the obvious ones but also
the doubts, fears, envy, impatience, and other weaknesses that beset
me and weigh me down. Help me repent of these sins and conquer
them, so that I might reach the mountain heights of Your Spirit.

Scripture Index